F**k You and Goodbye

Also by Matt Potter

Outlaws Inc.: Flying With The World's Most
Dangerous Smugglers

F**k You and Goodbye

Matt Potter

Constable • London

CONSTABLE

First published in Great Britain in 2014 by Constable

Copyright © Matt Potter, 2014

The moral right of the author has been asserted.

A CIP catalogue record for this book
is available from the British Library.

ISBN: 978-1-47211-007-7 (paperback)
ISBN: 978-1-47211-050-3 (ebook)

Typeset in Dante MT by SX Composing DTP, Rayleigh, Essex
Printed and bound by CPI Group (UK) Ltd, Croydon, CR0 4Y

Constable
is an imprint of
Constable & Robinson Ltd
100 Victoria Embankment
London EC4Y 0DY

An Hachette UK Company
www.hachette.co.uk

www.constablerobinson.com

The rising into place is laborious, and by pains men come to greater pains; and it is sometimes base, and by indignities men come to dignities. The standing is slippery, and the regress is either downfall, or at least an eclipse.

Francis Bacon, *Essay XI: Of Great Place*

Contents

Prologue: The Quitter's Tale

History is written by the winners. It's the survivors – the faithful servants, the insiders, the ones who stick around, who can adapt to almost any condition – who get to write the official histories.

They publish the memoirs. They park in the directors' spots, erect the statues; the new governments; wipe out the pockets of resistance; recruit new starters; set agendas; talk on documentaries and retrospectives.

Yet theirs – the official version – is never the whole story. There's another side that we only glimpse through the cracks.

The quitter's tale offers a far more compelling, and often a more honest take. It's one of self-deception, loyalty, bloody knives, betrayal, honour, disgrace, morality, disgust, love, thwarted ambition, duty, dread, and shattered hopes. (If future archaeologists unearth our HR filing cabinets, they'll conclude that we were all Shakespeares.)

So parting shots can speak to us as history. But they appeal to the amateur psychologist, the wannabe forensic surgeon, the gumshoe at the core of every journalist too.

I collect them. I've even ghostwritten a few for other people. Like most hobbies, this was one I slipped into without noticing. I've always been good at putting things into words, and it started with me amending, then supplying, job applications, begging letters, complaints and letters of resignation for a few close friends. Along the way, it's taken in official statements from rock bands, Brazilian bankers, businesspeople and everything in between.

You get to know some odd things. Like the fact that most resignations never make it beyond the draft stage. It's a kind of cheap therapy: the would-be resigner finds it comforting, empowering even, to know what they could say if they needed to; to feel the power they could call on as a last resort. I know plenty of people who keep a copy in their pocket, or their desk drawer, just in case. Pre-empt a bad day. The Ace in the hole for any tricky conversation.

There are themes, resignation types, that crop up again and again.

There's the dissection – a kiss-off as coolly devastating as a forensic accountant's investigation of a flailing, corrupt multinational. There's the genuine, heartfelt tribute. More common is the coded fuck-you: unfailingly polite, positive, glassy-eyed and *totally* equivocal. Very British.

The most fun are always the incendiary bombs. That's when they just let go and do the multidirectional splatter-gun thing on an employer who's been asking for it. Who doesn't love hammering those out at the end of a long day?

They tell a secret story of our own time, too, You notice the patterns – how they blossom and cluster around economic curves, wars, new technologies; how they change when society changes. Without noticing, when we write ourselves out of a story, we plug into something larger than ourselves. The resignation statement is a very

– maybe uniquely – personal take on the way a given story is unfolding. War in Iraq? The crisis in journalism? The collapse of communism? Vietnam? The rise of spin? Each era gets the resignations it deserves.

History and human nature: the low-level view, through the prism of the individual who decides to serve notice.

They become a rabbit-hole down which you discover a very different version of the world you think you inhabit. This version of the story isn't written down in books years later: it is told at the time of greatest crisis, in short, desperate and often quickly composed parting shots, by men and women who can no longer hold on and hope for the best. For them, the resignation letter is a passport to a new life.

For the first time, they are beyond the reach of their superiors. They can say what they've been bottling up and damn the consequences. And when enough of them say it – or the right people listen – then just for a moment, the winners' hold over history loosens. Empires fall, walls tumble, societies revolt.

This isn't something that insiders – from corporations to governments – like to hear. And who can blame them? Every damaging resignation letter, every cornered truth attack, every out-of-control speech by a former friend, is more than just an inconvenience, to be countered with positive spin and internal memos: it's an open challenge to the official version of the story, the perfectly controlled brand. They are breaks in an otherwise perfectly planned, smoothly executed narrative of the powerful. Holes in the program code. A rare, irresistible chance to hack into history's shiny, unstoppable operation.

They are the *memento mori*. The terror that forces tyrants behind walls. Resignations remind us, publicly, of the one thing we do not want to hear from history's ousted and outraged.

Today, me. Tomorrow, maybe you.

But whatever the motivation, a letter of resignation is never, ever *just* a letter of resignation, functional, forgettable. It's the ultimate rushed autobiography; the only chance most of us will ever get to compose something like our memoir – at least for the professional self who is now departing. In the face of anything from corporate frustration to public ridicule, private treachery or moral outrage, this is our one and only chance to tell our side. It is history as written on the spot by those who reject the official version.

For better or worse, our resignations are also the only famous last words we'll ever utter and then stick around to enjoy. For some, they are professional edge-play; a flirtation with the fantasy of eavesdropping on our own mourners. A little workplace death-tripping.

For some, it offers a last chance to explain themselves, and to damage the people who forced them out. For others, it's a desperate last attempt to stop the voices – to stem the flow of criticism, escape scrutiny, overthrow the order, blow the whistle, or thwart the law. Image consultants, crisis management PRs, lawyers, writers-for-hire like me, get called in to help with those. But as you'll see, the truth has a way of whispering its dark secrets between the lines of even the most careful spin.

For more, it can be the moment when, all other options exhausted, they finally face themselves. And whoever we choose to be in our resignations, we'd better be ready to live with that person for a long time afterwards.

This, after all, is the document nobody ever wants to write; it is a witness testimony we would rather not give.

Only this time – to use a phrase that crops up time and again in the statements themselves – we are left with no choice.

★ ★ ★

This brings us to the deepest mystery of the resignation letter. Amid the carnage and the coverage that follows – amid the post-mortems, investigations, tribunals, cover-ups, revolutions, career moves and crisis management campaigns – one question is always the same.

It is the question that the letters themselves try in vain to answer, over and over again – even as they explain, analyse, protest and bear witness to a million other details.

The question is: Why?

All the forces in the universe stack up against unburdening ourselves in a resignation letter. Professionally, it can be suicide. In practical terms, it is often self-defeating. Self-help books coach against unleashing its force; colleagues and confidantes urge caution, self-restraint. And yet we do it, and damn the consequences. We have no choice but to speak – in sorrow, love, grief, cold anger, thirst for revenge, wounded pride, the pain of injustice, loyalty, pangs of regret, throes of vengeful madness, deluded righteousness, panic, black distress, isolation, ecstasies of martyrdom, and a million other shades of human extremity – we need to say our piece even as we leave the stage.

So what will you say, when it's your turn? It's a question

that haunts us all, even in our private moments online. (Just type 'resignation letter' into Google and you'll find more than 33 million matches – almost double what you'll find for universal ordeals like 'childbirth', 'old age' or even 'bereavement'. What's more, of these worldwide discussions of resignation letters, the vast majority are tutorials and examples.)

We bide our time at meetings, composing devastating goodbyes to our colleagues and paymasters. Even as we know we will never utter them, our mouths hold the shape of the words. They are our secret power. So we keep them close, and hone them through PowerPoint presentations and dressings-down.

Personally, I find something wonderful – redemptive even – in all of this. We can't choose whether we go or not, but we can choose how we go.

It's the stuff of life and death; of the great religions, of art and poetry and mythology, of the band on the *Titanic*, of cowboys dying with their boots on. *Will we do it right when our turn comes?*

Maybe, in the end, that's what I hope this book can do for everyone who reads it. The untold history of some of our key moments is all very well. But when it comes down to it, all these great, moving, vicious, magnanimous, deluded, honest, sensational, sad, desperate, spectacular, angry, betrayed, hopeful, calculating, beseeching, vengeful, tired, self-erasing, self-aggrandizing, triumphant letters are all from people just like you and me, all trying to figure out how to deal with a bad situation in the best way they can.

The raw basics of existence.

Sometimes they've only themselves to blame. Sometimes

it's the other guy. Sometimes, well, things just didn't work out. And if the way they've found their exit can help you figure out how to find yours, then good for you.

Personally, I've got a feeling that, for me, they hold the key to something more. Maybe this book is my attempt to find out what it is. Wish me luck.

Now, if you'll excuse me, I've got some correspondence to catch up on.

Matt Potter, August 2014

1:

The Truth Bomb

Species gradually become better adapted to their immediate environment, fitter for survival. In spite of this, nemesis eventually claims them, and species become extinct.

– Paul Ormerod, *Why Things Fail*

'You want the truth? You can't handle the truth.'

– Jack Nicholson, *A Few Good Men*, 1992

It is 4.40 a.m. on a Wednesday, in the freezing winter of 1989/90. I am a 'Grey', an undocumented foreign worker. First job of the day: to shovel up and incinerate the day-old turds, food, sports sections and litter that fellow workers have left in holes and half-built fireplaces and between unfinished walls across the building site.

This winter, while Berliners dance on top of a broken wall with sledgehammers and banners, we have been building new walls. They rise in thick forests of development to the West – in Düsseldorf, Cologne, wherever the trucks take us. Paid in cash (two Deutschemarks an hour – about 60p), untraceable, invisible, without permits and subjected to appalling casual hazards, we are the navvies of the new free Europe; a morphing crew of nobodies from semi-developed economies: Poland, Yugoslavia, Turkey, Central Asia, Romania and, in my case, Slough. I'm luckier than most – I'm odd-jobbing; paying my way like this until the next thing starts. Still, that means I'm unqualified. So I get to dig holes, mix cement and torch human shit.

As I stamp my numb feet and stoke my fire of barbecue lighters, tabloids, cigarette packets and excrement, a tabloid page catches my eye, curling and yellow as the flames lick its margins. It is a story about what Communist Party members would do now they had no party. I scan the page as it folds into ash. These people crossing West in the photograph, just walking away from the confused-looking border cops. What will they do tomorrow? Have they even thought about it?

In the cold, dark wind, stinking flames and headlights, I realize there's something I have to do.

I shamble through the mud towards a Portakabin by the gate. Once inside, I calmly – and not unhelpfully – suggest to the foreman a few alternatives for my share of burning turds. As I tell him I won't be coming back, I point out a few of the dangers of the site – things he might want to look into. There are risks my colleagues are taking that they really shouldn't have to. The foreman looks terrified as I resign. I can't figure out why. I'm talking calmly, rationally – even trying, as I react to his expression, to be chummy, to calm him. It seems to make it worse. He shrinks back as if he's being given pointers on occupational safety by a ghost.

It is starting to rain. I head for the van where I can see two colleagues sitting and eating breakfast rolls, to tell them I'm off. None of us can figure out what's up with the foreman. A Yugoslav – there are still Yugoslavs – suggests he didn't like my 'truth bomb' about the site. Someone else floats the idea that he'd always thought I was one of the Poles, and was freaked out by the sudden transformation into a heavily accented Brit. Then the plumber arrives with coffee and gossip. It seems the foreman was afraid I'd try to shake his hand in 'those turd gloves'.

The Yugoslav's phrase stayed with me, though. From the nightly scenes in Berlin and Bucharest to political scandals at home, resignations, walk-outs and refusals suddenly seemed to be driving history.

Crowds were no longer chanting, but booing. They weren't enlisting in great marches forward like the posters told them to, but sauntering off. The great post-war systems were moving inexorably towards their own destruction. This was the triumph of entropy, not progress.

A world created not by ideas, chemistry, numbers, God, inventions or bullets, but by people handing in their notice.

I had never really understood before why powerful people – employers, regimes and so on – were so afraid of other people declaring, on an individual basis, that they wanted out. But here was 'truth bombing' as a humiliating public theatre of defiance. The hecklers in front of Ceauşescu's palace; climbers on the Wall; corporate whistleblowers; disaffected ministers; mismanaged shelf-stackers – all part of one mass, all moving in accordance with the same laws.

In the land of the committed believer, the contracted belonger, the opter-out is a grave threat indeed.

With hindsight, the 1990s' great theme *was* refusal; the decade's core act was not the salute, but the shrug.

The ironic and uncommitted, were about to take over the world.

In Britain more than anywhere, the coming decade was to be a fruitful time for creative, public quitters.

On my return in 1990, I started collecting resignations and analysing their backgrounds in earnest. It wasn't easy, simply because there were suddenly so many flying around. Thatcherism was imploding, with Michael Heseltine and Geoffrey Howe taking turns at playing Mark Antony and Brutus with their own parting shots. Then, as recession hit Britain and the West, and the eighties achievers' party hit the buffers, it was business's turn. These were not the quiet goodbyes of yesteryear, but great, furious, splattering media events. The dawning of a great age of corporate dissent.

Across the West, the slackers wandered off the career path with a shrug – their anti-aspiration the mirror image of all those refuseniks in the East now discovering the joys of consumer society – while *Adbusters'* subversive 'truth in advertising' defacement campaigns echoed the theatrical marginalia of the Berlin Wall's Eastside Gallery. Self-empowerment was in, and suddenly no soap opera, cabinet meeting, movie, international summit or AGM was complete without a grandstanding declaration of independence.

Climactic, public resignations became a powerful international currency from Wall Street to Hollywood. The era's defining movies – *Slacker* (1991), *The Firm* (1991), *Glengarry Glen Ross* (1992), *A Few Good Men* (1992), *Groundhog Day* (1993), *Clerks* (1994), even *Jurassic Park* (1993), all feature stars plotting and rehearsing their eventual break from the hypocrisy, villainy or empty repetition of their professional roles.

(Surely a candidate for least likely resignation speech in history is that of the Tyrannosaurus Rex in *Jurassic Park*. Richard Attenborough's park boss, micro-managing every aspect of the lives of the revenue-generating animals inside his hermetically sealed biodome, is as clear an early-1990s everyboss or Iron Curtain dictator as ever lived, with his insistence that everyone could be bought, and his creation of minutely surveilled spaces for workers, human and reptile alike. It's great fun to watch it now as Berlin Wall or corporate allegory: the *literal* iron curtain keeping humans and dinos apart! Jeff Goldblum's ominous soliloquy on chaos! The heroes' suspicion of being co-opted into branded ideology! It's no coincidence that when they rebel, the animals not only wreck the commercial plan, but vandalize his company's iconic logo. As T. Rex tears apart the logos on the branded Jurassic Park hoardings in the final scene, he becomes the movie's anti-corporate hero; its Adbuster; he hands in his notice with a roar of independence that brings the whole venture crumbling down. The inhabitants have wrestled their own land back.)

By 1993, 'getting on' in your job had come to look, at least in pop-cultural terms, very much like being suckered. Irvine Welsh's sarcastic jab at aspirational eighties consumerism in his bestseller of that year, *Trainspotting* – lifting the slogan of the iconic Katherine Hamnett/Wham T-shirt that symbolised the decade's worst go-for-it platitudes – became a pop-culture mantra, appearing on albums, club singles, and finally on T-shirts of its own: 'Choose life. Choose a job . . . Choose rotting away at the end of it all, pishing your last in a miserable home, nothing more than an embarrassment to the selfish, fucked-up brats you spawned to replace yourself. Choose your future.'

Pop culture's superstars were Homer Simpson and Kurt Cobain, its key image the swimming baby chasing a dollar. Beck vowed he wasn't 'going to work for no soul-sucking jerk' (1994), while Rage Against The Machine created the ultimate 90s chorus with 'Killing In The Name's' 'Fuck you, I won't do what you tell me.' (1992).

The 1990s revolution was not about the fall of communism: it was about the realization by people all over the world that being a committed swallower of the post-war company line didn't deliver what it promised. The contract was a dud.

The hour of the workplace dissident, the self-immolating truth-bomber, had come at last.

In that first heady rush of ornery possibilities, resignation letters of all kinds flowered forth. But of all the letters, speeches and releases that followed – vituperative, misjudged, embarrassed, principled – the explosive, dissident thud of the truth bomb was by far the most visible – and the most loaded.

From Steve Jobs's electrifyingly bitter 1985 resignation from Apple to Geoffrey Howe's legendary takedown of Margaret Thatcher, the truth bomb's terrible power is in the way it hijacks the news – blowing a hole in the corporate facade, tearing down the 'happy workers' posters.

For employers, just like governments, the threat truth-bombers pose is very real indeed. They are a constant internal threat, a more damaging, less governable office counterpart to hackers, activists and protesters.

In some cases, the damage can rival that inflicted by a terror attack, at least in financial terms. As I began to collate my notes for this book, senior executive Greg Smith resigned from investment bank Goldman Sachs with an explosive, beans-spilling open letter – one he had given to the *New York Times* for free on the condition that they gave him their op-ed page and ran it on the morning of the day he planned to resign. So as dawn broke on 14 March 2012, the phones began ringing at 200 West Street, Lower Manhattan.

'Today is my last day at Goldman Sachs,' he began. 'After almost 12 years at the firm – first as a summer intern while at Stanford, then in New York for 10 years, and now in London – I believe I have worked here long enough to understand the trajectory of its culture, its people and its identity. And I can honestly say that the environment now is as toxic and destructive as I have ever seen it.'

So much for credentials. But it was his unpacking of what he saw as the investment bank's culture that was heard around the world.

How did we get here? The firm changed the way it thought about leadership. Leadership used to be about ideas, setting an example and doing the right thing. Today, if you make enough money for the firm (and are not currently an ax murderer) you will be promoted into a position of influence.

What are three quick ways to become a leader?

a) Execute on the firm's 'axes', which is Goldman-speak for persuading your clients to invest in the stocks or other products that we are trying to get rid of because they are not seen as having a lot of potential profit.

b) 'Hunt Elephants.' In English: get your clients – some of whom are sophisticated, and some of whom aren't – to trade whatever will bring the biggest profit to Goldman. Call me old-fashioned, but I don't like selling my clients a product that is wrong for them.

c) Find yourself sitting in a seat where your job is to trade any illiquid, opaque product with a three-letter acronym.

Today, many of these leaders display a Goldman Sachs culture quotient of exactly zero per cent. I attend derivatives sales meetings where not one single minute is spent asking questions about how we can help clients. It's purely about how we can make the most possible money off of them. If you were an alien from Mars and sat in on one of these meetings, you would believe that a client's success or progress was not part of the thought process at all.

[. . .] Over the last 12 months I have seen five different managing directors refer to their own clients as 'muppets', sometimes over internal e-mail. Even after the SEC, Fabulous Fab, Abacus, God's work, Carl Levin, Vampire Squids? No humility? I mean, come on. Integrity? It is eroding. I don't know of any illegal behavior, but will people push the envelope and pitch lucrative and complicated products to clients even if they are not the simplest investments or the ones most directly aligned with the client's goals? Absolutely. Every day, in fact.

It astounds me how little senior management gets a basic truth: If clients don't trust you they will eventually stop doing business with you. It doesn't matter how smart you are.

These days, the most common question I get from junior analysts about derivatives is, 'How much money did we make off the client?' It bothers me every time I hear it, because it is a clear reflection of what they are observing from their leaders about the way they should behave. Now project 10 years into the future: You don't have to be a rocket scientist to figure out that the junior analyst sitting quietly in the corner of the room hearing about 'muppets', 'ripping eyeballs out' and 'getting paid' doesn't exactly turn into a model citizen [. . .]

I hope this can be a wake-up call to the board of directors. Make the client the focal point of your business again. Without clients you will not make money. In fact, you will not exist.

Weed out the morally bankrupt people, no matter how much money they make for the firm. And get the culture right again, so people want to work here for the right reasons. People who care only about making money will not sustain this firm – or the trust of its clients – for very much longer.

This is what it sounds like when a Master of the Universe channels the famous 25-page stream-of-consciousness memo written by Tom Cruise's sports agent in *Jerry McGuire*. (There's even a scene in Martin Scorsese's fictionalized biopic of former stockbroker Jordan Belfort *The Wolf Of Wall Street*, in which Belfort, played by Leonardo DiCaprio, and his mentor at J.L. Rothschild appear to pay direct homage to that line about benefiting the clients.)

There was nothing casual or *ad lib* about Smith's letter, however. Primed for publication via a number of secret meetings with the *New York Times*, the full letter feels almost breathtakingly calculated. Smith is careful to mention no names; to deal in non-specifics; to call out only 'analysts', 'people', and 'leaders'. Smith 'doesn't know of any illegal behaviour', but no regulator in the world could read this note and conclude that the firm didn't need an impromptu visit or two.

Cynics suggested it was a little rich for someone of director level to be moaning about a culture that had served them rather well. They pointed out how Smith's self-portrait was almost too wholesome (he sneaks in his degree, references to his integrity, and the following sentence: 'My proudest moments in life – getting a full scholarship to go from South Africa to Stanford University, being selected as a Rhodes Scholar national finalist, winning a bronze medal for table tennis at the Maccabiah Games in Israel, known as the Jewish Olympics – have all come through hard work, with no shortcuts'). Within 24 hours, a spoof piece, 'Why I Am Quitting Death Star – by Darth Vader' was doing the rounds.

But in the end, none of it mattered. This was a truth bomb as Hollywood blockbusters prefer them, with heroes and villains wearing hats of the appropriate colour just to make it easy for the passing trade, beyond the constituencies of high finance, corporate America, or news. And as it happened, the American public was more than ready for some bloodletting from an investment community that had sailed through the three years since the crash a little too slickly.

Caught on the hop, the bank's response was flat-footed. First, they played for time, then attacked Smith. It was standard stuff: they portrayed him as a relative junior (job title notwithstanding). But the damage was done. Shares in Goldman Sachs were down $2 billion by the end of the day. In the wake of his departure, extracts from the *Jerry McGuire* script reportedly began circulating on Goldman Sachs' internal messaging system.

So how does *one letter* do all that?

One consequence of globalization for blue-chips like this is the remote nature of ownership, client and stakeholder relationships. These people – only half listening, often far-flung – can't help but make decisions based on perception.

The stakes are high. So high that, along with recovery plans for things like 9/11-style attacks on their head-quarters, fires, flood, acts of God and system hacks, companies and public bodies are forced to account for 'reputational damage' in their risk strategies, attack drills and corporate insurance policies. The consequences of a resignation alone may not be great, but the consequences of a truth bomb like Smith's can be greater, in terms of zeroes, at least, than those of a real attack.

These quitters are acutely conscious that they are also rejecting the system through the manner in which they leave their job.

Resigning is a political act.

This is not new. Feudalism tied employment to notions of social duty – something codified in medieval Church and Aristocratic notions of a neoplatonic Great Chain of Being: from God at the top, everything, from orders of angels to animals, plants and humans (King downward through the social order) had its pre-ordained place. Getting ideas above one's station as, say, a land worker could be dangerously close to heresy.

This odd idea has, against all odds, survived the industrial revolution and the replacing of religion with economic theory.

Since the 1800s, employers have become an essential link between state and people, in economic, pastoral and surveillance terms. Unhappy workers in London, LA or Moscow were identified and blacklisted as 'potential agitators' throughout the twentieth century. MI5 reported to Prime Minister Edward Heath in 1972 that 'the Communist Party's attitude to industrial disputes is tactical and it exploits rather than creates them, preferring to work through union leadership'. And the Cold War, with its emphasis on technological advancement and economic superiority often saw the most innocuous workplace information classed state-sensitive in ways we find almost impossible to imagine today. Union organizers were routinely monitored by MI5, the CIA, the KGB and Stasi, who fed information back to management.

Those days seem dark and distant indeed. Yet even today the NSA's PRISM electronic surveillance system works with the collusion of the very tech firms and mobile service providers we trust not to share our data with governments. The Occupy protests of 2010 were defeated by police, secret services, banks and employers working together to monitor, profile and pressure protesters. Countries from Canada to Thailand now use drones to monitor and film private employees turning out on protests and picket lines.

Against a backdrop of a global crackdown on whistle-blowers, the blurring of private business with military adventure, and the secret lifetime blacklisting of 'unco-operative' workers by construction firms, expressing reservations and quitting is often just a heartbeat away from defection. And telling truth to power can start to look a lot like rebellion.

* * *

Workplace rebellion and resignations have form in terms of bringing about wholesale political change. Letters to the boss are dangerous things.

Czech brewery worker and playwright Václav Havel spent much of his life in prison or under house arrest – like Patrick McGoohan's Number Six in *The Prisoner*: nominally free to do as he pleased, only surveilled, and unable to travel. Where McGoohan's character thrusts a wad of papers at his secret-service handlers and resigns, Havel's explosive documents were the satirical, slightly slackerish 'anti-communist' plays he wrote – plays that often had to be copied out by hand and passed around in the form of letters and secret packages.

Havel's most famous character is Vanek (a barely disguised Havel), forever trapped in a job and doomed to enumerate its hypocrisies from within – forever declaring like Number Six that he is 'not a number . . . I'm a free man', and forever met with derision, amusement or (worse) nothing at all.

But Havel's own travails became famous too. The more trouble these open letters of workplace dissatisfaction got him into, the more famous he became. In the late seventies, *The Power of the Powerless* – his manifesto for mentally resigning from dead-end state jobs or even the whole belief system, when you couldn't physically leave – was copied out by hand and passed along shop floors. You might call it the first workplace resignation meme.

The Power of the Powerless contains an account of the fate of a brewer called 'Š', and illustrates the potential pitfalls of telling the truth. Š is the best worker at the brewery but is disillusioned by the inefficient way it is run by the politically powerful managers: 'They were bringing the brewery to ruin and not only did they fail to react to any of Š's suggestions, but they actually became increasingly hostile toward him.' His letter attempting to improve the situation is described as a 'defamatory document'. Labelled an anti-communist 'political saboteur', he is thrown out of the brewery. 'By speaking the truth, Š had stepped out of line, broken the rules, cast himself out, and he ended up a subcitizen, stigmatized as an enemy. He could now say anything he wanted, but he could never, as a matter of principle, expect to be heard.'

But *The Power of the Powerless* is not just a case study in why organizations should probably pay more attention to their 'dissidents'. It is fantasy resignation email memes passed between frustrated office workers today. Its power was not in anything it did, but what it showed was possible. Communist Czechoslovakia's insistence on a single narrative – call it ideological soundness or call it all singing from the same hymn sheet – made the essay, writing it, receiving it and talking about it, more than thrilling, amusing and illicit. It made it a powerful rallying call for everyone else who felt what the authorities in *The Prisoner's* village called 'unmutuality'. By 1980, translated copies had begun circulating in Poland's huge factories and shipyards – the mechanized, industrial heartlands of the Eastern Bloc. In its pages the fledgling Solidarity pro-democracy union found it had a ready-made battle plan. The momentum built through the 1980s, with the famous graffiti that spread across an ideologically and financially bankrupt East: 'They pretend to pay us, so we pretend to work.' By December 1991, the game was up: Soviet leader

Mikhail Gorbachev read out his own resignation letter – a classic in itself, which I'll come to later – and wound up the USSR as a going concern. Within months, Václav Havel was Czech president.

In search of an acceptable term for this popular outbreak of polite refusal, an English translator for the Czech dissidents called Rita Klimova came up with 'The Velvet Revolution'. The Slovaks' went with 'The Gentle Revolution'.

But something about the word was too confrontational for the way Czechoslovakians, for example, were simply shrugging and walking out of Party meetings *en masse*. It wasn't a revolution at all, not in the way that the Russian, French or American revolutions had taught us to understand the word. It was just the biggest mass resignation in history.

★ ★ ★

The idea that history could be driven by something as workaday as a resignation – by opting out of anything from getting up on a wet Monday to an economic philosophy is heady and addictive. For the casual historian, it also reveals some tantalizing clues to the way we see ourselves, and our allegiances.

Historically, truth attacks were the preserve of deposed and defeated leaders – the asymmetrical warfare equivalent of urban guerrilla graffiti or the YouTube speeches given from hiding by Osama bin Laden. Sauk Native American leader Chief Black Hawk took the part of the British against the United States in the War of 1812, in the hope that he would be able to stop US encroachment onto Sauk territory, and a Native American army known as the British

Band in the Black Hawk War of 1832. After the latter, he was hunted down by American agents and paraded as a prisoner through towns and cities on his way through Washington DC to prison in Virginia. Stepping down as leader of his people, Black Hawk gave the template resignation speech of the time.

I fought hard. But your guns were well aimed. The bullets flew like birds in the air, and whizzed by our ears like the wind through the trees in the winter. My warriors fell around me.

The sun rose dim on us in the morning, and at night it sunk in a dark cloud, and looked like a ball of fire. That was the last sun that shone on Black Hawk.

He is now a prisoner to the white men. He has done nothing for which an Indian ought to be ashamed. He has fought for his countrymen, the squaws and papooses, against white men, who came year after year, to cheat them and take away their lands. You know the cause of our making war. It is known to all white men. They ought to be ashamed of it. Indians are not deceitful. The white men speak bad of the Indian and look at him spitefully. But the Indian does not tell lies. Indians do not steal.

An Indian who is bad as the white men could not live in our nation; he would be put to death, and eaten up by the wolves. The white men are bad schoolmasters; they carry false books, and deal in false actions; they smile in the face of the poor Indian to cheat him; they shake them by their hands to gain their confidence, to make them drunk, to deceive them, and ruin our wives. We told them to leave us alone, and keep away from us; they followed us, and beset our paths, and they coiled themselves among us, like the snake. They poisoned us by their touch. We were not safe. We lived in danger. We were becoming like them, hypocrites and liars, adulterous lazy drones, all talkers and no workers.

The white men do not scalp the head; but they do worse: they poison the heart.

Farewell, my nation! Farewell to Black Hawk.

At first glance, Black Hawk's statement feels almost ancient. There is a sense of occasion; of a stage, and of speaking to history. Even in defeat, this sounds like a privileged voice. After all, the man was a public figure and the commander of an army. Black Hawk knew it, too. The following year, in captivity, he began planning an autobiography. The book was published in 1833 under the rather spectacular title *The Autobiography of Ma-Ka-Tai-Me-She-Kia-Kiak, or Black Hawk, Embracing the Traditions of his Nation, Various Wars In Which He Has Been Engaged, and His Account of the Cause and General History of the Black Hawk War of 1832, His Surrender, and Travels Through the United States. Also Life, Death and Burial of the Old Chief, Together with a History of the Black Hawk War.*

The memoir was an instant bestseller. He dedicated his book to his captor, US commander Brigadier General H. Atkinson, with a message that sheds light, not just on his resignation address, but on the reason we feel compelled to resign with statements today.

Before I set out on my journey to the land of my fathers, I have determined to give my motives and reasons for my former hostilities to the whites, and to vindicate my character from misrepresentation.

There was just one problem with this unburdening. Black Hawk's words were mediated, in ways that make them rather slippery. Unlettered, he dictated his memoir to an amanuensis, who worked with an editor to order the events, and to render the language more in tune with the middlebrow public's reading tastes.

More seriously, the book appears to have been signed off by an employee of the Government's Indian Agency.

Did Black Hawk deliver the gently regretful justification we read now, full of respect for brave US warriors and phrases like 'many moons'? Or is this what a Bin Laden video would look like, had it been made more palatable to the ear of a middlebrow DVD-store family audience in the Mid-West, scripted and signed off for release by the CIA and distributed through Blockbuster? Was it propaganda?

Fundamental to the resignation as testament is the ability to side step mediation – to go wildly and deliberately 'off message'. Of all the technologies to have transformed the way we resign – rolling news, the internet, email, surveillance – the most basic must surely be the blackboard. The popular uptake of resignation politics coincides with urbanization, the weakening of age-old hierarchies in the face of things like elected representation and complex labour markets. But our ability to create and deliver them, alone, unmediated and uncensored, is the direct result of universal literacy. 'Writes' equals rights.

In October 1924, a struggling author and poet from the American Deep South resigned from his job as Postmaster of the University of Mississippi to pursue his dream of being a novelist. It's a choice all would-be writers and artists have to make somewhere along the line, and despite the fact that only his poetry had brought him real praise to date, and he had nothing to fall back on, William Faulkner was determined. So far, so everyday. But what was highly unusual was the way he framed that resignation. In contrast to the somewhat timid dance of valediction characteristic of writers conscious that they might need to return cap in hand one day, Faulkner's resignation feels every bit as waspish – not to mention as final – as an outraged publisher's rejection slip.

'As long as I live under the capitalistic system, I expect to have my life influenced by the demands of moneyed people,' wrote Faulkner. 'But I will be damned if I propose to be at the beck and call of every itinerant scoundrel who has two cents to invest in a postage stamp.'

On the surface, and at this remove, this feels like a piece of ventriloquism: Faulkner in character, testing out a voice he would return to again and again in his fiction. But that's not it at all. Throughout his career, Faulkner's prolific output was, he admitted, driven by the need of an obscure novelist from a literary backwater to earn money. And that knowledge – that this wasn't a piece of play-acting by a well-off, middle-class writer, but something akin to an act of financial self-immolation – makes his invocation of 'the capitalistic system' so extraordinary.

This wasn't about leaving a job. This was about smashing – or at least, rejecting – the 'capitalistic system'. And in 1924, it was by no means clear that capitalism would prevail in America or anywhere else. Marx's *Das Kapital* – in which the evolution of economic 'systems' from feudal, through capitalist to socialist was described for the first time – was still a hot read. The Bolshevik Revolution of 1917 had been received enthusiastically by many in the West, too. So Faulkner's 'As long as I live under . . .' is less of a given than it appears today. In a Mississippi Delta of segregation, plantations and sharecroppers, that system must have seemed to have a tenuous foothold at best.

And capitalism is not the ancient bedrock it sometimes appears. For many hundreds of years – until late in the industrial age, in the case of Russia – the employee had been a belonging, a serf. The serf appeared in the Lord of the Manor's inventory; to be bought and sold, but also protected by their lord; and a woman could not marry elsewhere without the suitor (or another lord of another manor) paying her Lord compensation for the lost asset – it is via the Latin *'servus'* (slave), through Old French *'servise'* (slavery/servitude), and the Old English *'syrfe'*, and serf itself that we get the modern word 'service'.

The change, when it came, was not one brought about by enlightenment – Lords of the Manor didn't suddenly realize they shouldn't buy and sell other people. It was caused instead by urbanization, and the increasing use of money as an index of value. So where before, the lord of the manor protected whole communities in the knowledge that they would help him at harvest time, now he could simply pay peasants the going market rate to bring in his crops, and not bother with the whole year-round protecting bit. (The first use of the word 'contractor' pops up in 1540, as legal serfdom in Britain entered its terminal decline.)

Suddenly, workers were a human resource – or, to use

the phrase common until the 1980s, 'human capital'. You couldn't just hoard them; you had to *use* them, swap them, make them profitable, or someone else might do it better.

In this one term, we can trace the history of two powerful twentieth-century figures: the sharecropper, whose difference from the serf resides only in the extent to which his relationship with the land and his master is mediated by money; and our contemporary figure of ridicule, the wage-slave or the drone. Tom Joad or Willie Loman.

The universe that will produce both figures is the one in which Faulkner is writing. Part resignation, part prophecy, part critique, and containing his consciousness of his own place within the wider economic narrative, Faulkner's letter could not have been written ten years earlier. In that sense, it's a sort of Rosetta Stone for twentieth-century resignations.

But how you reject the system depends on which system you're rejecting. At almost the same time, on the other side of the world, one of Faulkner's contemporaries was asking to be counted out from a very different relationship of patronage and human capital – and taking his life in his hands as he did so.

Of all the bosses to assail with a righteously pissed-off letter of resignation, they don't get much bigger than Soviet leader Josef Stalin. Russian playwright and novelist Mikhail Bulgakov was a star of the Soviet Union. His play *Days of the Turbins* had been the talk of Moscow, with Stalin declaring himself a fan, and reportedly seeing it 15 times during its Moscow run. But by 1929, he had fallen foul of the censors. His plays were turned down for production, his novels shelved. Notionally free (like Havel) to do as he pleased, but never, on principle, to be performed or published, his sense of helplessness grew as he continued to produce works nobody would ever be allowed to read. Finally, having exhausted all options with his employers at the Cultural Department of the USSR, in July 1929 the blacklisted Bulgakov lost patience. From his apartment in Moscow, he wrote a personal letter of resignation to Stalin himself. Though he later claimed to have written the note in a fit of mental agony, never intending to post it, it nevertheless found its way into the mail. The writer was playing a dangerous game, and if posting his letter was a mistake, it was a potentially fatal one: Bulgakov had also copied in his managers at the department, blowing the whistle on the runaround he had received in having his works passed for publication or performance. The note ended with his resignation as a citizen, demanding his own deportation from the country of his birth, so that he could be a writer somewhere else if the Soviet Union couldn't use him.

For the attention of: The General Secretary of the Party, J. V. Stalin
cc: President of the Central Executive, M. I. Kalinin
cc: Head of the Cultural Department, A. I. Svidersky
cc: A.M. Gorky
From: Writer Mikhail Afanasyevich Bulgakov
(Moscow, B.Pirogovskaya
35/a, Qr 6, T.2-03-27)

This year it's going to be ten years since I started my literary enterprise in the USSR. Out of these ten years, I dedicated the last four to drama, writing four plays. Of them, three plays (*Days of Turbins, Zoya's Flat* and *Crimson Island*) were produced by the state theatres of Moscow, and the fourth one – *The Escape* – was accepted by Moscow Art Theatre for staging.

While the theatre was working on the play, it was banned.

Now I have heard there's a ban on staging of *The Days of Turbins*, and one on staging *The Crimson Island* too. *Zoya's Flat* was taken off after the 200th show last season, on the instructions of the authorities. So by the current theatrical season, all my plays appear to have been prohibited, including *The Days of Turbins*, which has completed 300 shows.

So, here's the situation up to this point: my novella *Notes on the Cuffs* is banned. The collection of satirical stories *Diaboloid* was banned from being reprinted. My collection of short sketches was denied publication. *Moves of Chichikov* was refused a permit to be staged. And the publication of the novel *The White Guard* in the journal *Russia* was nixed too, as the journal itself was banned.

While I was publishing my works, critics in the USSR paid more and more attention to me. Every single work of mine – be it fiction or drama – was deprived of even a single encouraging remark. In fact, the more my name became popular in the USSR and abroad, the more antagonistic the state press got towards me. Eventually their remarks turned into hysterical abuse.

All my works received monstrous, unfavourable criticism; mud was thrown on my name not only in the periodicals but also by such publications as *The Great Soviet Encyclopedia* and *The Literary Encyclopedia*. Helpless to defend myself, I requested permission to go abroad, even just for a short while.

My request was also rejected.

My works *The Days of Turbins* and *Zoya's Flat* were stolen and taken abroad. In Riga, one of the publishers wrote his own ending on my novel *The White Guards,* and published under my name a new book with an illiterate, nonsensical ending. They started plundering the prestige that was due to me abroad.

Then my wife Lyubov Evgeniya Bulgakova applied again for permission to go abroad alone for settling my financial affairs over there, while I offered to stay back as a hostage.

We were not allowed to do that.

Many times I have requested that my manuscripts be returned to me from SPU and either I was refused or I did not receive any answer to my applications.

I requested permission to send my play *The Run* abroad, in order to save it from theft beyond the boundaries of the USSR.

I was not allowed to do that.

By the end of this tenth year, my strength is overtaxed. I am unable to survive any longer. Banned, hounded, now knowing all too well that I shall no more be printed or staged in the USSR, driven towards a nervous breakdown, I have decided to approach YOU and request for your efforts to persuade the Government of the USSR to BANISH ME BEYOND THE BOUNDARIES OF THE USSR ALONG WITH MY WIFE L. E. BULGAKOVA, who joins me in this request.

M. Bulgakov

Moscow, July 1929

One can imagine how he felt after posting that. In his prose, Bulgakov acts out the way he keeps running into career brick walls; they knock his measured sentences back and back until he explodes into block-cap demands. And while Bulgakov in the letter does things you can visualize and for which he is accountable (applying for permissions, requesting manuscripts), he uses the passive voice for everything the authorities do ('All my works received monstrous criticism . . . mud was thrown . . . my request was rejected . . . we were not allowed . . . .'), so that they feel faceless, unaccountable and diffuse. The cumulative effect on the reader is an almost suffocating sense of powerlessness. This is not just a sign-off letter; it's a virtuoso performance in itself.

The letter – or seeing themselves cc'd on it – seems to have shocked his bosses. On 18 April Bulgakov was relaxing at his home when the telephone rang. Answering, he was told by an unfamiliar voice that a 'Comrade Stalin' was waiting to be put through. Shocked, Bulgakov answered that that was fine, and listened in silence as Stalin told him: 'We received your letter, I read it along with some comrades. You will get a proper answer to it . . . But is it true that you are requesting to be allowed to go abroad? What, have we pestered you so much? Where would you like to work? In the Art Theatre?' Bulgakov managed to squeak out a 'Yes.'

'Very well,' replied Stalin. 'Submit your application there.' Then he added, with a tone so friendly it must have been utterly chilling: 'I feel that they will agree.'

And indeed Bulgakov was offered a job at Moscow Art Theatre (something his party bosses had been considering anyway, they claimed – entirely coincidentally, of course). While his work continued to encounter censorship and censure – to the point where Bulgakov had to reconstruct his masterpiece, *The Master and Margarita*, from memory after torching the manuscript in a fit of impotent frustration – it is widely believed that this letter, and Stalin's intervention, prevented his arrest and possible assassination.

The letter also prefigures another accidental – or unwilling – dissident. The way Bulgakov went over the heads of his party-member bosses and appealed to their boss makes him a kind of prototype for 'Š', Václav Havel's blocked and frustrated brewer. Bulgakov and Š found themselves pushed into roles they never wanted; forced into reluctant rebellion by a rigid and unresponsive command structure. Today, they might work for private corporations, or government agencies and be called whistleblowers. But when the media and the authorities to whom you are forced to take your grievance are themselves your persecutors, the options are slim indeed.

Bulgakov was lucky. Unlike Š, he was famous. He had connections. But the sense that one is wasting one's time, buried alive somewhere deep in a structure that keeps one in a vegetative state, is not confined to totalitarian regimes.

By 1943, journalist Eric Blair, aka George Orwell, was working in a steady job broadcasting for the BBC India service. But on 24 September 1943, he resigned with a letter to the BBC's Eastern Editor, Laurence Rushbrook Williams, that opened with disarming candour, 'For some time past I have been conscious that I was wasting my own time and the public money on doing work that produces no result.' Thanking the BBC and his immediate bosses for the leeway and understanding they had shown him, he soon cut to the chase. The note is a concentrated dose of everything that makes Orwell's journalism, even his fiction, so powerful – namely, its refusal to manipulate. Spare and plain, it shrugs at sentimental patriotism in the same way Havel would refuse to engage with the language of totalitarianism. The crucial lines are devastating, even now. He calls the BBC's mission – the broadcasting of British propaganda to India – 'almost hopeless' and signs off:

> I myself prefer not to spend my time on them [broadcasts] when I could be occupying myself with journalism which does produce some measurable effect.

Earlier that month, civil disobedience had broken out in France, and wavering Italy had fallen to the Allies. Just a week before, the headlines had been full of the Salerno Mutiny, in which some 600 soldiers of the British Army's X Corps refused orders to join a new posting alongside the US Army in southern Italy.

And whether or not Orwell had that week's BBC reports in mind when he wrote this note, it's rich with the feeling that entropy had a hold of the British Empire; that whatever happened next could just as well happen as a result of people leaving, not joining, a cause. For Orwell that entropy plays as large a part in history as energy; resignations are every bit as good as rallies; and, in his case, carrying on with useless work is as political a life choice as, say, joining a revolution.

The sense in Orwell's resignation that history may be left to take care of itself as the forces that shape it simply run out of puff, is right at the heart of one of the most influential – yet least known – resignations of the twentieth century.

Vietnam veteran jet-pilot Captain Ron Keys resigned from the US Air Force with an epistolary flamethrower aimed at his commanding general in 1979. Keys had become increasingly disturbed by the way the USAF was going about its business. Like Bulgakov he later claimed that the letter was only written as part of an exercise, and was posted by accident, to his mortification. If that's true – if it was effectively a 'dear diary . . .' scrap, one of those notes you write on waking in the small hours to exorcise your worries – then the trapped, silent-scream quality in it is even more poignant.

To: General Wilbur Creech, commander in chief, US Tactical Air Command.
From: Captain Ron Keys

Dear Boss,

Well, I quit. I've finally run out of drive or devotion or rationalizations or whatever it was that kept me in the Air Force this long . . .

I've been on temporary duty to every dirty little outpost on democracy's frontier that had a 6,000-foot strip. I've been gone longer than most young jocks have been in – and I don't mind the duty or the hours. That's what I signed up for. I've been downtown and seen the elephant, and I've watched my buddies roll up in fireballs – I understand – it comes with the territory. I can do it. I did it. I can *still* do it – but I won't. I'm too tired, not of the job, just the Air Force.

Tired of the extremely poor leadership and motivational ability of our senior staffers and commanders. (All those Masters and professional military educators and not a leadership trait in sight!)

[. . .] We have a fighter pilot shortfall – didn't you hear? So now we have lower quality people with motivation problems, and the commander won't allow anyone to jettison them.

If you haven't noticed, that leaves us with a lot of people in fighters, but very few fighter pilots [. . .] Result: most operational squadrons aren't worth a damn. They die wholesale every time the Aggressors deploy – anybody keep score? Anybody care?

Certainly not the whiz kid commander, who blew in from 6 years in staff, picked up 100 hours in the bird, and was last seen checking the grass in the sidewalk cracks. He told his boys, 'Don't talk to me about tactics – my only concern is not losing an aircraft . . . and meanwhile, get the grass out of the sidewalk cracks!' – and the clincher – integrity. Hide as much as you can . . . particularly from the higher headquarters that could help you if only they knew. They never will though – staff will see to that: 'Don't say that to the general!' or 'The general doesn't like to hear that.' I didn't know he was paid to *like* things – I thought he was paid to run things . . . how can he when he never hears the problems? Ah well, put it off until it becomes a crisis – maybe it will be overcome by events. Maybe if we ignore it, it won't be a problem. (Shh, don't rock the boat). [. . .] I listened to a three-star general look a room full of us in the face and say that he 'Didn't realize that pencil-whipping records was done in the Air Force[. . .] It was embarrassing – that general looked us in the eye and said, in effect, 'Gentlemen, either I'm very stupid or I'm lying to you.'

I about threw in the towel right there – or the day TAC fixed the experience ratio problem by lowering the number of hours needed to be experienced [. . .]

And that's why I'm resigning. Long hours with little support, entitlements eroded, integrity a mockery, zero visible career progression, and senior commanders evidently totally missing the point (and everyone afraid or forbidden to inform them.) I've had it – life's too short to fight an uphill battle for commanders and staffs who won't listen (remember Corona Ace?) or don't believe or maybe don't even care.

So thanks for the memories, it's been a real slice of life . . . But I've been to the mountain and looked over and I've seen the big picture – and it wasn't of the Air Force.

But it was read, and went what today we would call viral. It quickly became famous within the American military, inspiring a rash of copycat resignations that soon became an air-force convention of operational critiques known as 'Dear Boss notes'. These letters, written by frustrated, angry, soon-to-be-ex-servicemen across the American armed forces, lift the 1979 original, often down to opening paragraph and structure, while just slotting in new examples of incompetence and institutional failure, as if they were filling in the blanks on an Air Force test form. It's an odd tradition, and there's an 'I am Spartacus' quality about the way they invoke the original as they add their own critique. Yet despite the way they just add new, personal touches to the template letter, they can be savage, moving and very funny – occasionally by accident. One

2009 USAF Dear Boss note sounded positively divaesque: 'Since I first put on a uniform, we're on our third Air Force emblem, third different flight suit, second battle dress uniform (third if you include the Velcro nametag debacle).'

Keys' letter, the 1979 resignation that spawned them all, is long. There's a fair bit of airman-speak in it. But at its core is a dazed, disgusted litany of everyday madness. Its surreal roll-call of high-command illogic conjures up some inkling of what Joseph Heller's novel *Catch-22* would have been like had it been written by Tom Cruise's character in *Top Gun*.

There are so many great lines in the full letter, worthy of a great screenplay, or one of those surreal, amphetamine-fuelled Dylan songs from the 1960s: 'Either I'm very stupid or I'm lying to you'; 'I'm too tired, not of the job, just the Air Force'; 'I didn't know the General was paid to like things'; 'A lot of people in fighters, but very few fighter pilots.'

Part of what makes these lines jump off the page – part of what makes the letter read so much like a screenplay – is the way Keys brings such a host of different voices in, mimicking so many different characters as he writes. Try reading it out loud, and pretty soon you're play-acting the whole motley company of Air Force characters as they wind Keys up and bear the brunt of his ripostes. This is a one-man fringe production; a Punch & Judy show of blockers, fools, yes-men and incompetents. In this at least, it is the antithesis of Bulgakov's note. Authority isn't grey and faceless here: it's vivid, grotesque and infuriatingly proud of itself.

And stuck in the middle of all these clowns and jesters is Keys, the hard-bitten pilot with his exasperated, rhetorical questions, his answers bursting into shouts, and his obsessive, circling variations on 'I've had enough and I quit.'

For those with the ears to listen as the Cold War entered its lurching, punch-drunk finale, Keys' letter should also have sounded a warning. Even this short quotation is littered with the despairing cries of someone who knows he's howling into the void. 'Anybody care?', 'Didn't you hear?' 'In case you haven't heard' – Of course, nobody in command hears, or knows, or seems to care, because everybody is too afraid to speak out. In the wake of the Edward Snowden and Private Manning cases, anyone doubting the motives and methods of whistleblowers in the armed forces should read Keys' 'Dear Boss' letter in full, and ask why the tradition it established took hold so readily. These are letters to nobody; whistles blown in a void, by airmen who have no recourse but to speak out and walk away. I quit. I've had enough. I'm resigning. Here's why.

But life is never quite that simple.

As it happened, the whistle was heard. General Creech saw the letter. Keys was duly summoned and consulted. Big changes to operational procedure were made. Keys went on to a distinguished career, rising as high as the man to whom he had addressed his letter 'Dear Boss'.

There is a final twist to the story. Had Keys known how he would eventually leave the Air Force, he might have gone through with his initial resignation. General Ronald Ellis Keys retired in 2007 after the 'USAF nuclear weapons incident', in which six live nuclear bombs went missing for thirty-six hours. It transpired that Keys' men had unwittingly flown six nuclear warheads from North Dakota to Louisiana without authorization – or even knowing what they were.

Quite by accident, America – and the world – was arguably closer to a full-scale thermonuclear event than at any time in its history, and the man whose 1979 letter had nailed the operational incompetence of the Air Force's top brass was the officer in command. It's funny how life works out.

But the template was established. The blast of the truth bomb must be heard to ensure maximum effect. And no one was watching more closely than Grenada-born, LSE-educated economist Davidson L. Budhoo.

Budhoo had been a senior staffer at the International Monetary Fund (IMF) for twelve years when he resigned with his own 'Dear Boss' letter to its managing director Michel Camdessus in May 1988. Budhoo's contention was that the IMF, which supposedly existed to alleviate poverty, had been overtaken by a secret agenda to convert all countries to freewheeling capitalism, and Budhoo claimed that its economists had committed statistical fraud in Trinidad and Tobago – at massive human cost – to achieve that aim. It is full of the late twentieth century's unease, and the sense that by sticking with a job, you are propping up the system. It is the feeling, born of the world wars, the Nuremberg trials, the Civil Rights struggle, that not to object is to be an accomplice. And by that logic, resignation and revolt are indeed one and the same.

Dear Mr Camdessus,
    Today I resigned from the staff of the International

Monetary Fund after over 12 years, and after 1000 days of official fund work in the field, hawking your medicine and your bag of tricks to governments and to peoples in Latin America and the Caribbean and Africa. To me, resignation is a priceless liberation, for with it I have taken the first big step to that place where I may hope to wash my hands of what in my mind's eye is the blood of millions of poor and starving peoples. Mr Camdessus, the blood is so much, you know, it runs in rivers. It dries up too; it cakes all over me; sometimes I feel that there is not enough soap in the whole world to cleanse me from the things that I did do in your name and in the name of your predecessors, and under your official seal.

It's a heck of a landing for a resignation – the equivalent of starting a movie with an almighty explosion – and you can almost feel the blood draining from the faces of Camdessus and the other IMF staffers. His full letter – a list of charges stretching to over 100 pages – detailed that fraud. But the way in which he set out his position became a sort of resigner's charter. Though it was effectively buried by the IMF publicity machine – whose briefings against Budhoo smothered press coverage – it set the blueprint, inspiring everyone from communist-bloc rebel movements to successive waves of IMF refuseniks and Naomi Klein.

But I can hope, can't I? Certainly I can hope. I can hope there is compassion and indignation in the heart of my world, and that people can stand up and take notice of what I have to say, and listen to your reply. For you will have to reply, because the charges that I make are not light charges – they are charges that touch at the very heart of western society and western morality and post-war inter-governmental institutionalism that have degenerated into take and sham under the pretext of establishing and maintaining international economic order and global efficiency.

[. . .] Will the world be content merely to brand our institution as among the most insidious enemies of humankind? Will our fellowmen condemn us thus and let the matter rest? Or will the heirs of those whom we have dismembered in our own peculiar Holocaust clamor for another Nuremberg?

I don't mind telling you that this matter has haunted me; it has haunted me particularly over the past five years. It has haunted me because I know that if I am tried I will be found guilty, very guilty, without extenuating circumstance.

But beyond the question of guilt, there is a far more operational matter that bothers me; it is this: what devil is there in us that will allow us to go this far into a shame and an ignominy without screaming out a protest as human beings and as men of conscience? How could we have allowed ourselves for so long to defend the indefensible?

When I ask myself that question I become disoriented. I become disoriented because I cannot cope with the consequences of the answer that I know will surface one day.

Even as Budhoo's letter goes on to list increasingly specific charges of corruption and malfeasance against the IMF, it remains hugely theatrical – in parts, its purple prose sounds almost camp. But its power is in its high rhetoric. Like Ron Keys' letter, Budhoo's is uncontrolled, verging on a stream of consciousness. He voices questions to himself; imagines a clamour of voices trying to shut him up as he speaks. But he won't shut up. This isn't unadorned truth spoken clinically, but a personal crisis of conscience – a breakdown on paper. Something that's been kept quiet for way too long.

But rather than just deliver it to his boss, copying it to others, or even sending it to a newspaper, Budhoo went the whole hog. He published the entire letter as a book, and delivered it, bound and printed. It's clear that it was theatrical because Budhoo wanted it to be: this was whistleblowing as public theatre. By 1996, it had become a play: *Mr. Budhoo's Letter of Resignation from the IMF (50 Years Is Enough)* had its off-Broadway run in New York's East Village, receiving a glowing notice in the *New York Times*. Perhaps the intervening years and the Cold War's end had changed the context enough for Budhoo's message to become palatable: as Naomi Klein notes drily in *The Shock Doctrine*, 'The short theater review was the only time Budhoo's name was ever mentioned in the *New York Times*.'

In retrospect, it's not surprising that Budhoo's original blast against free market expansionism fell on deaf ears here in the West. After all, this was the moment the Soviet Union began to collapse – perestroika was introduced in January 1987, and candlelit protests were breaking out across the Eastern Bloc. 'We' were the good guys, and 'we' were winning. This was no time for a malcontent to piss into the tent.

In fact, things were rather less peachy than they might have looked on this side of the Iron Curtain too. The US deficit was at an all-time high, and both sides' sudden realization that they needed to save cash was already sweeping away the entire global system of puppet-states

– patronized by both capitalism and communism – into which the IMF had been co-opted.

In May 1988, the very month Budhoo wrote his letter, the USSR withdrew from Afghanistan; meanwhile, the Iran-Contra affair (in which the US secretly sold arms to Iran in the hope of funding anti-communist Contra rebels in Nicaragua) was publicly unpicking confidence in the way America policed world conflict and world trade. UN Secretary General Kurt Waldheim had just been exposed as a former Nazi. The public sense of disillusionment was high. Budhoo wasn't a lone prophet or a maverick: he was another canary in the coal mine.

More cracks began to appear as both East and West started to doubt the icons of their faith. Publicly, the US Army had made a commitment that every effort would be made to find and repatriate the estimated 2,000 American servicemen still missing, *Deer Hunter*-style, in the jungles of Vietnam. The US government had secured the return of 591 POWs in 1973, as part of a peace accord, but amid the news that 83% of US service personnel strongly believed comrades were still imprisoned in the jungles, the government set up a dedicated office – POW-MIA – to continue to search for more. But anything more than rumour proved agonizingly difficult to establish. Soon, veterans' publications began printing long-standing rumours of a cover-up. The Government knew full well that soldiers were still prisoners in Vietnam, went the theory. But POW-MIA was a fig leaf – a dummy organization, set up to make it look like they were trying to bring them back and save their embarrassment. In reality, it said, politicians had no intention of pressing the Vietnamese for anything, for fear of destabilizing the region – and the country's communist backers, China – again. As the years went by, and even the cold war that had mapped out the north-south Vietnam split ended, first pressure groups, then servicemen, then departmental insiders began to doubt the Army's efforts – or that missing POWs were really President Bush's 'highest national priority' after all.

Still, Colonel Millard 'Mike' Peck felt he could change things. A highly decorated veteran of over 20 years' army service, he'd heard the rumours – the negativity whenever anyone in his old unit mentioned POW-MIA. But he was a committed, tenacious and persuasive man. He worked hard as head of the US Army's search operation. Then, after only eight months in the job, on the freezing morning of February 12, 1991, Colonel Peck stopped hammering at the typewriter in his Washington, DC office, and sat back. He plucked the last piece of paper from the machine, fastened it to four completed pages. With a bit of work, he found that large tacks could fix the letter to his door like a sign. With a few jolts of the stapler, it was done. Then, still in uniform, he walked out of the building, never to return. This is the note he left behind.

DATE: 12 FEB 1991
ATTN: POW-MIA
SUBJECT: Request for Relief
TO: DR

As a Vietnam veteran with a certain amount of experience in Indochina, I was interested in the entire POW-MIA question, and willingly volunteered for the job, viewing it as sort of a holy crusade . . . My plan was to be totally honest and forthcoming on the entire issue and aggressively pursue innovative actions and concepts to clear up the live sighting business, thereby refurbishing the image and honor of DIA. I became painfully aware, however, that I was not really in charge of my own office, but was merely a figurehead or whipping boy for a larger and totally Machiavellian group of players outside of DIA . . .

What I witnessed during my tenure as the cardboard cut-out 'Chief' of POW-MIA could be euphemistically labelled as disillusioning . . . That National leaders continue to address the prisoner of war and missing in action issue as the 'highest national priority' is a travesty. From my vantage point, I observed that the principal government players were interested primarily in conducting a 'damage limitation exercise', and appeared to knowingly and deliberately generate an endless succession of manufactured crises and 'busy work' . . .

The mindset to 'debunk' is alive and well . . . Practically all analysis is directed to finding fault with the source. Rarely has there been any effective, active follow through on any of the sightings, nor is there a responsive 'action arm' to routinely and aggressively pursue leads . . . The sad fact, however, is that this issue is being controlled and a cover-up may be in progress. The entire charade does not appear to be an honest effort, and may never have been . . .

I feel strongly that this issue is being manipulated and controlled at a higher level, not with the goal of resolving it, but more to obfuscate the question of live prisoners, and give the illusion of progress through hyperactivity . . . From what I have witnessed, it appears that any soldier left in Vietnam, even inadvertently, was, in fact, abandoned years ago, and that the farce that is being played is no more than political legerdemain done with 'smoke and mirrors', to stall the issue until it dies a natural death . . . For all of the above, I respectfully request to be relieved of my duties as Chief of the Special Office for Prisoners of War and Missing in Action . . . So as to avoid the annoyance of being shipped off to some remote corner, out of sight and out of the way, in my own 'bamboo cage' of silence somewhere, I further request that the Defense Intelligence Agency, which I have attempted to serve loyally and with honor, assist me in being retired immediately from active military service.

MILLARD A. PECK
Colonel, Infantry

Peck's memo caused a national sensation. Though he would later tell a closed Congress hearing that he had never envisaged his resignation going quite so public, the 'Peck Memorandum' was timed with devastating precision, as the First Gulf War raged and the American public grew concerned about the possible capture of US soldiers.

Peck's note may be a cry of anguish like Budhoo's and Key's, but as a piece of drama it is far more carefully scripted – and by a man clearly used to putting in concise, persuasive bulletins. The full memo was divided into 20 discrete paragraphs, each with its own chapter heading: Cover-Up; The Crusade; The Harsh Reality; The Stalled Crusade; Everyone Is Expendable; Smoke And Mirrors; High-Level Knavery; One Final Vietnam Casualty; A Farewell To Arms. They even begin to sound like the 20 episode titles of a TV thriller series – *The X-Files* or *The Fugitive*, perhaps. And like a drama, the letter builds with a strange and irresistible momentum through its five acts, from scene-setting through nagging suspicion and demotivation, to intimations of something genuinely sinister, the big reveal, and escape.

The full memo is an oddly unsettling read too, even more than Budhoo's: Peck's letter plays the same games of suspense and reveal with the reader. From taking a job that 'appears' challenging to the beginning of the 'charade', Peck creates an atmosphere of all-encompassing doubt worthy of Alfred Hitchcock. Like the Department, his memo becomes its own terrifyingly inscrutable game of smoke and mirrors. Nothing is what it seems. The government's commitment to MIA soldiers? A deception. The Director of the National League of Families? 'One wonders who she really is and where she came from'.

When Peck finally begins to talk cover-ups and conspiracies, the letter itself has prepared us, and we go with him. And when he uses the metaphor of the Viet Cong bamboo cage, it doesn't feel like a metaphor at all . . . at least not now in 2014, as US military and intel whistleblowers suffer in their own greater or lesser bamboo cages.

This departure, following those of Keys and Budhoo, reads like the third act in the Cold War's end. He even provides the era's best epitaph – though he was talking about the MIA effort in Vietnam, it's tempting to think his eyes were on the present – with a paragraph called 'The Stalled Crusade'.

The backdrop to his resignation provides clues. While the newly post-communist East recoiled at the slow-drip revelations of what its state security could do to citizens at home, there was a similarly chilling trickle in the West. Only this one was largely focused on the sleaze and mendacity surrounding Western diplomacy and corporatism abroad.

Brand West was as complex and mendacious as Key's Budhoo and Peck had warned.

It is no coincidence that, after maintaining a roughly two-year cycle since 1961, the James Bond franchise lay low from 1989 all the way through to 1995, as public appetite for flag-waving foreign policy propaganda hit an all-time low. From the shades of grey of *The X-Files* to the ironies of Schwarzenegger's *True Lies* and *The Last Action Hero*, military and intelligence heroes were compromised and complex in a way they hadn't been since the countercultural depictions of the 1960s; without the black-and-white of Communism, the confusion of Somalia and the Balkans showed Western foreign policy itself had turned postmodern. In the words of Fox Mulder, 'Trust no one.' Released into this sudden climate of suspicion, self-doubt and insecurity, Peck's memo supplied its very own cast of 'Smoking Man' style suspects.

'Many of the puppet masters play a confusing, murky roles,' he wrote.

> For instance, the Director of the National League of Families [of American Prisoners and Missing In South East Asia] occupies an interesting and questionable position in the whole process. [She] actively sabotages POW-MIA analyses or investigations . . . She apparently has access to top secret, codeword message traffic, for which she is supposedly not cleared, and she received it well ahead of the DIA intelligence

analysts . . . One wonders who she really is and where she came from.

Peck's memo seemed to prove everything that any shade of the American political spectrum wanted it to prove: from the fecklessness of government in the run-up to George Bush Sr's presidential re-election push, to an untrustworthy military and the cheapness of a soldier's life, or the need for greater punishment for leaks.

While the accusations against the NLF's Director were rebutted as 'ludicrous', the Pentagon opened an investigation. Peck was called upon to testify to the senate by Republicans convinced that the Bush administration was party to a cover-up.

Partly, the memo was incendiary because so much of its content *felt* true, rather than because it was. Soldiers – especially those in a failed war – do conveniently slip down the agendas of approval-hungry administrations. The military is a Leviathan. Governments do break promises. We want to believe.

US government officials blamed the Vietnamese for the uncanny 'smoke and mirrors' feeling around the hunt for MIA servicemen. The longing by families for leads on their missing sons, they pointed out to the *New York Times*, 'spawned a number of scams by unscrupulous Vietnamese, including an odious trade in human bones and offers to provide help in locating servicemen in return for sponsorship for permanent residency in the United States.'

By any reckoning, Peck's resignation worked in generating the shakedown, the transparency and the popular awareness he felt was needed. His ability to focus on deeper truth, whatever the petty circumstances, is the difference between an easily dismissed rant and something genuinely, powerful. It's where the resignation statement can rise out of its specifics, and become a manifesto. A rallying cry. Even art, in a way.

Mark Schlueb left the US *Akron Beacon Journal* newspaper in March 2001. Schlueb was getting his retaliation in early: he had heard, along with a number of others, that he was in the frame to be let go. On his way out of the door, he dashed off this personal email to his employer, newspaper magnate and Knight Ridder publishing CEO Tony Ridder.

Dear Mr Ridder,

I wanted to write and tell you what a fine time I've had working for the *Akron Beacon Journal*. (That's a newspaper your company owns in Northeast Ohio.) I've only worked here since last June, but I've had an opportunity to uncover plenty of great stories, and put them into what I consider the best newspaper in Ohio. (Ohio is a state in the Midwest.) All the while, I've been able to work with the most talented group of writers and reporters with whom I've ever had the privilege to associate. It's been very inspiring – in fact, my desk is only about 20 feet from John S. Knight's old typewriter, which is now kept behind glass.

Of course, you're cutting these fine people off at the knees, you asshole. How do you expect the dedicated and loyal reporters at the *Beacon Journal* to keep putting out a quality paper when you're eliminating nearly a quarter of the reporting staff? You faceless corporate hacks take a break from your golf game long enough to scream that circulation must stay up, but then you order arbitrary budget cuts that force the elimination of entire sections of the Sunday paper. And when that's not enough, you order layoffs that eliminate the very employees who have helped keep circulation from falling. Seriously, the kid who changes the oil in my car could run Knight Ridder with more foresight than you.

I brought my wife and two children to Akron – a thousand miles from our native Florida, where I had a secure job and other offers – to work at the *Beacon Journal*. The editors here were able to attract me with the excellent reputation they and John S. Knight had built over a period of decades. In just a few months, you've managed to wreck everything they built. How many top-notch reporters will choose to move to Akron, if they would face the prospect of working at an understaffed, demoralized newspaper?

Maybe I should have seen this coming. After all, it wasn't that long ago that Knight Ridder budget cuts gutted the *Miami Herald*. Remember what happened then? There was a mass exodus of talented reporters, and the *Herald* is a shadow of its former self.

Don't worry about me; I'll land on my feet. I don't regret coming here, even though I've been laid off now.

In fact, my only regret is that you haven't come to visit the *Beacon Journal*. I would have loved to piss on your shoes.

Schlueb has you from the outset – specifically, the hilarious, lethal parentheses. Those mock-helpful explanations alone speak more elegantly of Schlueb's (and all of our) perceptions of out-of-touch bosses and absentee boards than the whole catalogue of corporate failings he then lays at Ridder's door.

But there's more to Schlueb's attacks than most. This is

a letter you can feel coming alive as it's hammered out: you can feel the change as Schlueb's letter starts to tell *him* what it wants to say. That first paragraph is the sound of Schlueb trying to bend rapier wit and sarcasm to his purpose; to maintain a sense of poise and dignity for the last ten minutes of his employ. But the letter has other ideas.

The line that opens the second paragraph – 'Of course you're cutting these people off at the knees, you asshole' – is an almost ecstatic surrender to the more immediate joys of anger and contempt. And it's the little things that yield the richest rewards: the weighted, almost chatty pause in 'Of course', for example, is the pull-back for the punch that makes the whole letter work. It keeps things cold and urbane, where a lesser writer would have descended into impotent rage.

Still, it's the final line that always gets quoted. Of course it does: it's magnificent. It's such an unanswerable explosion, a final splatter of disgust – it somehow manages to enact the thing it describes. But what lifts this resignation from angry blast to virtuoso performance is its sense of well-intentioned exasperation. Schlueb feels like one of those *Twilight Zone* characters who sees the future, tries to warn people what's coming, then throws up their hands as the world refuses to listen.

(It also recalls the wonderful resignation note that editor N. Ravi sent to his board on the *Hindu* newspaper in India: 'A combination of megalomania and a crass disregard of the values that *The Hindu* has always stood for has brought the institution to this sorry state. It is shocking that some of the board members should want to run a media institution like a company producing plastic buckets.')

These days, Mark Schlueb is genuinely baffled at how a note fired off so quickly and with so little thought all those years ago could have achieved such lasting fame. In the immediate aftermath, he made a fair point that no blue-collar worker's resignation would be passed around quite so much by a media establishment that often seems to notice news about itself most of all. Today, he says he doesn't regret writing the letter, but does regret its lasting fame: 'now, 12 years later, when you Google my name, despite the hundreds (thousands?) of news stories I've written, that letter is the fourth link. So I've been trying to put it in the rearview.'

Unsurprisingly, Schlueb landed on his feet as he predicted – imagine any editor-in-chief turning down a journalist who writes like that – as a senior reporter for the *Orlando Sentinel*. In 2005, acclaimed investigative reporter Laurie Garrett left US paper *Newsday* with a 1,500-word blast. Addressed to her colleagues, the radius was higher, and wider. Today, it reads like a visit from the Ghost of Crisis Meetings Yet To Come.

'You have been through so much pain and difficulty over the last year, all of which I monitored closely and with considerable concern, that I don't want to disappear from the *Newsday* scene without saying a few words. Indulge me.

Ever since the Chandler Family plucked Mark Willes from General Foods, placing him at the helm of Times Mirror with a mandate to destroy the institutions in ways that would boost dividends, journalism has suffered at *Newsday*. The pain of the last year actually began a decade ago: the sad arc of greed has finally hit bottom. The leaders of Times Mirror and Tribune have proven to be mirrors of a general trend in the media world: They serve their stockholders first, Wall St. second and somewhere far down the list comes service to newspaper readerships. In 1996, I personally confronted Willes on that point, and he publicly confirmed that the new regime was one in which even the number of newspapers sold was irrelevant, so long as stock returns continued to rise.

The deterioration we experienced at *Newsday* was hardly unique. All across America news organizations have been devoured by massive corporations, and allegiance to stockholders, the drive for higher share prices, and push for larger dividend returns trumps everything that the grunts in the newsrooms consider their missions. Long gone are the days of fast-talking, whiskey-swilling Murray Kempton peers eloquently filling columns with daily dish on government scandals, mobsters and police corruption.

The sort of in-your-face challenge that the Fourth Estate once posed for politicians has been replaced by mud-slinging, lies and, where it ought not be, timidity. When I started out in journalism the newsrooms were still full of old guys with blue collar backgrounds who got genuinely indignant when the Governor lied or somebody turned off the heat on a poor person's apartment in mid-January. They cussed and yelled their ways through the day, took an occasional sly snort from a bottle in the bottom drawer of their desk and bit into news stories like packs of wild dogs, never letting go until they'd found and told the truth. If they hadn't been reporters most of those guys would have been cops or firefighters. It was just that way.

Now the blue collar has been fully replaced by white ones

in America's newsrooms, everybody has college degrees. The *His Girl Friday* romance of the newshound is gone. All too many journalists seem to mistake scandal mongering for tenacious investigation, and far too many aspire to make themselves the story. When I think back to the old fellows who were retiring when I first arrived at *Newsday* – guys (almost all of them were guys) who had cop brothers and fathers working union jobs – I suspect most of them would be disgusted by what passes today for journalism. Theirs was not a perfect world – too white, too male, seen through a haze of cigarette smoke and Scotch – but it was an honest one rooted in mid-20th century American working class values.

Honesty and tenacity (and for that matter, the working class) seem to have taken backseats to the sort of 'snappy news', sensationalism, scandal-for-the-sake of scandal crap that sells. This is not a uniquely Tribune or even newspaper industry problem: this is true from the Atlanta mixing rooms of CNN to Sulzberger's offices in Times Square. Profits: that's what it's all about now. But you just can't realize annual profit returns of more than 30 percent by methodically laying out the truth in a dignified, accessible manner. And it's damned tough to find that truth every day with a mere skeleton crew of reporters and editors.

This is terrible for democracy. I have been in 47 states of the USA since 9/11, and I can attest to the horrible impact the deterioration of journalism has had on the national psyche. I have found America a place of great and confused fearfulness, in which cynically placed bits of misinformation (*eg:* Cheney's 'If John Kerry had been President during the Cold War we would have had thermonuclear war.') fall on ears that absorb all, without filtration or fact-checking.

Leading journalists have tried to defend their mission, pointing to the paucity of accurate, edited coverage found in blogs, internet sites, Fox TV and talk radio. They argue that good old-fashioned newspaper editing is the key to providing America with credible information, forming the basis for wise voting and enlightened governance. But their claims have been undermined by Jayson Blair's blatant fabrications, Judy Miller's bogus weapons of mass destruction coverage, the media's inaccurate and inappropriate convictions of Wen Ho Lee, Richard Jewell and Steven Hatfill, CBS's failure to smell a con job regarding Bush's Texas Air Guard career and, sadly, so on.

What does it mean when even journalists consider comedian Jon 'This is a fake news show, people!' Stewart one of the most reliable sources of 'news'?

It would be easy to descend into despair, not only about the state of journalism, but the future of American democracy. But giving up is not an option. There is too much at stake.

I would remind my *Newsday* colleagues that during the bleak period that commenced with the appointment of Willes, and persists today, some great journalism has been done at the paper. A tiny, dedicated team of foreign correspondents has literally risked their lives to bring readers fresh, often ground-breaking news from the battlefields of Iraq, Afghanistan and the Middle East. *Newsday* readers are on top of details about the sorry state of fiscal governance in Nassau County, scandals in Suffolk County, Bloomberg's plans for the west side of Manhattan, and the sad state of politics in Albany. We still have some of the best film and performing arts criticism in the country, an aggressive photo department, tough sports columnists, under-utilized specialty and investigative reporters and a savvy business section.

So what is to be done?

I have no idea what Tribune corporate leaders in Chicago have up their sleeves for *Newsday*, the *LA Times*, *Baltimore Sun*, *Chicago Tribune* and the other media outlets under their control. Despite rumors that are rife in the newsrooms, you are also in the dark. And you should remember that. During times of hardship as extreme as those we have experienced at *Newsday* it is easy to become paralyzed by rumors, unable to think clearly about the work at hand. After all, people have lost their jobs, and some were removed from the building by armed guards, with only moments' notice. Every *Newsday* employee is justified in his or her concern about just how lean Chicago plans to make the newspaper machine.

But rumors only feed fear, and personal fear is rarely stimulus for good journalism. Now is the time to think in imaginative ways. *Salon* and *Slate* have both gone into the black; in nations like Ukraine and South Africa courageous new forms of journalism are arising; some of the blogs that clog the internet are actually quite good and manage to keep politicians on their toes. Opportunities for quality journalism are still there, though you may need to scratch new surfaces, open locked doors and nudge a few reticent editors to find them. On a fundamental level, your readers desperately need for you to try, over and over again, to tell the stories, dig the dirt and bring them the news.

Les Payne has often correctly pointed out that *Newsday*'s problems have never been rooted in the institution's journalism: Rather, they have been business issues. We have never been accused of fostering a Jayson Blair, a bozo who accepted $250,000 from the Bush Administration to write flattering stories, an investigative reporting team that relied on a single source for a series that smeared the life of an innocent man, acted as a conduit for the Department of Defense for weapons of mass destruction disinformation, or any of the other ghastly violations of the public trust that have recently transpired. *Newsday*'s honor has, by its own accounts, been besmirched by a series of lies committed on the business/advertising/circulation side of the company. (And few news organizations have covered on its pages their own shortcomings as closely as has *Newsday*.)

All of us have been forced to pay a price for those grievous actions. But nobody has charged that *Newsday*'s journalistic enterprise has failed to abide by the highest ethical standards.

Newsday has always had more talent than it knew how to use. So go ahead, Talent: Show them your stuff. I'll be reading.

This is a whistle blown not just for an organization, but for an industry, even a society – resignation as dissidence on a grand scale.

Garrett draws a clear line from what's happening in the *Newsday* office all the way to the future of democracy itself – via a meditation on the submission and disappearance of the working class, the collusion of Big Money and Government, and the title of Lenin's 1902 manifesto for revolution, *What Is To Be Done?* Faulkner would have been proud.

Like all great resignations, Garrett's is a potted history of its time, milieu and society, from someone free enough to speak, critical enough to see, and informed enough to hit home.

Garrett also mentions the Bush administration's manipulation of the news agenda. She calls out the White House, Jayson Blair and more by name. But post-9/11, collusion of news industry and government had become, simply, the way things got done. Corporate structures were playing henchman to state power over the individual once more; Havel's figure of the 'watcher', the workplace spy and propagandist, had been outsourced to Big Media. One wonders what Laurie Garrett would make of Silicon Valley's recent work for the NSA.

The revolving door between administration and private sector means that while some resignations speak truth to power, others are more ambivalent. Revealing a recent close call with cyber-Armageddon that the White House had apparently sought to keep low-profile, this 2003 office memo from Richard Clarke, George W. Bush's Special Advisor on Cybersecurity, was sent out to all Administration department heads. It was leaked online almost immediately.

With the completion of the National Strategy to Secure Cyberspace and the stand up of the Department of Homeland Security, it is a good juncture for me to end my 11 years in the White House . . .

The events of the last weekend demonstrate yet again how vulnerable our society is to cyberspace attacks.

The Sapphire Worm was essentially a dumb worm that was easily and cheaply made . . . Nonetheless, the results of the worm were significant.

It spread to hundreds of thousands of machines in less than 15 minutes. It disabled some root servers, the heart of internet traffic. Although it was aimed at servers, it caused routers to flop and cease to function. Some airline flights were delayed or cancelled. Some banking functions ceased. A national election/referendum in Canada was canceled. Workers were sent home at some major US companies.

With slight modifications, the results of the worm would have been more significant. More sophisticated attacks against known vulnerabilities in cyberspace could be devastating.

As long as we have vulnerabilities in cyberspace and as long as America has enemies, we are at risk of the two coming together to severely damage our great country . . .

I have enjoyed working with you to raise awareness about terrorism and more recently about cyberspace security. Thirty years after beginning federal service, I hope now to learn how to contribute to these issues as a private citizen.

This is where those deeper truths become clear and present dangers, and where the resignation becomes an overt call for action: departure as manifesto for change. Or perhaps as future lobbyist's speculative business card. Every resignation dramatizes something. But where the likes of Ron Keys and Mike Peck set scenes and told stories, Clarke's world turns on faster cycles. There is no time for stories, just copy – ready to paste straight into the morning editions. Clarke's letter reads like an editorial column – even down to the sweeping, editorial 'we': shorthand for the ready-made constituency of readers. Indeed, Clarke himself disappears after the opening lines, as his resignation assumes a newspaper's state-of-the-nation op-ed tone.

His theme, of course, is the favoured theme of cyber security professionals everywhere: that it's scary out there, and that people should spend more time and money on cyber security. (He once famously said, 'If you spend more on coffee than on cybersecurity, you'll be hacked; what's more, you'll deserve to be hacked.'

'Accidental' wider circulation is a theme of the truth attack. Like Bulgakov and Keys, Clarke claimed never to have intended for his resignation to connect as it did. Ostensibly written to colleagues anxious to secure budget share, it argues a point only worth making to outsiders. Perhaps the puzzle as to how the letter 'leaked' so swiftly isn't that hard to solve after all. To no one's surprise, having announced his resignation with a high-profile letter to policymakers about the need for more cyber security, he segued into a position as a corporate risk analyst.

But resignations as press events, orchestrated through leaks and advance briefings, aren't just a government ploy. They're increasingly popular amid boardroom disputes, too.

After increasing levels of disagreement and acrimony among the Disney board, Walt Disney's heir Roy Edward Disney resigned from the company in 2003 with a letter to then-chairman Michael Eisner, which he released simultaneously to the press for them to print wholesale. It contained more spectacular fireworks than the company brochure. Though I should point out that by including his letter, I make no suggestion that any of his charges had merit.

Like so many truth bombs, underlying it was the feeling that his voice was being silenced; that no one was listening. Roy Disney started with this – effectively justifying his decision to go public and go explosive.

> For whatever reason, you have driven a wedge between me and those I work with even to the extent of requiring some of my associates to report my conversations and activities back to you. I find this intolerable.
>
> Finally, you discussed with the Nominating Committee of the Board of Directors its decision to leave my name off the slate of directors to be elected in the coming year, effectively muzzling my voice on the board.

He then cut to the meat, with a list of seven points that make devastating reading even today.

> [This] Company, under your leadership has failed during the last seven years in many ways:
>
> 1. The failure to bring back ABC Prime Time from the ratings abyss it has been in for years and your inability to program successfully the ABC Family Channel. Both of these failures have had, and I believe will continue to have, significant adverse impact on shareholder value.
>
> 2. Your consistent micro-management of everyone around you with the resulting loss of morale throughout the Company.
>
> 3. The timidity of your investments in our theme park business. At Disney's California Adventure, Paris and now in Hong Kong, you have tried to build parks 'on

the cheap' and they show it and the attendance figures reflect it.

4. The perception by all of our stakeholders – consumers, investors, employees, distributors and suppliers – that the company is rapacious, soul-less, and always looking for the 'quick buck' rather than long-term value which is leading to a loss of public trust.

5. The creative brain drain of the last several years, which is real and continuing, and damages our Company with the loss of every talented employee.

6. Your failure to establish and build constructive relationships with creative partners, especially Pixar, Miramax, and the cable companies distributing our products.

7. Your consistent refusal to establish a clear succession plan.

The end is where it really delivers. These are all charges you could make against a number of other companies, of course, but Roy Disney reminds us that this isn't any other company. It's been around a long time; his family was there at the start; and he has nameless masses on his side.

In conclusion, Michael, it is my sincere belief that it is you who should be leaving and not me. Accordingly, I once again call for your resignation or retirement. The Walt Disney Company deserves fresh, energetic leadership at this challenging time in its history just as it did in 1984 when I headed a restructuring which resulted in your recruitment to the Company.

I have and will always have an enormous allegiance

and respect for this Company, founded by my uncle, Walt, and father, Roy, and to our faithful employees and loyal stockholders. I don't know if you and other directors can comprehend how painful it is for me and the extended Disney family to arrive at this decision.

This isn't a resignation so much as a siege engine. Just look at those charges: wonderfully slow-burning and non-specific: lack of soul; cheapness; loss of trust; negative perceptions; timidity; intransigence; lack of clarity. There's little there you can convincingly refute, partly because – with the exception of the first charge – there's nothing there but *feeling*.

Of course, it was never meant to be a business case or a set of figures. These are charges designed to prey on the doubts and vanities of the other shareholders. And prey on them they did. Eisner survived Disney's parting shot with the backing of shareholders – but Disney was implacable. The press, which he had excited so expertly with his duel-target resignation statement, could smell blood on the boardroom carpet. Within a year, the departed Disney was back, leading a coup that deposed Eisner as chairman, though he continued to serve as CEO.

★ ★ ★

If Roy Disney was playing Banquo's ghost at the board-room table, the next resignation was more like a visit from Jacob Marley, treating the Scrooges of America's invest-ment community to a chillingly accurate vision of their own future – complete with earthly unhappiness and looming oblivion.

On 17 October 2008, as the financial crisis brought stock markets around the world tumbling, hedge-fund boss Andrew Lahde (a man whose letters had hitherto been signed 'The Hedge Fund Manager With a 1000% Return') resigned from his own company Lahde Capital. He did so with an emailed public information memo – to investors and prospective investors – that took more than one rather unexpected turn, and nailed corporate practices, mindsets, lifestyles and personalities across America with the informed, dead-eyed accuracy of the insider . . . and then got *really* unusual.

Lahde had seen what, speaking to me in 2013 from his refuge on the West Coast, he calls the dominoes falling. He'd long suspected the collapse, or something like it, was coming, and spent the late summer closing positions and getting his investors their returns. He'd also been planning his exit: He had never thought of investing as a career. It was an operation. It always had an end. The question was how.

Lahde used to send weekly newsletters to his investors. A few funnies, the odd heads-up, and some idea of what he was doing with the money. But by October, he was fried. He wanted out. The operation was over. So he began to write.

When his email popped up on his investors' inboxes early that crisp, autumnal Manhattan day, they assumed he had another tip for them. And he did. Only this one was almost certainly not the kind they were hoping for.

Today I write not to gloat. Given the pain that nearly everyone is experiencing, that would be entirely inappropriate. Nor am I writing to make further predictions, as most of my forecasts in previous letters have unfolded or are in the process of unfolding. Instead, I am writing to say good-bye.

Recently, on the front page of Section C of the Wall Street Journal, a hedge fund manager who was also closing up shop (a $300 million fund), was quoted as saying, 'What I have learned about the hedge fund business is that I hate it.' I could not agree more with that statement. I was in this game for the money. The low hanging fruit, i.e. idiots whose parents paid for prep school, Yale, and then the Harvard MBA, was there for the taking. These people who were (often) truly not worthy of the education they received (or supposedly received) rose to the top of companies such as AIG, Bear Stearns and Lehman Brothers and all levels of our government. All of this behavior supporting the Aristocracy only ended up making it easier for me to find people stupid enough to take the other side of my trades. God bless America.

There are far too many people for me to sincerely thank for my success. However, I do not want to sound like a Hollywood actor accepting an award. The money was reward enough. Furthermore, the endless list of those deserving thanks know who they are.

I will no longer manage money for other people or institutions. I have enough of my own wealth to manage. Some people, who think they have arrived at a reasonable estimate of my net worth, might be surprised that I would call it quits with such a small war chest. That is fine; I am content with my rewards. Moreover, I will let others try to amass nine, ten or eleven figure net worths. Meanwhile, their lives suck. Appointments back to back, booked solid for the next three months, they look forward to their two week vacation in January during which they will likely be glued to their Blackberries or other such devices. What is the point? They will all be forgotten in fifty years anyway. Steve Balmer, Steven Cohen, and Larry Ellison will all be forgotten. I do not understand the legacy thing. Nearly everyone will be forgotten. Give up on leaving your mark. Throw the Blackberry away and enjoy life.

So this is it. With all due respect, I am dropping out. Please do not expect any type of reply to emails or voicemails within normal time frames or at all. Andy Springer and his company will be handling the dissolution of the fund. And don't worry about my employees, they were always employed by Mr. Springer's company and only one (who has been well-rewarded) will lose his job.

I have *no* interest in any deals in which anyone would like me to participate. I truly do not have a strong opinion about any market right now, other than to say that things will continue to get worse for some time, probably years. I am content sitting on the sidelines and waiting. After all, sitting and waiting is how we made money from the subprime debacle. I now have time to repair my health, which was destroyed by the stress I layered onto myself over the past two years, as well as my entire life – where I had to compete for spaces in universities and graduate schools, jobs and assets under management – with those who had all the advantages (rich parents) that I did not. May meritocracy be part of a new form of government, which needs to be established.

On the issue of the U.S. Government, I would like to make a modest proposal. First, I point out the obvious flaws, whereby legislation was repeatedly brought forth to Congress over the past eight years, which would have reigned in the predatory lending practices of now mostly defunct institutions. These institutions regularly filled the coffers of both parties in return for voting down all of this legislation designed to protect the common citizen. This is an outrage, yet no one seems to know or care about it. Since Thomas Jefferson and Adam Smith passed, I would argue that there has been a dearth of worthy philosophers in this country, at least ones focused on improving government. Capitalism worked for two hundred years, but times change, and systems become corrupt. George Soros, a man of staggering wealth, has stated that he would like to be remembered as a philosopher. My suggestion is that this great man start and sponsor a forum for great minds to come together to create a new system of government that truly represents the common man's interest, while at the same time creating rewards great enough to attract the best and brightest minds to serve in government roles without having to rely on corruption to further their interests or lifestyles. This forum could be similar to the one used to create the operating system, Linux, which competes with Microsoft's near monopoly. I believe there is an answer, but for now the system is clearly broken.

Lastly, while I still have an audience, I would like to bring attention to an alternative food and energy source. You won't see it included in BP's, 'Feel good. We are working on sustainable solutions,' television commercials, nor is it mentioned in ADM's similar commercials. But hemp has been used for at least 5,000 years for cloth and food, as well as just about everything that is produced from petroleum products. Hemp is not marijuana and vice versa. Hemp is the male plant and it grows like a weed, hence the slang term. The original American flag was made of hemp fiber and our Constitution was printed on paper made of hemp. It was used as recently as World War II by the U.S. Government, and then promptly made illegal after the war was won. At a time when rhetoric is flying about becoming more self-sufficient in terms of energy, why is it illegal to grow this plant in this country? Ah, the female. The evil female plant – marijuana. It gets you high, it makes you laugh, it does not produce a hangover. Unlike alcohol, it does not result in bar fights or wife beating. So, why is this innocuous plant illegal? Is it a gateway drug? No, that would be alcohol, which is so heavily advertised in this country. My only conclusion as to why it is illegal, is that Corporate America, which owns Congress, would rather sell you Paxil, Zoloft, Xanax and other addictive drugs, than allow you to grow a plant in your home without some of the profits going into their coffers. This policy is ludicrous. It has surely contributed to our dependency on foreign energy sources. Our policies have other countries literally laughing at our stupidity, most notably Canada, as well as several European nations (both Eastern and Western). You would not know this by paying attention to U.S. media sources though, as they tend not to elaborate on who is laughing at the United States this week. Please people, let's stop the rhetoric and start thinking about how we can truly become self-sufficient.

With that I say good-bye and good luck.

All the best,

Andrew Lahde

You can almost hear the clanking of chains – ghostly ones and golden handcuffs – and the horrified gasps of the other hedge fund managers.

This is as close to storming the barricades as you can get while simultaneously walking away in disgust. Tracked down through acquaintances on the phone (he won't say where), Andrew Lahde recalls that he'd been running on empty, frantically trying to close out positions remaining on investments in the days before he quit. There are other stories around the email, too. One was that the reason Lahde invited George Soros to form an alternative to capitalism was that if he'd set himself up as the man to do it, as it's thought he initially planned to, he'd have been a marked man for the authorities in those paranoid, post-9/11, post-meltdown days. But the power of Lahde's public resignation is as a manifesto. Coming from the hedge-fund star of the credit crisis, it's devastating.

There's something intensely poetic here too. It's got an icy stillness at the heart of it, and the same weird ecstasy as Schlueb's letter – the sense of the fog lifting, of fingers dancing on the keys and of an ecstatic prickling in the scalp.

This sense of controlled clarity is almost scary – especially to anyone still toiling away in the anthill. It's signally not a 'rant' or a 'meltdown' or any of the things it got called on TV at the time. It's what every great resignation should be: a moment of self-realization, and an escape. Step outside the daily race, and it looks so much smaller. Throw away your BlackBerry. Business is not a lasting legacy. Give up on leaving your mark. We will all be forgotten. Vanity, all is vanity.

Perhaps someone needs to make Lahde's story into

a film for it to have the full cultural impact it deserves. Would it star Tom Hanks, Kevin Spacey or Will Smith? As a central soliloquy, this resignation could have come from Sam Mendes' *American Beauty*. Lahde tells me he had offers. Maybe someday, one of them will be worth his time. For now, it's a great, thrilling read.

Lahde's resignation enjoyed brief and intense fame. But, in the way of these things, within days it was drowned out by the white noise of punditry, rebuttals and indignant ripostes. He regrets, he says, the way people – not least legalization groups – chose to focus on the 'marijuana thing'. Today, as the first wave of the Great Recession falls back, it is almost completely forgotten.

Lahde himself remains obscure, referring in our conversation to a large island where he hid out, and making contact initially through intermediaries. He tells me at one point that he hasn't talked to a journalist since it happened. But maybe Andrew Lahde's parting shot will ricochet back at us one day. As the global economy continues to struggle, the bodies keep falling and the system fails to fix itself, it still feels like an unexploded device planted at the heart of the free market. Of all the resignations in this book, perhaps this is the one that could still make the jump from archive to prophecy at any minute.

Andrew Lahde makes it look easy. But this next resignation, less than a year later, shows just how difficult it is to hit the target square on. Even when the target is a giant American accountancy firm.

* * *

In some ways, this resigner had it easier – hedge-funders

aren't exactly sympathetic figures, and Lahde's occasional sneers make him a target – but just look what happened. This email, attributed to an unknown PricewaterhouseCoopers auditor in Philadelphia, hit inboxes round the world on Monday, 31 August 2009 according to the first audit and accountancy blogs to report it; though *Life Of An Auditor* at least remained agnostic on the question of its veracity.

Genuine or not (or, as is often the case somewhere in between – a heartfelt resignation that was never enacted), the sense of claustrophobia is palpable. The writer skewers what he sees as his workplace's circular logic and self-regarding practices. Yet there's an uneasy sense that he may be part of the problem. Even in his resignation letter, there's no sense of a new beginning or even a world beyond the grey cubicle walls.

As many of you now know this Friday will be my last day with PwC so I wanted to say good-bye and thank you for everything.

My decision to leave was not a snap decision as it may have seemed but a well thought out process. It started one night in the audit room as I was helplessly attempting to focus on some inane, completely irrelevant task so I could leave when the green card carrying cleaning lady came into my cage to empty my garbage when my decision was made. I realized that I was actually jealous of her job. I would have gladly emptied the garbage cans in the whole building over any of the nonsense I was doing on my computer.

See, at the end of her shift she has made a difference, she has added value, be it minimal, of removing the refuse from the employees' cubes. At the end of the day she sees the empty garbage cans and knows that she accomplished something. When trying to apply this mindset to my own work I found it to be impossible. At the end of my shift, I will have documented a control, that was only created for the sake of having a control, and my work will get picked apart by anal retentive managers, but ultimately find a home in a cabinet somewhere, only to see the light of day again when it is thrown out in 7 years when it is deemed to be irrelevant.

I have added zero value to the client, zero value to my own company, and it has made me routinely daydream about ways to off myself. I find it very hard to be motivated when I know the end result of my work has no impact on anything but simply must be completed because PwC audit guide says it must be completed.

What makes this entire process worse is the fact that those around you insist that this work is crucial to the world's existence and it is essential that you never use abbreviations, that your sheets must be as colorful as possible, and all lines must be drawn with a ruler or else it is clear that PwC will come apart from its hinges. I must have missed out on the brainwashing session that PwC provided all senior associates and managers that taught them how to turn obsessive compulsive up a notch.

Anyway . . . that was how I came to decide that public accounting was not really for me.

A couple other pieces of advice for my co-workers and the company as I part:

I would greatly encourage some kind of weight loss challenge to be implemented firm-wide. The herd of water buffalo you call your work force is embarrassing and a bit gross. When I call a co-worker over from 2 cubes down and they are legitimately out of breath when they get to my cube it may be time to knock off 10 or 80 pounds. The company seems to encourage this obesity; each busy season we get a giant package full of pixie sticks, chocolate and assorted sweets. As much as I would enjoy type 2 diabetes, I think I'll pass.

Do not ever, ever, *ever* put one male on a team with all females unless you want him to quit and or commit a hate crime. This is inhumane. One can only endure so many conversations about *Grey's Anatomy*, weddings, and handbags before they wish for a cancerous tumor in their armpit.

I think the joke is old already, enough with the Sarbanes-Oxley. It was fun while it lasted but there is no way anybody can honestly think that this bullshit is necessary. Oh you want me to pull a sample of the HR file to make sure everyone's birthday and hire date is accurate? Yea I'll jump right on that, and trust me I'll *definitely* let you know if there is an exception and not just make up answers that result in me doing less work.

You can easily cut some costs and get rid of the HR department. I'm pretty sure you can train a monkey to send out the available list and a timesheet reminder every two weeks.

For all its ham-fistedness (it's impossible to read the bits about snacks, female colleagues and *Grey's Anatomy* without wincing) the resignation is strangely poignant – beyond even the normal level of poignancy guaranteed by an accountant nursing fantasies of suicide as he watches his bin being emptied. Inside its maddening, padded-cell stanzas, there's a truth attack wanting to get out.

In its moment of fearless unburdening, it's a sort of 'Dear Boss' for public accounting. Just one problem: the resigner's gun-sights aren't trained on incompetent US Air Force commanders, but on the notoriously exacting – and infinitely less pulse-quickening – accounting standards of the US Public Company Accounting Reform and Investor Protection Act, aka the Sarbanes-Oxley Act. Which may explain why it never achieved quite the same traction.

Resignations at law and accountancy firms make less sexy copy than at governments, banks and media organizations, so it's just possible that the resignation did indeed detonate, and few outside the company heard it. It was the tree that fell and never made a sound; the seed on stony ground. We aim for Andrew Lahde, we end up David Brent.

The despair – the nagging feeling that one is resigning in a void, and one's truth bomb will be a dud – is what makes this resignation special. As for Sarbanes-Oxley, it was introduced in 2002 as a way to prevent a corporate accounting scandal like Enron ever happening again, which itself is somewhat funnier – and darker – post-2008. And as for Enron, we'll be hearing more of them in a later chapter.

In contrast, the feeling that one is changing history lies behind the most spectacular truth bombs. That your words themselves will make something happen. That's how it was for one depressed, demotivated British tabloid journalist in 2011. On 4 March, *Daily Star* journalist Richard Peppiatt sent an email he had been mulling over for days, having been brought to what he calls 'a bad place' by journalistic practices at the newspaper. He copied in his employers, and the media desk at a competing national newspaper. He planned the move minutely, even down to contacting the *Guardian* to see if they would report the resignation for greater impact.

It was a huge fuse to light. The paper had promised to print his letter. But as the email pinged into his bosses' inboxes, and other breaking news stories took over the attention of the *Guardian*'s editors, Peppiatt seemed to have been hung out to dry. Leaving his office and ignoring phone call after phone call to his mobile, he could only wait, and sweat on what looked increasingly like a moment of madness – a truth bomb that would go off prematurely, wiping out his own promising career but leaving his foe unharmed.

The letter is a masterpiece, and Richard Peppiatt has kindly allowed it to be reproduced in its full glory here.

Dear Mr Desmond,

You probably don't know me, but I know you. For the last two years I've been a reporter at the *Daily Star*, and for two years I've felt the weight of your ownership rest heavy on the shoulders of everyone, from the editor to the bloke who empties the bins.

Wait! I know you're probably reaching for your phone to have me marched out of the building. But please, save on your bill. I quit.

The decision came inside my local newsstand, whilst picking up the morning papers. As I chatted with Mohammed, the Muslim owner, his blinking eyes settled on my pile of print, and then, slowly, rose to meet my face.

'English Defence League to become a political party' growled out from the countertop.

Squirming, I abandoned the change in my pocket and

flung a note in his direction, the clatter of the till a welcome relief from the silence that had engulfed us. I slunk off toward the tube.

If he was hurt that my 25p had funded such hate-mongering, he'd be rightly appalled that I'd sat in the war cabinet itself as this incendiary tale was twisted and bent to fit an agenda seemingly decided before the EDL's leader Tommy Robinson had even been interviewed.

Asked if his group were to become a political party I was told the ex-BNP goon had replied: 'Not for now.'

But further up the newsprint chain it appears a story, too good to allow the mere spectre of reality to restrain, was spotted.

It almost never came to this. I nearly walked out last summer when the *Daily Star* got all flushed about taxpayer-funded Muslim-only loos.

A newsworthy tale, were said toilets Muslim-only. Or taxpayer-funded. Undeterred by the nuisance of truth, we omitted a few facts, plucked a couple of quotes, and suddenly anyone would think a Rochdale shopping centre had hired Osama Bin Laden to stand by the taps, handing out paper towels.

I was personally tasked with writing a gloating follow-up declaring our postmodern victory in 'blocking' the non-existent Islamic cisterns of evil.

Not that my involvement in stirring up a bit of light-hearted Islamaphobia stopped there. Many a morning I've hit my speed dial button to Muslim rent-a-rant Anjem Choudary to see if he fancied pulling together a few lines about whipping drunks or stoning homosexuals.

Our caustic 'us and them' narrative needs nailing home

every day or two, and when asked to wield the hammer I was too scared for my career, and my bank account, to refuse.

'If you won't write it, we'll get someone who will,' was the sneer *du jour*, my eyes directed toward a teetering pile of CVs. I won't claim I've simply been coshed into submission; I've necked the celeb party champagne and pocketed all the freebies, relying on hangovers to block out the rest.

Neither can I erase that as a young hack keen to prove his worth I threw myself into working at the *Daily Star* with gusto. On order I dressed up as a John Lennon, a vampire, a Mexican, Noel Gallagher, Saint George (twice), Santa Claus, Aleksandr the Meerkat, the Stig, and a transvestite Alex Reid.

I've been spraytanned, waxed, and in a kilt clutching roses trawled a Glasgow council estate trying to propose to Susan Boyle (I did. She said no).

When I was ordered to wear a burkha in public for the day, I asked: 'Just a head scarf or full veil?' Even after being ambushed by anti-terror cops when panicked Londoners reported 'a bloke pretending to be a Muslim woman', I didn't complain. Mercifully, I'd discovered some backbone by the time I was told to find some burkha-clad shoppers (spot the trend?) to pose with for a picture – dressed in just a pair of skintight M&S underpants.

Forget journalistic merit, I heard this was just an ill-conceived ploy to land an advertising contract with the chain. Admittedly, that was unusual. Often we hacks write vacuous puff pieces about things you own. Few would deny there's one hell of an incestuous orgy of cross-promotion to leer at down at Northern & Shell HQ [Desmond's company].

Never mind that it insults the intelligence of amoebas

when your readers are breathlessly informed the week's telly highlights include *OK! TV* and *The Vanessa Feltz Show*.

I suspect you see a perfect circle. I see a downward spiral. I see a cascade of shit pirouetting from your penthouse office, caking each layer of management, splattering all in between.

Daily Star favourite Kelly Brook recently said in an interview: 'I do Google myself. Not that often, though, and the stories are always rubbish. There was a story that I'd seen a hypnotherapist to help me cut down on the time I take to get ready to go out. Where do they get it from?'

Maybe I should answer that one. I made it up. Not that it was my choice; I was told to. At 6 p.m. and staring at a blank page I simply plucked it from my arse. Not that it was all bad. I pocketed a £150 bonus. You may have read some of my other earth-shattering exclusives. 'Michael Jackson to attend Jade Goody's funeral.' (He didn't.) 'Robbie pops pill at heroes concert.' (He didn't either.) 'Matt Lucas on suicide watch.' (He wasn't.) 'Jordan turns to Buddha.' (She might have, but I doubt it.)

I know showbiz is the sand on which your readership is built. And while I didn't write tittle-tattle dreaming of Pulitzers, I never knew I'd fear a Booker Prize nomination instead.

You own the *Daily Star*, and it's your right to assign whatever news values to it you choose. On the awe-inspiring day millions took to the streets of Egypt to demand freedom, your paper splashed on 'Jordan . . . the movie.'

A snub to history? Certainly. An affront to journalism? Most definitely. Your undeniable right? Yes, sir.

But what brings me here today is those times you

dispense with those skewed news values entirely by printing stories which couldn't stand up to a gnat's fart.

It's those times when you morph from being a newspaper owner into the inventor of a handy product for lining rabbit hutches. While the *Daily Star* isn't the only paper with a case to answer, I reckon it's certainly the ugliest duckling of an unsightly flock.

Its endemic lack of self-perception really is something to behold. It only takes a comedian to make an ironic gag about racism and your red top is on hand to whip up a storm, demanding the culprit commit *hara-kiri* beside Stephen Lawrence's shrine.

Yet turn the page and Muslims are branded 'beardies' or 'fanatics', and black-on-black killings ('Bob-slayings', as I've cringingly heard them called in your newsroom) can be resigned to a handful of words, shoehorned beneath a garish advert.

Outraged, we brand other celebrities sexist, demanding such dinosaurs be castrated on the steps of the Natural History Museum.

Then with our anger sated it's back to task, arranging the day's news based on the size of the subjects' breasts.

Were this the behaviour of an actual person they would be diagnosed schizophrenic and bundled into the nearest white van. But because the mouthpiece is a newspaper, it's all supposed to be ok. Well, here's some breaking news – it's far, far worse. When looking for the source of this hypocritical behaviour, I didn't have to go far.

The *Daily Star* seems to set out its editorial stall as a newspaper written for, and fighting for, the (preferably white) working class.

Yet as a proprietor you recently dropped out of the Press Complaints Commission, leaving those self-same people with no viable recourse if they find themselves libelled or defamed on your pages.

Your red-top drones on about British jobs for British workers, yet your own reporters' pay has been on ice so long it was last seen living in an igloo and hunting seals.

A great swathe of your readership lives in the north of England, yet you employ just one staff reporter outside London. One. I guess it makes the same sense to you up there in your ivory tower as it does to me down here on my high horse. I get it, I do.

Because no one has time for subtlety of language, of thought, when they're scrabbling to pump out a national newspaper with fewer staff hacks than it takes to man a yacht.

When you assign budgets thinner than your employee-issue loo roll there's little option but for *Daily Star* editors to build a newspaper from cut-and-paste-jobs off the *Daily Mail* website, all tied together with gormless press releases. But when that cheap-and-cheerful journalism gives the oxygen of publicity to corrosive groups like the EDL – safe in the knowledge it's free news about which they'll never complain – it's time to lay down my pen.

Peppiatt then echoes Jeff Goldblum's warning on chaos theory in *Jurassic Park*. Whatever you think you're controlling might be the thing you're unleashing.

You may have heard the phrase, 'The flap of a butterfly's wings in Brazil sets off a tornado in Texas.' Well, try this:

'The lies of a newspaper in London can get a bloke's head caved in down an alley in Bradford.'

If you can't see that words matter, you should go back to running porn magazines. But if you do, yet still allow your editors to use inciteful over insightful language, then far from standing up for Britain, you're a menace against all things that make it great.

I may have been just a lowly hack in your business empire, void of the power to make you change your ways, but there is still one thing that I can do; that I was trained to do; that I love to do: write about it.

The letter sent, Peppiatt holed up inside his flat. As the hours ticked by, he went into full fugitive mode, avoiding calls and hate messages from people he believed were ex-colleagues, and wondering whether he'd done it all in vain.

Finally, days later, the *Guardian* printed the letter in full. It quickly went viral – going from the media pages to national news, then international. It swept across social media and the internet.

The lid was blown off the UK newspaper industry. With phone-hacking evidence building over at News International, this letter – a spectacular journalistic *cri de coeur* from an employee who had taken all he could take – set the agenda for the coming clean-up.

Ironically, in some ways this parting shot was the making of Peppiatt. Called to give evidence to the Leveson Inquiry into media standards, he became the voice of conscience for the news industry. His one-man stage show, *One Rogue Reporter*, is a success. A film based on it premiered in the summer of 2014.

★ ★ ★

Newspapermen, captains of industry and commanding officers are ideally placed to detonate their truth bombs over a wide area. It's less often that a humble shopworker resigns with so much panache that they have to go into hiding after moving to Korea.

On 22 July 2011, a store-buyer for the Whole Foods organic supermarket in Toronto reached boiling point. With his position giving him access to email lists across the company, the employee, whose name was kept out of the press in the aftermath at his own request, wrote a long email, cc-ing everyone, picking out a number of colleagues and line managers for special comment.

The email is fascinating for the way in which the writer's rage keeps derailing his own speech. At times, it's almost as if there are two voices fighting for control of the resignation: the calm, rational employee levelling constructive, intelligent criticism at the organization, and a raging, vengeful Id. It's systematically organized, almost an inventory or a shopping list of grievances . . . only the system keeps breaking down as the writer gets carried away.

It begins with an apocryphal quote often attributed to nineteenth-century philosopher Edmund Burke: 'All that is necessary for the triumph of evil is that good men do nothing.' It then meanders through a cocktail of revolutionary and anti-brand rallying cries before settling scores with various 'cowardly wieners'.

But there's another reason it's so hypnotic, so worth visiting and revisiting: of all the letters in this chapter, it is perhaps the most honest, unmediated record of the conflicting feelings we all have, even as we commit to pressing 'send'.

The buyer sets out his stall with a little panache. It begins with slacker sentiment, down to the disparaging reference to the faux-Nirvana that real grungers love to hate:

> My experience at Whole Foods was like an increasingly sped up fall down a really long hill. That got rockier with every metre. And eventually, just really spiky . . . with fire, acid and Nickleback music.

Then he hits the gas, tearing a hole into the company's values with no fewer than twenty-one ways the company fails to live up to them. For me, there's something quite masterful in the repetition – twenty-two times, to be exact – of the innocent 'Oh . . .' question, juxtaposed with company value.

> Oh, you buy poorly made, ugly t-shirts for your employees that will just be thrown in the trash and pretend they're gifts when they're really just advertising tools? (Supporting team member happiness and excellence, Caring about our communities and our environment) . . .
>
> Oh, you've somehow created the worst computer program I've ever used to run your entire buying system? IRMA is some Windows 95 era stuff, guys. I could design a significantly better interface in 30 minutes on a pad of paper. I know several students who could create a superior program in their spare time. Was someone actually hired to create that thing? Was it the Realplayer dudes? Even Captain Picard

couldn't facepalm hard enough to express the amount of failure in that . . . that, thing . . . (Supporting team member happiness and excellence) . . .

Oh, you ambush employees using two managers when you want to write someone up? No warning. No representation. All reasons and excuses fall on deaf ears. (Supporting team member happiness and excellence) . . .

This is the sound of the excited flourish of the detective, unmasking the perpetrators, pointing the finger of guilt, and exposing the whole sorry sham. But the resignation's third act is where things really hot up. Clearly relishing his new role as an anti-corporate version of *The Equalizer*, our hero focuses on specifics, and simultaneously seems to forget what he was doing. What started as a noble call to resist, or at least a critique of the company, becomes a shitlist. With clinical relish, he begins picking off colleagues with over a dozen personally addressed passages.

Dear [NAME REDACTED] . . . The fact that you still have a job is also a massive failure by your department's leaders as well. I'd be ashamed of being such push-overs who refuse to support good people if I were them. Quite ashamed.

And then, for good measure, an aside to the top brass that recalls Keys' point about the General not being 'paid to like things':

Do you guys realize that the store NEVER looks as good as it does when you arrive? When word spreads that you're coming to inspect the store almost every team leader begins running around like Brampton teens on PCP. They whip their employees into a frenzy. They sweep anything under the bed that they think you won't like. They attempt to make the store look like nobody ever shops there. This stops us and them from doing actual productive work which in turn impacts sales and creates a lot of pointless stress. Then you arrive, hand out your almighty advice. The team leaders grovel at your feet . . . Then you leave and they put everything back the way it was . . .

That seems to get the anger out of his system. As the writer winds down, he's the conscious sharer of enlightened best practice once more.

[You] work at a grocery store. Go ahead and relax . . . Whole Foods will try to make you feel like they are doing you a huge favour by employing you. It's really a mutual agreement or transaction. Don't fall for the guilt trips. Call in sick if you need to, etc. There are laws in place to stop them from taking advantage of you. And if you're thinking, 'This is just the way it is. Suck it up!' you're the biggest part of the problem. I'm afraid we can't be friends.

Just enjoy life. It's pretty short, you know?

Good luck.

As for the author, he was tracked down by reporters for *Gawker* – who broke the story, printing the letter in full – weeks later, in South Korea. He claimed that the letter was 'a collaborative effort. Quite a bit of it is from other employees. I just edited it to keep them anonymous'.

We are witnessing something deeper than one man's anger here, then; the letter is a barely controlled channel for a more popular rage. If it was collaborative then it recalls the origin of the phrase 'round-robin letter' – from seventeenth-century French *rubin-rond*, or round ribbon. The letters were circular-cut documents, in which signatories to a petition of protest against the Crown could add their names around the edge, in a non-hierarchical fashion, so as to conceal who had started the petition and who had simply joined its signatories late on. Like *Murder on the Orient Express*, it legitimizes the act by implicating more than one agent of vengeance.

Or maybe it's something less orderly, more disquieting. Perhaps the signatory is just the delivery boy, and this letter – this one resignation – is just the start. Burke was a staunch critic of the rise of mob rule and the Reign of Terror in eighteenth-century France. Suddenly that misattributed quote seems a little more appropriate.

★ ★ ★

The truth-bomb resignation can be a rallying cry that spurs the masses to action; or an entropic blast of negative energy that corrodes confidence in an organization.

Davison Budhoo's 1988 letter of resignation became something of a touchstone for disaffected servants of the IMF and World Bank programmes – the 'Dear Boss' of the white-collar economic capitalist classes. By 2012, Briton Peter Doyle was a senior economist at the IMF. His resignation letter is shorter than that of Budhoo, but no less damning – of the lack of strategy, of internal politics, of institutional incompetence and of the installation of its fêted head, Christine Lagarde. The surprising thing is how little within the IMF appears to have changed over twenty-five years, even as the world changed around it. For Trinidad and Tobago, read Greece. And for the developing economies taking a ducking in the ruthless world of the free market while their populations starve, read the European Union.

After twenty years of service, I am ashamed to have had any association with the Fund at all.

This is not solely because of the incompetence [managing the global economic crisis and the Eurozone crisis]. Moreso, it is because the substantive difficulties in these crises, as with others, were identified well in advance but were suppressed here . . . timely sustained warnings were of the essence. So the failure of the Fund to issue them is a failing of the first order . . . The consequences include suffering (and risk of worse to come) for many including Greece, that the second global reserve currency is on the brink, and that the Fund for the past two years has been playing catch-up and reactive roles in the last-ditch efforts to save it . . .

A handicapped Fund, subject to those proximate roots of surveillance failure, is what the Executive Board prefers. Would that I had understood twenty years ago that this would be the choice.

There are good salty people here. But this one is moving on. You might want to take care not to lose the others.

There is one important change from the IMF that Davison Budhoo nailed in 1988: the feeling that the failings at the heart of the organization have less to do with subservience to a political agenda than with the loss of any agenda or sense of purpose at all, beyond stolid self-perpetuation. Like so much in post-cold war politics, the IMF of Doyle's letter isn't an evil or immoral organization; it's a moribund one, paralysed by process, bias and established interest.

It's possible that Doyle's resignation address, together with those of Peppiatt, Lahde and Greg Smith, will one day be seen as the first warning shots across the bows of a wider system that had become too unequal, too rigid, too riddled with vested interest, in everything from economic policy to law to private wealth to press ownership. If they are, then there's another less celebrated letter that deserves to stand alongside them.

Los Angeles-based artists Catherine Opie and Barbara Kruger resigned from the board of the Museum of Contemporary Art on 15 July 2012 with a priceless – and witheringly funny – critique of the way cultural institutions follow the smell of money.

The early morning email was titled simply 'Resignation' and addressed to both Chairs and the Museum Director. 'We want the best for MOCA,' it began. 'We want it to remain the globally respected institution it has become.'

Then it nailed a world in which art is reduced to a cash cow and 'philanthropy' has come to mean a smart way for rich corporations and individuals to avoid paying tax.

> [This] is not about a particular cast of characters, about good actors and bad. It's a reflection of the crisis in cultural funding. It's about the role of museums in a culture where visual art is marginalized except for the buzz around secondary market sales, it's about the not so subtle recalibration of the meaning of 'philanthropy,' and it's about the morphing of the so-called

'art world' into the only speculative bubble still left floating (for the next 20 minutes). Can important and serious exhibitions receive funding without a donor having a horse in the race? Is attendance a sustaining revenue stream for museums? Has it ever been? These are questions we have been asking.

We do know that a major rethinking of the mechanisms and templates for cultural funding is long overdue. Parties and galas are ok, but sometimes these things called 'museums' have to have things called 'exhibitions'. Our concerns are with the art, the exhibitions, and how the money that makes the exhibitions possible is gathered and distributed.

It's an alternative history of culture since the 1980s in two paragraphs – from the recalibration of 'philanthropy' by institutions and corporations who smell small government (and tax-deductable advertising spend) on the wind, to the emptying of art of any value but price, and the problem of offering 'difficult' cultural propositions to a population that expects art 'on demand' like everything else.

But it's Opie and Kruger's refusal to offer easy answers that gives the letter its power to unsettle. All those lingering questions, all those suspended quotation marks, ironize the museum's pursuit of high-net-worth donors. The cool outsiders in the playground, it is their very detachment that makes the joiners and jocks feel ill at ease and self-conscious. There's something irreducible here. Kruger's art had always appropriated advertising and mass messaging to create something gnomic and teasing; Opie's had begun examining social spaces, roles and structures we take for granted. And in the midst of it, their letter refuses to become a polemic. It even sounds like a gallery caption for a piece. A performance, perhaps. A public resignation. What is it (not) about? What questions does it raise? Let's think about those public spaces we take for granted. Its hidden question is 'What are you going to do now you've become a commodity?' And it's one we're all going to have to answer if we're not careful.

Pieces like this, Lahde's and even Ron Keys' letter offer something quite exhilarating. They seem to exist in spite of everything: their writers have been co-opted, put in uniform, in roles; they are trained to speak off a menu of officially sanctioned responses to a very limited number of enquiries (USAF majors follow orders; artists-in-residence come to heel for a museum's donors). So going off-menu really is a refusal to play by the rules; to insist on what Dr Johnson called 'the appeal to nature' when faced with a judgement faultless on its own terms but phoney in feel. Like Lahde invoking health, families and a future free of phones or deals, this resigner insists that the corporate world live by the same standards of decency as the natural world, whatever HR says.

This appeal to greater authority than the person giving the orders taps into the reason these resignations feel so liberating.

If two world wars in the twentieth century showed that the difference between the employer and employee class was often the difference between life and death, perhaps the technologies they helped usher in also pointed to a conscription-free, high-movement future in which 'Stick it up your arse' was a viable alternative. 'No more jobs for life' cuts both ways, after all.

These sudden, but minutely planned blasts against the

system could be the only effective weapon in a hugely asymmetrical conflict, not just of ideologies but of feelings about what it means to live. For the zero-hours contractor, dissident, whistleblower and top-brass alike, the truth bomb is the great – maybe the only – leveller of odds. Perhaps, after all, Orwell was wrong in *Nineteen Eighty-Four*: the future isn't the vision of a boot coming down on a human face forever. It's the sound of the team induction meeting. And rebellion is the lonely, echoing sound of fingers rattling a keyboard in the small hours.

But while individuals could blow whistles to call attention to corporate wrongs, the Empire was striking back with its own uniquely subtle ways of silencing debate . . . and killing unwanted coverage.

2:

The Conversation Killer

'Be silent, or else let your words be worth more than silence.'

– Pythagoras

'I think I can reasonably claim a respite from the burdens of responsibility and the glare of publicity.'

– Reginald Maudling

'I would rather obey a fine lion . . . than two hundred rats.'

– Voltaire

Getúlio Vargas was a desperate man. He looked around the table at the members of his cabinet. A circle of stony faces looked back at him. He saw himself as they saw him now. A tense, pale and doomed man. A sweating liability. And maybe, just maybe, a killer.

As things stood, right now, he was still Brazil's president. But he could read the signs as well as anyone else here.

That someone had attempted to assassinate his main political rival was unfortunate. That they had botched the attempt and killed a serving Major in the Brazilian army was unforgivable. But he had not ordered it, had known nothing of the attack until the first reports. This was 1954

– these were dangerous times. In the days since the attempt, the streets, the media, the garrisons, even parliamentary sessions had been aflame with accusation and rumour. His allies were deserting him. Today, he'd lost the military. And now, this. His own cabinet.

President Vargas left the meeting, smiling his goodbyes, shaking hands as he went. He could fix this. He had one last plan. There was no way it could fail. Vargas walked through quiet corridors to his office. He sat at his desk and – with infinite care – wrote his resignation on a piece of letterheaded paper. Then he read it back. It was one heck of a resignation.

> Nothing remains except my blood. I gave you my life, now I give you my death. I choose this way to defend you, for my soul will be with you. My name shall be a flag for your struggle. I calmly take the first step to eternity, and leave life to enter history.

Then Vargas took his black Colt .45 from his drawer, leaned forward, and shot himself through the chest.

At that precise moment, the second political reign of Getúlio Vargas began.

Vargas's resignation note, and the dramatic manner in which it was delivered, stopped cold the rumours and conspiracy theories concerning his involvement in the botched assassination. Instead, suddenly he was the one conspired against, sinned against, all but assassinated. His opponents – now widely cast as his bloodthirsty persecutors – endured an uproar so great, so total, and so long-lasting, that they were consigned to political exile for many years.

A good resignation can start a dialogue or raise an issue, it can euthanize one too.

There is a darker class of resignation letter. One whose pleasures are far more subtle and complex than those of the truth attack. This is the conversation killer. It is the only known method for resigning in disgrace, failure or adversity, and not having anyone notice.

Broadly, there are two ways to kill a message as it is delivered.

The first is to create white noise and furore around it. This is a favoured tactic of the tobacco and gun-ownership lobbies. Insist on equal space for rebuttal in the name of 'balance'; delay the admission that tobacco causes cancer by calling the science into question and calling for 'further research'. Launch ad-hominem attacks, social media hashtags. Manufacture a 'media storm' in place of a verdict. President Getúlio Vargas took this approach to its extreme. Andrew Lahde and Richard Peppiatt both found themselves on the receiving end. More recently, we've seen governments use it around Edward Snowden and revelations of secret service overreach. The most famous case is the memo from a press officer in Tony Blair's cabinet suggesting the 9/11 coverage presented 'a good day to bury bad news'.

The second way is to have the message self-destruct even as it is conveyed. This is an art around which an entire industry has grown. PR-composed resignations, often seemingly open-handed and honest, are the slipperiest of all. They aspire to the condition of invisibility, not just for the letter, but for the writer too. Whether they are managed in traditional corporate terms or not, they are written in order to shield, not to disclose, the resigner and their organization.

It's the hallmark of the corporate non-apology. I've copywritten some myself. Here's how it's done. You write the statement, then go back through it and weaken it at the joints. Not enough to make it fall over; just enough to kill any nice turns of phrase; to remove any commitments to timeframes, concrete rebuttals or the allegations they address. Then you hand it to the company's Legal, Risk and Compliance team. At this point, more qualifiers will be added as subclauses, smack in the middle of sentences. Their additions will often be characterized by minor grammatical slips: so tiny that the casual reader will skip over them, while journalists will be reluctant to include them. An additional patina of legalese and passive-voice phrases will descend across it like an early morning mist.

These resignations deal in non-specifics. They move the conversation onto areas like press intrusion, protecting their families from unwarranted stress or not wanting to provide distractions from the many good things the organization does.

They refer – but only ever obliquely – to correcting mis-understandings, misjudgements and distortions. Yet they never use this very public forum to make the corrections. Rather than come out and put their case, or identify specific problems with the charges against them, they offer further conversation . . . only deferred, to some unspecified later date, when the heat is off.

The language of these statements has become part of our everyday discourse. It's in everything from train announcements to terrorist attacks. The most chilling example of this tactic of compliant self-erasure is the resignation letter of 7/7 London tube suicide bomber Sidique Khan from the primary school where he worked as a teaching assistant. Having taken months of sick leave and unauthorized leave of absence from his job in 2004, Khan resigned from his job as Mentor at Hillside Primary School, Leeds, in order to make final preparations for his attack. While the reason given is redacted from his letter, his leaver's form bears a tick next to the box marked 'Family Commitments'.

17.12.04

Dear [redacted],

I'm sorry I have not been in touch for a while, a lot has happened in the last few months. [REDACTED BY UK HOME OFFICE] and there is no definite time frame as to when I will return.

Unfortunately this letter is therefore a letter of my resignation from my post. It's been great working with you and I will be in touch when I return.

Yours Sincerely

Sidique Khan

Khan's letter speaks far more than it says – nine-tenths of its mass lie below the waterline, out of sight. Khan needed to disappear without causing suspicion. He had already travelled to Pakistan for training as a suicide bomber, and suspected he was under some form of surveillance. His letter was designed to be as bland as possible, and he uses all the classic smokescreen tricks used by writers who want their letter to self-destruct, even as it is read.

1. *Apology deflected:* Khan had been on extended sick leave, then had gone missing. He says: 'I'm sorry I have not been in touch for a while, a lot has happened'. Other letters use similar constructions, such as, 'I am sorry if those offended by my actions felt that . . .' These apologies are designed to placate, but alarm bells should ring. They are almost never sincere, and serve to close down the conversation about why they did what they did.

2. *Faux-helpfulness:* Information is volunteered, but is so fuzzy as to be useless: 'there is no definite time frame'.

3. *Don't call me, I'll call you:* Khan says he will be in touch on his return, signalling his wish to be left alone and implying that he will be back. This is the airline bomber's trick of buying a return ticket so as not to arouse suspicion. But it's also a way of suspending the recipient's instinct to enquire further.

In fact, there are some telling similarities with an earlier resignation by another man with much to hide. Guy Burgess resigned from the BBC to take up a Foreign Office position in 1944. When one knows Burgess was a Russian spy, manoeuvring into a position where he would be more able to access secrets, the possibility of return, goodwill and helpfulness floated in his letter read very differently.

I wish to send in my resignation to the Corporation in order to take up an appointment in the Foreign Office. Personally, it will be a real grief to leave the department and the division. I should like to emphasise this very strongly. Also to say that

> I should like to give any assistance that may be possible in
> the future to the department if this should be found useful.
> I very much hope that the formal full three months' notice,
> which contractually exists between me and the Corporation
> with regard to any non-military appointment, will not be
> rigidly insisted on . . .

According to his Russian handler from 1945, Burgess
would soon turn so much material over to the Soviets that
the Embassy of the USSR in London had to employ cipher
clerks to translate it on a nine-to-five basis. He certainly
seems keen to get started.

Such letters betray a smiling, somewhat glassy-eyed
and very British impenetrability. Today they speak in the
almost-but-not-quite, non-language of the online form; the
corporate automated communication.

These standard-form, non-communication 'enquiry
fielding' platforms set the tone for the 2000s – and Khan's
resignation – just as the smooth robotic voices of spaceship
interiors regulate the lives of science-fiction astronauts;
the endless push-button options with which your mobile
service funnels and neuters your rage into a series of
capitulations.

The phrase 'call centre' entered English in 1983, and
by the early 2000s, some 800,000 Britons were employed
reading scripted responses down phone lines. The conver-
gence between the languages of poll-driven political
discourse and target-driven customer service in that time
has been remarkable: it's now almost impossible to hear
a public figure resign, apologize or unveil a new policy
without spotting the tics of 'call recorded for training and

quality purposes' culture. Like the UK rail network's first automated service announcements, which spread over the same period, the voice is passive-offensive. Apologies are offered for any inconvenience that may have been caused. No admission of liability. Terms and conditions apply.

As this all-purpose sanitized messaging and response-control matrix spread, it was seized upon as a cookie-cutter model for press officers and spin doctors under pressure to act quickly in sticky situations.

At the same time, the number of sticky situations multiplied. The arrival of Sky News as Britain's first 24-hour rolling news channel in 1989 had sped up the news cycle. It coincided with the arrival of quick-response poll-driven policy pioneered by the Bill Clinton election campaign in 1992 and quickly adopted by both sides in the US. Suddenly, rather than convening over pizzas or whisky to knock something up ready for the morning's first edition, press officers were expected to respond then and there, on the fly. Driven by the sudden expectation that they would say something – anything – and offered a new vocabulary of non-specific equivocation by technology, they seized their chance. A new breed of releases arrived – statements and reports written and prepared by experts in order to seal off the communication and kill the story in their delivery.

This was the first generation to grapple with the demands of instant news at the top of the hour; of live reaction. It was the first to find ways to hack it, too. 'Spin', a perjorative slang term for 'deceive' in the 1950s, morphed into what presidential speechwriter William Safire in a 1996 *New York Times* column called 'a mockingly admiring [term for] "polish the truth"'.

From the unspoken Ts and Cs around President Bill Clinton's 'I did not have sex with that woman' to Michael Howard's legendary fourteen consecutive attempts to avoid answering Jeremy Paxman's question, the need for a new, templated, pre-prepared language of damage limitation became urgent as, public figures under pressure scrambled for safety.

In some areas of public life – large corporations, government departments, finance – this call-centre register become a tic; an involuntary habit. Nervous of comebacks, we began to qualify, dilute, cover our words as we wrote them; to write emails in the linguistic equivalent of self-erasing type. Communication became its opposite. Clear-cut resignations, like apologies, contracts and the small print beneath the advertising hoardings, became riddles.

Warren Buffett's Berkshire Hathaway hedge fund was notorious for releasing statements containing controversial or sensational information, and ending them with this head-smashingly circular sign-off from Buffett himself (from his release announcing a resignation amid allegations of impropriety):

> I have held back nothing in this statement. Therefore, if questioned about this matter in the future, I will simply refer the questioner back to this release.

This is the equivalent of 'If none of these apply, press 1 to go back to menu options'. Even something as uncontroversial as the British Ministry of Defence closing down its specialized UFO reports and investigations department, the Directorate for Defence Security, was announced on New Year's Eve in a bid for the press release not to be noticed by the press. (For the record, the statement said: 'The MOD has no opinion on the existence or otherwise of extra-terrestrial life. However, in over fifty years, no UFO report has revealed any evidence of a potential threat to the United Kingdom. The MOD has no specific capability for identifying the nature of such sightings.')

These are communications that aspire to self-erasure. Linguistic holding patterns, they defy you to resolve them, to force them to a point. They cannot be read, unless you can read between the lines.

The smokescreening business exploded in tandem with the increase in the speed at which answers were expected, And the lineage of the self-destructing resignation letter goes back far beyond any modern age of political spin and PR, and beyond poor Getúlio Vargas too. In fact, it coincides with an earlier, similar Big Bang for rapid-turnaround accountability: the birth of parliamentary democracy in Reformation England.

★ ★ ★

Written communication in politics had always been a dark, dangerous and explosive art – from the messengers of Classical times whose messages were tattooed on their heads, to be covered with hair until delivery, to the Middle Ages' hopelessly tangled and treacherous webs of treaties and undertakings, satirized by anamorphic skull between the two figures in Holbein the Younger's *The Ambassadors*. (The European Middle Ages' reputation as the first age of treacherous fine print may or may not have something to do with the rise of the legal profession. All but non-existent in the dark ages, at least formally, the practice of canon law saw a careers boom in the thirteenth century, with the Mayor of London introducing qualifications and regulation in 1280.) By the heyday of the Elizabethan Court, the need to protect yourself, not from what others said about you but from the possible future consequences of your own words, had reached a kind of paranoid hysteria of purloined letters and endless contractual conditions that prefigures the Nixon tapes and Cold War spymania.

This fever for disguising or encoding one's own written words only plunged further into lethal, trust-no-one insanity as the Civil War tested both secure communications and allegiances to their limit.

Yet the Age of Parliament, and the first publicly accountable body in British history, meant that suddenly, policy had to be announced publicly. Not only that: your proposal, defence or testimony could be interrogated, in something like real time, and often to your face. The day of assignations in Palace corridors and sealed commands to half a dozen Earls was over. The national political address had arrived. For any floundering authority figure, this was bad news indeed.

By April 1659, just seven months into his rule, Oliver Cromwell's son Richard had become the least popular man in England. Widely despised by the armies he purported to command as Lord Protector of England, Wales and Ireland, he presided over the newborn Parliament at a time of spiralling government debt, social unrest, political partisanship and popular mistrust of the ruling cadre.

If that sounds familiar, then today's political class

should probably start the engines of their escape launches about now. Cromwell tried bluster, denouncing malcontents and moaners; and then blamed underlings and generals for the mess, to save his skin. It was a disastrous miscalculation. Within days, his own troops surrounded Westminster, demanding his removal. He was caricatured as 'Tumbledown Dick, the national calamity'.

All of which turns his uncharacteristically meek, emollient resignation letter – an apparent exercise in 'drawing a line' and escaping the shitstorm – into something rather more mysterious.

In the letter, Cromwell fails to address directly the reasons for his resignation, but hints vaguely and repeatedly that even this letter is a hostage; that it speaks in words other than those he would have chosen. He comes close to declaring that the letter has been largely drafted for him to sign (he may already have been under house arrest when he wrote it), too:

I have perused the Resolve and Declaration, which you were pleased to deliver to me the other Night; and, for your Information touching what is mentioned in the said Resolve, I have caused a true State of my Debts to be transcribed, and annexed to this Paper: Which will shew what they are, and how they were contracted.

As to that Part of the Resolve, whereby the Committee are to inform themselves, How far I do acquiesce in the Government of this Commonwealth, as it is declared by this Parliament; I trust, my past Carriage hitherto hath manifested my Acquiescence in the Will and Disposition of God; and that I love and value the Peace of this Commonwealth much above my own Concernments: And I desire, that by this, a Measure of my future Deportment may be taken; which, thro' the Assistance of God, shall be such as shall bear the same Witness; having, I hope, in some degree, learned rather to reverence and submit to the Hand of God, than to be unquiet under it: And, as to the late Providences that have fallen out amongst us, however, in respect of the particular Engagements that lay upon me, I could not be active in making a Change in the Government of these Nations, yet through the Goodness of God, I can freely acquiesce in it, being made; and do hold myself obliged, as (with other Men) I expect Protection from the present Government, so to demean myself with all Peaceableness under it; and to procure, to the uttermost of my Power, that all in whom I have any Interest, do the same.

Richard Cromwell

Like the classic B-movie scene in which a kidnapping victim alerts a prying relative on the phone that something is terribly wrong by speaking in a weirdly forced, overly formal way and deliberately getting key names wrong, Cromwell's resignation was a coded dog-whistle to his supporters and friends, while appearing placatory to his captors.

The language is impersonal – Cromwell was usually a passionate, opinionated and eloquent letter-writer, and the cold legalese of his resignation was a clear signal that it was not really Richard Cromwell speaking here. It also ends abruptly, with no leave-taking – something Cromwell habitually included. He may be yours, but he is certainly not yours sincerely.

Over the centuries, it's tempting to discern a pattern by which each successive increase in communication speed and transparency claims its own high-profile scalp among those who fail to account for it.

Sometimes, you can feel the birth pangs of a new way of communicating in the resignations themselves. The most famous modern example of this coded resignation is King Edward VIII's letter abdicating the throne in 1936, and we owe it to the sudden arrival of newsreel and wireless coverage.

Both the original draft, written by Edward himself and vetoed by Prime Minister Stanley Baldwin, and the approved version that Baldwin considered less likely to cause national schism, constitutional unrest or even civil war, are revealing in their own way.

Within the space of twenty-four hours, Edward's letter went from a relatively plain-spoken and poignantly open-hearted plea for understanding to something else entirely. Here, from 9 December 1936, is Edward's vetoed draft announcement:

> Neither Mrs Simpson nor I have ever sought to insist that she should be queen. All we desired was that our married happiness should carry with it a proper title and dignity for her, befitting my wife. Now that I have at last been able to take you into my confidence, I feel it is best to go away for a while, so that you may reflect calmly and quietly, but without undue delay, on what I have said.

But Baldwin was keenly aware that the relay of this message instantaneously to millions contained the potential for a volatile post-Depression public to react in unpredictable ways. Cue Baldwin's intervention, the inevitable counsel of lawyers, and a redraft. This second draft was something far more robotic – the kidnap victim's monitored call again. The following day, Edward settled on his final letter of abdication. It's a mixture of legalese and waffle, and nothing of Edward is present.

INSTRUMENT OF ABDICATION

I, Edward the Eighth, of Great Britain, Ireland, and the British Dominion beyond the Seas, King, Emperor of India, do hereby declare my irrevocable determination to renounce the Throne for Myself and for My descendants, and My desire that effect should be given to the Instrument of Abdication immediately.

In token thereof I have hereunto set my hand this tenth day of December, nineteen hundred and thirty six, in the presence of the witnesses whose signatures are subscribed.

To Baldwin, this final letter, unaccompanied by any informal message or heartfelt valediction, was a victory. To anyone else its utter capitulation must have looked like a frustrated, indignant protest: OK, fine, I'm gone. And you can whistle for your seamless handover or soothing words of valediction. Fuck you. Stiff upper lip indeed.

The next time he addressed the nation, on the day his reign officially ended, he would do so as His Royal Highness, Prince Edward. The game over, the tone of his farewell to the people was moderate. Perhaps that's because, again, the text he had submitted had been rejected, edited and redrafted – this time by Baldwin's man, Winston Churchill. However, one barb aimed squarely at Baldwin was allowed through. In 2013, newly declassified Cabinet Office files revealed that the King's telephone was secretly being bugged throughout the wrangling over his resignation letter, on the orders of none other than the Home Secretary. Edward may have suspected as much. His final farewell began: 'At last I am able to say a few words of my own.'

★ ★ ★

For the resignation buff, this is gripping stuff: the resignation as crime scene, and as parlour game. It becomes a puzzle: can you tell what the writer is really saying? And what they really want?

But like any riddle, it can also be a sport. And as a sport, it owes its existence to the most famous resignation letter of all time; one now quoted every minute of every day as the tagline of a Hollywood wit.

Groucho Marx's 1949 letter resigning from the Friars Club said simply:

PLEASE ACCEPT MY RESIGNATION. I DON'T WANT TO BELONG TO ANY CLUB THAT WILL ACCEPT ME AS A MEMBER.

The message is often read as a throwaway remark, an inconsequential piece of off-the-cuff smart-arsery by a man who threw out one-liners for free. It is anything but.

In fact, it was a masterclass in killing a conversation and pre-emptively snuffing out questions. Marx had found himself enrolled at a club on the insistence of a friend, but despaired of the 'general clap-trap that you are subjected to from the All-American bores which you would instantly flee from if you weren't trapped in a clubhouse'. The morning after a particularly tedious exchange with other members, he fired off his resignation in a telegram, formulated, he later admitted, as a circular statement – a gnomic piece of inscrutability – specifically designed to bamboozle and pre-empt any attempts to urge him to stay or to delve into his real reasons for leaving.

Marx's two-liner, brief as it is, is a masterclass in the key tactics of any conversation-killing resignation letter. Letters and statements by everyone from Muammar Gaddafi to hedge-fund manager Warren Buffet have copied its beautifully inscrutable circularity, its persuasive, evasive, playfull non-speak.

As with all code-breaking work, it helps to know what you're looking for. Official notifications can appear spookily uniform – that's their MO – but look for the cracks. Sometimes, as with James Murdoch's resignations from News International and BSkyB (both included later) you can only see the stress lines appearing when you hold two up together.

Their inscrutability, their coded messages, control-freak openness and lists of junior contacts from whom further information could be solicited are intentionally, befuddling statements as jets of squid ink. They are not incendiary in their nature like other resignations, but dully explosive, like a canister of sleeping-gas launched through the office window. Nothing to see here, they say. This story is over. Like the three goats in the fairy tale, they urge you not to challenge them, but to await developments, for there will probably be another one along any moment.

It was not quite as easy as that, of course. In Britain, the twentieth century began with generalized suffrage, matured with the proliferation of a huge and powerful press establishment, and ended with twenty-four-hour rolling news and internet access. The increased stake of the ordinary people in what others – from government to industry – are up to has been matched by their curiosity and the ease with which they could find out.

What followed was an odd sort of resignations arms race that continues to this day, with the explosion of social media as a conduit between people, brands and organizations. The keener press and public are to find out what went wrong, and the quicker the interrogation cycle, the more effort the resigner or their company puts into making sure we don't find out. And the more 'crisis management PR' teams cloud the issue, the more tenacious we are in pursuing it.

Here in Britain, the next escalation of that arms race came at the height of another, more deadly arms race.

On 5 June 1963, the Conservative government's Secretary of State for War, John Profumo, resigned amid a growing scandal over his affair with the lover of the Russian attaché in London.

The Minister, married and with a position that gave him access to high-level classified documents and discussions around Britain's defence capability, had met a London 'good-time girl', Christine Keeler, at a house party at Cliveden, Lord Astor's mansion. He began an affair, not knowing that Keeler had also been seeing one Yevgeny Ivanov – aka Eugene – the Soviets' senior naval attaché in London.

When allegations of the affair surfaced that March – along with suspicions on the part of MI5 that the Soviets had been using the unwitting Keeler to try and extract information from the minister – Profumo denied everything in Parliament.

It was Profumo's bad luck that his indiscretions hadn't come three years earlier. In 1961, a small, cheaply produced magazine called *Private Eye* hit the news-stands for the first time. With its origins in a tiny periodical produced by Richard Ingrams, Christopher Booker, Willie Rushton and Paul Foot, and with funding from the likes of Peter Cook giving it muscle, *Private Eye*'s remit was satire – still an unfamiliar term. Its name too was ominous. The private eye, the editors explained, was the one who 'fingered the suspects'.

On 24 November 1962, what Booker called 'the rage for satire' hit television, in the form of the BBC's *That Was The Week That Was*. David Frost and Ned Sherrin's savage irreverence towards authority were a sensation, their lampooning of popular figures just what a sanctimony-sick public wanted. And, week after week, John Profumo found himself in the crosshairs.

In a disastrously miscalculated move which he hoped would stop the satirists, but which only inflamed speculation further, Profumo also announced that he would sue for libel anyone repeating the allegations outside of the Commons. The drip-drip of information continued; Profumo became a national laughing stock. In June he was forced to admit he had lied.

This is his resignation to Harold Macmillan.

Dear Prime Minister,

You will recollect that on 22 March, following certain allegations made in Parliament, I made a personal statement. At that time the rumour had charged me with assisting in the disappearance of a witness and with being involved in some possible breach of security.

So serious were these charges that I allowed myself to think that my personal association with that witness, which had also been the subject of rumour, was by comparison of minor importance only. In my statement I said there had been no impropriety in this association. To my very deep regret I have to admit that this was not true, and that I misled you and my colleagues and the House.

I ask you to understand that I did this to protect, as I thought, my wife and family, who were misled, as were my professional advisers.

I have come to realize that, by this deception, I have been guilty of a grave misdemeanour and despite the fact that there is no truth whatsoever in the other charges, I cannot remain a member of your Administration, nor of the House of Commons.

I cannot tell you of my deep remorse for the embarrassment I have caused you, to my colleagues in the Government, to my constituents and to the Party which I have served for the past twenty-five years.

Yours sincerely,

Jack Profumo

This is an unusual letter. At first glance, it appears to hold nothing back. On the subject of what happened in Parliament, of his regrets regarding his position, his party and Macmillan himself, Profumo speaks plainly and openly, accusing himself. 'I made . . . I allowed . . . I said . . . I have . . . I did.'

But when it comes to who misled his wife and children, something extraordinary happens. Profumo flinches, for the first and only time in the letter, and the passive voice appears. 'They were misled.' The paragraph never recovers. It stutters and stumbles forward, through a series of hesitations and qualifications. Then it stops. You can almost sense the relief as Profumo finds his footing again amidst the reassuring conventions of Parliamentary leave-taking.

In the letter, as in life, private emotions erupt into public discourse, and public discourse is ill-equipped to contain them.

By 18 October 1963, Macmillan, the PM to whom Profumo had addressed his resignation, was also gone – amid speculation that the ill health he gave as his reason for resigning had been precipitated by trying to limit the damage from the affair. The Conservative government was holed below the waterline, and by 1964 Harold Wilson's Labour government was in power.

As for the minister himself, after he resigned he took a menial job cleaning the toilets of a charity building in London's Tower Hamlets, a deprived borough in the East End. He never spoke of the affair in public again.

He might have wished he had adopted the same line as one of his successors in the next Conservative government.

Lord Lambton, Parliamentary Under-Secretary of State for Defence (RAF) in Ted Heath's government, was exposed in the *News of the World* in 1973 as an enthusiastic habitué of prostitutes, having been photographed in bed with one of his regulars by her husband, who took the photos to the paper. On searching his house, the police found cannabis.

Lambton's response on 24 May 1973 was a virtuoso resignation statement that was so astonishingly open – even by today's standards – that the press had nowhere else to take the story.

> This is a sordid story. I had a casual acquaintance with a call girl and one or two of her friends. But there has been no security risk and no blackmail and never at any time have I spoken of any aspect of my late job. All that has happened is that some sneak pimp has seen an opportunity of making money by the sale of the story and secret photographs to the papers at home and abroad. My own feelings may be imagined, but I have no excuses whatever to make. I behaved with credulous stupidity. I must repeat that there has been no high life vice ring, no security leak, no blackmail and, as far as I know, no politician of any party is remotely connected to these events. Thank you.

The letter's 'attack-as-defence' posture was so effective that it caused an upsurge of sympathy and even admiration – the phrase 'and one or two of her friends' recalls showbiz arch-cads like Leslie Phillips, David Lee Roth or Alan Rickman's Sheriff of Nottingham. It's the sort of line that image consultants would spend all night brainstorming into a statement today.

In today's crisis management PR terms, what happened next would be called an 'information dump'. Lambton followed his resignation statement with statements to the press, and to a security inquiry, that today sound more like precursors to our own celebrity penitents' soul-baring, line-drawing *Oprah* interviews than anything else.

He claimed at various times that he was driven to hi-jinks with prostitutes by the insanely high pressure of his job as a junior minister; by the demotivating dearth of stimulating, demanding tasks in his 'futile' day-job; and by 'faulty judgement' arising from a personality crisis (the result of his wrestling with questions around his use of his hereditary aristocratic title). He listed 'gardening' and 'debauchery' as two activities he indulged in enthusiastically in order to distract himself from this 'obsession'.

The security inquiry – its protocol had been established in the wake of the Profumo affair – duly found that he had no case to answer: 'There is nothing in (Lambton's) conduct to suggest that the risk of indiscretions on these occasions was other than negligible.' Lambton, mercifully winning his lifelong battle with responsibility and his title, retired to Tuscany and downgraded himself to Viscount Lambton.

* * *

As one politician was on the way out, another was on the way up. Despite low pilot aptitude scores and poor attendance, in May 1968 George W. Bush found himself promoted to jet pilot in the Texas Air National Guard, neatly sidestepping any question of draft to Vietnam.

After a further series of incidents (including a suspension from flying) that could have damaged a less lucky man – or perhaps a man whose father was less influential in the Republican Party – 'W' resigned with one haphazardly filled-out form in June 1974. Addressed to Air Reserve

Personnel Center/DPAAD with the subject line 'Tender of Resignation', it began: 'I, <u>George Walker Bush</u>, under AFR 35-41, paragraph 20-10, hereby voluntarily tender my resignation from all appointments held by me at this time.' The reason stated, 'Inadequate time to fullfill possible future commitments', is especially tantalizing when one knows the process of grooming him as an oilman and Republican mover had already begun. The timing – Vietnam was winding down – is equally thought-provoking.

Bush's trajectory, and that confident, upwardly mobile farewell, is worth contrasting with the resignation of, and dishonourable discharge given to, another US Air Force pilot whose off-duty behaviour also fell short, but was of less distinguished stock.

Kelly Flinn was a heroine and a role model. The youngest of five children from St Louis, Missouri, she had wanted to fly since attending Space Camp one summer at NASA's Huntsville, Alabama base. After training on bombers at Air Force Academy, she became the first female B-52 pilot in the US Air Force. She resigned with a general discharge – also called a 'less-than-honourable discharge' – rather than face military criminal trial. Those charges, including disobeying an order, making a false statement, conduct unbecoming of an officer and fraternization, stemmed from an affair with a married civilian – a football coach also working at Minot Air Force base. Amid widespread concerns about gender double standards in the forces, Flinn initially fought the case, and when the Air Force mobilized a legal, PR and crisis management team against her, Flinn responded in kind. After a short but brutal 'PR war' that damaged all parties in the affair, Flinn wrote this resignation statement to Sheila E. Widnall, Secretary of the Air Force in the Clinton administration. However complex a character Flinn is, when she writes about 'wanting to be forgiven for my human fault', one can't help but think of George Bush Sr's more fortunate son. Flinn's is a very effective and moving letter. Here are a few lines:

May 23, 1997

It is extremely difficult, if not impossible to put into words my love for the Air Force and devotion to the Air Force. It is with heartfelt agony and the deepest sadness I have ever felt that I submit my resignation from the Air Force.

I truly love the United States Air Force, and would like the opportunity to continue to serve my country. I realize that I have made mistakes and errors in judgment . . . It is a huge personal loss for me, to be asking to resign from the United States Air Force. [It] feels like a part of me has died. If given a choice, I would prefer to receive some form of non-judicial punishment, return to flight status, and continue to use all of the training I have received to benefit the Air Force and my country . . . I would never intentionally do anything to bring discredit upon the Air Force. I truly fell deeply in love with a man who led me down the path of self destruction and career destruction [. . .]

I only want to serve my country and to be forgiven for my human faults. I don't think it's too much to ask. I only wish that someone in my chain of command would have asked what was happening in my life. Then they would have learned of the fear and the darkness in which I was living . . . [I] did not stand up for myself as a human being. That will never happen again. [. . .]

The whole letter is an oddly artless, ham-fisted letter to issue in the context of a high-stakes PR war with the US Air Force and US Government. Flinn repeats herself, forgets what she was saying, splurges out declarations of love for the Air Force, and blurts awkwardly worded condemnations of her former lover. I've seen this happen before, and it means one of two things. Perhaps she'd decided to go it alone, and not taken her PR team's advice on rewrites (sometimes this happens because the PR team's meter reading has exceeded the client's budget). Or maybe 'artless' is part of the strategy to win public sympathy. A cut-glass letter from a high-powered pilot would go over the head of Joe Public. This has been left full of the linguistic tells of the underdog – the opposite of the fast-and-loose, privileged, yeehawing Young Dubya archetype – on purpose.

Because there was a second future role at stake here. As well as being a member of US service personnel, Kelly Flinn was something of a celebrity. As the first female B-52 pilot, she was on Air Force recruitment posters throughout the country, and played a central part in nearly every one of the USAF's equal-opportunities recruiting drives. By 1997, she was very much Brand Flinn. That brand became even more powerful as she battled against an almost proudly sexist institution in what many considered to be a stacked case. After all, as another pilot pointed out: 'The question she was asked would never have been asked of a male pilot, because affairs are deemed acceptable for males, and no-one wants to put a male in a position where he has to lie about sex and then run the risk of being discharged.'

With lurid details seeping out that spring on the nightly network news, Brand Flinn was holed. It was time to limit damage, to restore the brand's sheen and to build its value again. And if the letter seems familiar, it's because the template it follows is not that of the corporate resignation, but the Hollywood/Washington confessional. This is a resignation for prime-time, not the politics show.

'I am not asking to be absolved', 'I fell deeply in love with a man who led me down the path of self destruction', 'the fear and darkness in which I was living' and 'I did not turn to anyone for help when I should have' are all part of the lexicon of American celebrity redemption and career fightback, from disgraced televangelists to Mel Gibson, and philandering politicians to Lance Armstrong. (We'll get to them later.)

But the resignation is also a job application in waiting – a news sound-bite friendly CV. It includes a statement of her worth, her training, her capabilities, her passion for the job: she sounds like a real catch. And, of course, there's her capacity to learn from her mistakes. Even as she leaves, she's not thinking of herself, but of how reinstatement would have offered more value to her employer.

A high-profile book deal saw *Proud to Be: My Life, the Air Force, the Controversy* dominate the chat-show circuit that same November. Interview previews even sounded like the pitch for a Hollywood film. ('She rose higher and fell harder, but Kelly Flinn's story is universal . . . we share her horror as the love she dreamed of turns into a nightmare and she must battle the military's sex police behind closed doors,' went her publisher's blurb, calling her life 'a combination of *Top Gun* and *The Scarlet Letter.*') There was, it's worth noting, nothing artless in her ghostwriter's copy this time.

Flinn's next, well-paid job in private-sector aviation saw her promoted to captain. It still didn't get her groomed as a future president like George W, though. Even skill, celebrity and a good agent can only get you so far.

Only a fool underestimates the capacity of a well-executed resignation to open some doors; or at least to reposition the resigner as the valuable commodity in the equation – perhaps the one party in the affair who will go on to greater things. A little personal ego helps, too. Newcastle United suffered a poor run of results at the start of the 1999–2000 Premiership season, but there was uproar when the manager dropped Tyneside's talismanic goal-scorer Alan Shearer and captain Robert Lee. 'There's not much to say,' said thinking-man's footballer Ruud Gullit on 28 August 1999, when he resigned as manager. 'I want to notify everyone in this room that I resigned from Newcastle United.' He read the following prepared statement to the room, as flashbulbs popped:

The reason for my resignation is partly for the bad results we have had in the last couple of weeks but the biggest reason is something that I am going to explain to you now . . .

When all the players will be fit I still think that this team is capable of doing very good things, therefore I wish Newcastle United a very prosperous future with more luck than all the previous managers have had.

The main reason why I came to England four years ago was that I wanted to have my own private life back. The years at Chelsea I enjoyed very much because I really have the feeling that I could be myself again. The feeling of walking along the street minding my own business, being able to shop, being able to go to the cinema, being able to go out, being able to be like anyone else.

These things seem very ordinary for someone who doesn't know what it is like to be me. These things are worth more to me than any treasure. The moment I came to Newcastle the journalists asked me if I understood how big the job was and I thought I knew, now I know what they really meant by that. In this last year my private life has been invaded in a bad way. I cannot see the point why my family has to suffer for my profession. For me my family always comes first and therefore I took this decision to resign . . .

As a player I could express the joy I had inside me and as a manager I could express that to my players, this resulted in two medals that I treasure very much. The feeling of being twice at Wembley in a final has given me in this short period of management and coaching a great satisfaction . . .

I would like to thank [my PA, and players, and the] Malmaison Hotel who have been really good to me during my stay in Newcastle. And I want to thank all the restaurants where I have been to for their marvellous food and hospitality . . .

And last but not least, I would like to thank Freddy Shepherd and Freddie Fletcher for their support and energy and the belief they gave me . . . I hope one day they can fulfil their dreams to make this club one of the best clubs in Europe. Newcastle Football Club has come from a small club to a club of international standing and it is partly because of them . . .

Thank you for your attention, and I will go on a long holiday with my family.

It's a thoughtful, balanced piece from a man clearly more eloquent and magnanimous than most football managers. But there's more going on here than perhaps even Gullit realizes. On first reading, it seems to be a classic piece of public resignation rhetoric – he is leaving because of tabloid intrusion into his private life, which is a shame because he is a football legend who achieved great things for the club. There is no mention of the ongoing feud with Alan Shearer.

Still, it leaves a rather odd impression, something you can't quite put your finger on. And that's down to some rather exquisite moments. The plug for the Malmaison and the statement 'These things are normal for anyone who doesn't know what it is like to be me' are worthy of Alan Partridge. But they're part of something larger (and rather odd) that happens throughout. The paparazzi, the Malmaison, the marvellous food at 'all the restaurants', his personal secretary, his forthcoming long holiday . . . Gullit seems to be peppering his resignation with reminders that he's the one living the high-status, globetrotting dream. This isn't going to rain on his parade.

It's also an exquisitely weighted exercise in diplomatic cattiness. For all their occasional awkwardness, Gullit's statements were well thought-out and carefully put together. He had the help of a PR team (almost all football statements are at least partly crafted by PR companies in Soho) but he remains a rare example of a thinker in the football fraternity. This may be his finest hour. Read closely, and what first seems like a sincere valediction is actually so full of equivocation and qualification – perhaps subconscious – that it leaves you with the impression that the club he's leaving is steered by two dreamers and is pretty much going nowhere without him – at least, unless they get 'more luck than *all* previous managers have had' (italics mine).

But for all Gullit's unconscious equivocation – and the Alan Shearer-shaped hole at the heart of his resignation statement – it's fairly heart-on-the-sleeve stuff. If you're looking for messages so coded that they practically self-destruct on the lips, look to Wall Street. Because nobody plays resignation find-the-lady with more brazenly hole-filled statements than the Americans.

Throughout the 1990s, Texas-based energy, commodities and services giant Enron looked like the perfect company. It was *Fortune* magazine's most innovative company no fewer than six years running. Its revenue for the year 2000 topped $101 billion. It was, surely, one of the world's strongest and best-run companies, even awarding statesmen like Nelson Mandela, Mikhail Gorbachev and Colin Powell its own prize, modelled on the Nobel, for 'distinguished public service'.

There was just one problem: the whole company was built on a lie.

In 2001, it was revealed that Enron's apparent success was a sham, its figures the result of a sophisticated deception. As the Enron accounting scandal unfolded into the biggest corporate collapse in American history, its cache of internal emails – archived by the authorities when a police raid seized the machines and servers – traces a precipitous curve from 'I am resigning for purely personal reasons' to resigning due to 'multiple inquiries and investigations'.

One breathtaking email sent to board members even

'attached . . . a list from the Enron Corporate Secretary's Office of the Enron companies where you are a board member and/or an officer, noting your title', so difficult was it to keep track, and so urgent was the need to resign from as many as possible before the shit hit the fan. A reply, sent at 5.30am, simply asks, 'Should I resign from all of these companies immediately?' The two emails here, from main culprits Kenneth Lay and Jeffrey Skilling, illustrate the speed of the Board of Directors' journey from low-key containment to capitulation at the hands of the law.

Jeffrey Skilling, President, Enron
14th August 2001
To: all staff
I am resigning for personal reasons. I want to thank Ken Lay for his understanding of this purely personal decision, and I want to thank the board and all of my colleagues at Enron.

Kenneth Lay, CEO, Enron
4th February 2002
To: All staff
I want to see Enron survive and successfully emerge from reorganization. Due to the multiple inquiries and investigations, some of which are focused on me personally, I believe that my involvement has become a distraction to achieving this goal. My concern is for current and former Enron employees and other stakeholders, and I feel that it is in their best interest for me to step down from the Board.

If the measured tone of the two resignations here was intended to calm and reassure, it had the opposite effect. It was already becoming clear that Enron had been engaged in some sleight of hand, and that many of its executives had been less than honest with shareholders or employers.

Even as Lay pressed 'send', Enron's offices and servers were under investigation. In that context, smooth corporatese begins to look like blinkered denial. They're trapped – corporate darlings for so long that they've never developed another register; one to use when things go wrong. Their faces are frozen in the dealmaker's grin, like Hallowe'en masks with US Presidents' grinning faces on them.

Jeffrey Skilling is currently serving fourteen years of a twenty-four years and four months sentence in a high-security prison in Colorado on multiple felony charges. Kenneth Lay was found guilty of ten felony counts in 2006. He died of a heart attack while awaiting sentencing. Even the innocent board members appear to find themselves haunted by the episode. One is now Vice-President of a global communications and infrastructure company. His biography on their website says: '[Redacted] most recently served as Vice President and General Counsel of a global business unit of a multinational diversified energy services company, headquartered in Houston.'

The case cast a long shadow on the corporate resignation, as companies became obsessed by the power of reputational damage. This fear also made them hostages to the unpredictable power of the resigner. As they rushed to comply with new and stringent accounting laws introduced to ensure there would never be another Enron, companies looked at how they could protect themselves from their own misdeeds. They also looked at how they could deal with whistleblowers. A 'crisis communications' industry that had grown up to manage genuine crises was now called upon to hand-hold whenever someone quit. They didn't come cheap and reputational damage was now a business risk factor on the insurance policy, along with fire, earthquake, non-payment and the loss of key clients. Soon, it had budgets, degrees and business books of its own, with names like *Managing Reputational Risks: Curbing Threats, Leveraging Opportunities* (2003) and *Reputational Risks: A Question of Trust* (2006).

At the same time, a change swept through the culture of the high-profile kiss-off. Two big cases in California show just how scared of resignations bosses had become – and how far they were prepared to go to control them. On 5 September 2006, a *Newsweek* investigation revealed that Hewlett Packard (HP) chairwoman Patricia Dunn had instructed the US engineering and tech giant's general counsel to hire freelance spies to investigate board members and several journalists. The aim was to find the source of a leak from HP, but things quickly spiralled out of control. After the spies themselves recruited yet more private detectives, who impersonated HP board members and journalists in order to get access to their phone records, the story broke and the scandal engulfed the company.

Perhaps mindful of the sensitivity around corporate dirty tricks in the wake of the Enron trials, HP quickly hired PR specialists Sitrick and Company to 'manage' their media relations during the crisis. Dunn's resignation letter – as part of a press release from the company in which she got to speak last – is the fruit. There's more to it than one would think at first sight.

I have resigned today at the request of the board. The unauthorized disclosure of confidential information was a serious violation of our code of conduct. I followed the proper processes by seeking the assistance of HP security personnel. I did not select the people who conducted the investigation, which was undertaken after consultation with board members. I accepted the responsibility to identify the sources of those leaks, but I did not propose the specific methods of the investigation. I was a full subject of the investigation myself and my phone records were examined along with others. Unfortunately, the people HP relied upon to conduct this type of investigation let me and the company down. I continue to have the best interests of HP at heart and thus I have accepted the board's request to resign. I look forward to appearing before Congress next week to answer their questions and help the company put this unfortunate event behind it.

Sitrick's writers are talented people – some of the best. Hewlett Packard's a big client paying them top dollar for a very important job on a top-of-the-hour story. So how come the resignation is so confusing and vague? The words all make sentences, but the sentences don't work together. In some cases, they actually appear to go against each other. There's no thread at all – effects don't always follow causes. Is not selecting the people a good thing or a bad thing? An admission or mitigation? It's hard to hold onto the narrative even a second or two after reading it.

Writing badly enough to be unquotable, but not badly enough to be memorable, is a skill damage-limitation PRs use all the time. It's not easy, either – it's a bit like playing golf just well enough for your boss to enjoy it, while making sure he beats you. Its purpose is to kill the story.

Think of it from any PR and reputation-management agency's point of view. Patricia Dunn could have issued a statement that was far more convincing, and much more sympathetic. It would have been *better* as prose. But it would have been *worse* as a piece of crisis communication. That statement would have become part of the story. People would have reported it, shared it. Newspapers would have printed it in full. It would have made sense, and been coherent, and therefore people could have argued with it or backed it. The name Hewlett Packard would have been associated with the dirty tricks campaign for hundreds of thousands more column inches, and millions more Google search matches. After rolling news, the wireless, TV satire and parliamentary debate, the idea that SEO is a determining factor in corporate governance shouldn't be that surprising.

This way, whatever else the statement does, it represents a conversational dead end, online and elsewhere, without ever saying so.

There was to be another twist. Less than four years later, it was the turn of Dunn's replacement Mark Hurd to become mired in scandal – this time around a sexual harassment claim brought against him by a former soft-porn star and beauty queen named Jodie Fisher who had been working at HP. Again, a powerful crisis management team was called in to help with his resignation letter.

Work such as this pays big fees, even by US corporate standards. One company who pitched to draft the resignation was APCO, a Washington DC lobbying firm whose PR and global strategy payrolls include a former US Ambassador to the UN, director of communications for the French Prime Minister, Baron Hutton of Furness – aka John Hutton, cabinet minister under Tony Blair and Gordon Brown. APCO was overt in its promise: they could supply a resignation that would kill the story.

Next, they defined the stakes for a botched resignation. APCO's pitch presentation to the HP board at its landscaped Californian HQ pulled out all the stops. It included the dramatic delivery of 'live' magazine, newspaper and TV news mock-ups, all showing calamitous news reports of the kind that would appear in the national media – if HP didn't take them on. It all led up to the final recommendation: Hurd had to go, and APCO had to handle it. Hurd and his employer, both anxious for their own rapidly falling stock, willingly took the bait and paid up.

When it appeared, Hurd's resignation went one better than Dunn's. It was one of three short items on a routine press release on performance.

HP today announced that Chairman, Chief Executive Officer and President Mark Hurd has decided with the Board of Directors to resign his positions effective immediately.

'As the investigation progressed, I realized there were instances in which I did not live up to the standards and principles of trust, respect and integrity that I have espoused at HP and which have guided me throughout my career. After a number of discussions with members of the board, I will move aside and the board will search for new leadership. This is a painful decision for me to make after five years at

HP, but I believe it would be difficult for me to continue as an effective leader at HP and I believe this is the only decision the board and I could make at this time. I want to stress that this in no way reflects on the operating performance or financial integrity of HP. The corporation is exceptionally well positioned strategically. HP has an extremely talented executive team supported by a dedicated and customer focused work force. I expect that the company will continue to be successful in the future.'

The CEO of one of the world's biggest companies had pestered a retired porn star at the workplace, spirited her off on first-class jets to luxury hotels on expenses ($75,000 for one claim), and settled her harassment case at a late-night meeting before the company's investigators had been given a chance to speak to her.

Yet you could so easily miss that entirely. The statement reads like a supplementary piece to a main release that, in fact, never took place. There's no sense of Hurd's reason for resigning. There is no denial, no admission, nothing material. To turn his apology into something this insubstantial without sounding evasive is a craft. And it's full of nice touches that a PR professional might recognize; even the part that most closely approaches his reason for resigning is stuffed with so many extraneous words that no headline writer or journalist can isolate a quote from it.

For APCO, it was a job well done: it was a sad story written in vanishing ink. You have to applaud the effort, but to a journalist, resignation statements like this can be infuriating. Of course, you report it anyway. But when you have to pitch the story, you know the material isn't going to do you any favours.

None of this is rocket science, but it's easy to get wrong, too. A case study of what might have been had APCO not been so good at being dull came on 13 June 2008, in Silicon Valley. Three years after merging his company with Yahoo!, Flickr founder Stuart Butterfield resigned from the Yahoo! board in entirely happy circumstances. When asked for a written statement, he responded with a winningly self-effacing note that he hoped would minimize the fuss around his departure. His mistake was making it funny. Butterfield's rambling email was written in character. The character he chose was that of an elderly Wild West tinsmith and animal herder.

As you know, tin is in my blood. For generations my family has worked with this most useful of metals. When I joined Yahoo! back in '21, it was a sheet-tin concern of great momentum, growth and innovation. I knew it was the place for me . . .

By the time of the internet revolution and our expansion into Web Sites, I have been cast adrift. I tried to roll with the times, but nary a sheet of tin has rolled off our own production lines in over 30 years.

In my 87 years service, I've accomplished many feats, shared in the ups and downs, made great friends and learned a tremendous amount . . . but there is a new generation now and it would be unfair not to give them a chance. Those that started in the make-work programs of the depression, on the GI programs in the late '40s and even those young baby boomers need their own try without us old 'uns standing in the way.

So please accept my resignation, effective July 12. And I don't

*need no fancy parties or gold watches (I still have the one from '61
and '76). I will be spending more time with my family, tending to
my small but growing alpaca herd and of course getting back to
working with tin, my first love.*

Your old tin-smithing friend and colleague,

Stewart Butterfield

The note was leaked to Silicon Valley media almost
immediately, then beyond, becoming part of the folklore
in a community not known for the humour and playfulness
with which it approaches severance.

Like Marx, the genial Butterfield – who went on to
found a new company, Tinyspeck – has found himself
under siege at events from people desperate to know the
ins and outs behind the note. Like Schlueb, he is haunted
by that one note, casually dashed off. Google him, and
there it is.

In that sense it backfired. A more detailed, more boring
summary – the Hewlett Packard method – would have
meant having to talk less about it in future. As it is, he has
to dissect it every time he appears at a press conference
and over late-night emails to people like me, half a decade
later.

Curiosity is one thing. But for embattled public figures
facing serious questions, disappearing is never simple.
In his resignation to President George W. Bush on 6
November 2006, US Defense Secretary Donald Rumsfeld
– architect of the wars in Iraq and Afghanistan – got it
so wrong that he managed to reignite everything from
Fawlty Towers 'Don't mention the war' headlines to calls
for his impeachment.

Again, the issues were evasiveness and responsibility. The problem was that the thing Donald Rumsfeld didn't want to mention by name – Iraq – remained right at the heart of his statement, shouting, 'Look at me.'

> With my resignation as secretary of defense comes my deep appreciation to you for providing me this unexpected opportunity to serve.
>
> I leave with great respect for you and for the leadership you have provided during a most challenging time for our country. The focus, determination and perseverance you have so consistently provided have been needed and are impressive.
>
> It has been the highest honor of my long life to have been able to serve our country at such a critical time in our history and to have had the privilege of working so closely with the truly amazing young men and women in uniform. Their dedication, professionalism, courage and sacrifice are an inspiration.
>
> It is time to conclude my service. As I do so, I want you to know that you have my continuing and heartfelt support as you enter the final two years of your presidency.

The statement itself is interesting chiefly for that hole that seemed to enrage and exasperate most of the world the week of release. But also because Rumsfeld himself is tantalizingly absent from his own resignation. Where he says 'I', it is to talk about what he thinks of Bush, leadership, the country, its young men and women – anything but 'I'. Rumsfeld cannot bring himself (or perhaps is too canny to try) to assess his own contribution; or to ask for others' assessment. The final impression is of an *éminence grise* – always floating behind the scenes, never quite in the firing line.

But the archives reveal hidden depths to even this most shallow of resignations. Rumsfeld had tendered his resignation to George W. Bush twice before. Both attempts to resign were made in May 2004 in the wake of the exposé of abuses at Abu Ghraib prison in Iraq. The first simply says, 'You have my resignation any time you feel it would be helpful to you.' The second, a longer note in which he pressed his case, was explicit in recognizing the abuses meted out to Iraqis by US service personnel, and his feelings of responsibility. Unlike the 2006 letter, both were handwritten, informal and private. So what stopped him referring to his job, the war or anything else in 2006?

Perhaps, like HP's crisis management team, he knew any hint of justification in his public letter would draw fire. Unlike them, he lacked the skill to cover the hole. And so Rumsfeld left the public stage, not with a whimper, but with a bang. Just three years later, Erik Prince of Blackwater/ Xe Services – the private military company whose actions in Iraq had become the focus of outcry about its methods and the deaths of civilians on Rumsfeld's watch – himself resigned with a letter that appeared to take Rumsfeld's as its template. There was pride, confidence in the future, new challenges, a one-sentence gloss of the company's history – and, perhaps knowing that he was speaking to the record, and it was all a game of search and reputation management after all – a blithe refusal to acknowledge what everyone was really thinking.

Sometimes the people who try to sidestep questions

with their resignations should know better. When Andy Coulson moved from editing the *News of the World* to a position as Prime Minister David Cameron's media strategist and spokesman, he may have hoped he had left his past behind. It didn't turn out that way, and as the phone-hacking inquiry gathered steam, he resigned with this statement.

21 January 2011

I can today confirm that I've resigned as Downing Street director of communications.

It's been a privilege and an honour to work for David Cameron for three-and-a-half years. I'm extremely proud of the part I've played in helping him reach No 10 and during the coalition's first nine months.

Nothing is more important than the Government's task of getting this country back on its feet. Unfortunately, continued coverage of events connected to my old job at the *News of the World* has made it difficult for me to give the 110% needed in this role.

I stand by what I've said about those events but when the spokesman needs a spokesman, it's time to move on.

I'll leave within the next few weeks and will do so wishing the prime minister, his family and his brilliant and dedicated team the very best for what I'm sure will be a long and successful future in government.

'When the spokesman needs a spokesman' is a beautiful, pearl-like phrase, and could only have come from a highly successful tabloid editor. It's got that same sense of the common man's bafflement in the face of official logic that informs pieces on Eurocrats demanding straighter bananas and officials employed to administrate official administration. What it says is, I recognize I must go. What it *really* says is: the world's gone mad.

There are other flashes of the former tabloid street-fighter here too. 'Standing by' what you've said is the standard Fleet Street legalese response to challenges on the grounds of accuracy. It says, we think we're telling the truth. It *really* says, we're not going to tell you any more.

If the rest of it reads a little like one of the Prime Minister's own classic announcements – plumply proud, full of the slightly awkward overstatements around keenness, commitment, gung-ho spirit and the common-touch phrasing of aspirational Middle England – then that's hardly surprising, as Cameron was reading out Coulson's words all those years.

For all the joys of his final statement, if Coulson thought he had cauterized the wound around phone hacking, he was wrong. Smokescreening like Coulson's only works in a high-turnaround, short-attention-span environment like the media. In court, his circular statements were mercilessly and methodically unpicked. While other defendants in the hacking trial, including Rebekah Brooks, were cleared, Coulson was convicted of conspiracy to intercept voicemails. On 4 July 2014 he was sentenced to 18 months in prison. Other cases against him continue.

The more attempts at 'drawing a line' and 'moving on' one sees flounder – even in experienced hands like Coulson's – the more baffling it is that anything but disclosure and suture is ever even considered. But sometimes situations develop too fast for those at the centre to judge where they'll lead. Sometimes, they think they'll get away with it. So when a lewd picture of New York Congressman Anthony Weiner was posted on his own Twitter account, he claimed to have been hacked, and repeatedly denied any involvement. As the writer Graham Lineham observed, "My account was hacked" is the modern equivalent of "A witch did it".'

As Weiner stuck to his guns in the face of mounting evidence, bizarre TV interview followed bizarre TV interview. At one point, he pulled a trusty Donald Rumsfeld technique, pretending he couldn't hear questions being asked by an interviewer inches away from him with a microphone. Still, the momentum built.

Then, suddenly, the game was up. On 7 June 2011, his guilt conclusively proved, he resigned from the House of Representatives with a well-overdue 'line-drawing' public statement.

I have not been honest with myself, my family, my constituents, my friends and supporters, and the media.

Last Friday night, I tweeted a photograph of myself that I intended to send as a direct message as part of a joke to a woman in Seattle.

Once I realized I had posted it to Twitter, I panicked, I took it down, and said that I had been hacked. I then continued to stick to that story, which was a hugely regrettable mistake. [. . .]

I'm deeply ashamed of my terrible judgment and actions. I'll be glad to take any questions that you might have.

But even there, things did not go as planned. Hecklers, including one from a radio station, had been attracted to the circus, and interrupted his statement with cries of 'Bye bye, pervert!' and 'Are you fully erect?' – even hijacking his closing offer of a Q&A, in atonement for the way he'd stalled reporters before. In seeking to control the narrative so tightly throughout, Weiner had unwittingly been feeding the trolls all along.

Weiner's story is more than a cautionary tale about media management, though. A fascinating post-script came in 2013, as Weiner (who had now taken to calling himself 'Carlos Danger' in his sex messaging in an ill-advised attempt to remain inconspicuous), found himself engulfed in a fresh sexting scandal that blew apart his campaign for Mayor of New York. Talking to a *GQ* reporter after the wrap party for the failed mayoral campaign in 2013, Weiner summed up the Conversation Killer's credo with a piece of remarkable insight that pinpoints what Hewlett Packard's people were able to do, and his were not.

> 'It's weird: When you're in this, everyone [in the media] is trying to be the viral moment. I was trying *not* to be.'

Few have been more canny in this regard than Dominique Strauss-Kahn, with his 2011 resignation from the International Monetary Fund. With allegations of rape hanging over him in the US, and sordid claims around his sexual conduct leaking out in France, he appeared to use his letter of resignation to claim innocence, and to position himself as a family man with a great work record. Crucially, he did so with a series of carefully chosen phrases. Each of them could be quoted alone and out of context, or even partially quoted, without giving the press their 'viral' moment.

> It is with great sadness that I feel compelled today to present to the Board my resignation as Director of the IMF.
>
> My thoughts go first to my wife – whom I love more than anyone – to my children, my family, my friends.
>
> At this moment, my thoughts are also with my colleagues in the IMF. Together we have achieved such a remarkable amount in just over three years.
>
> To all of you, I wish to reiterate that I reject most categorically all the accusations that are levelled at me.
>
> My intention is to protect this institution, which it has been my honour to serve with dedication, and I intend especially – especially – to devote all my strength, time and energy to proving my innocence.

The charges were later dropped. Strauss-Kahn's reputation as a man may never recover from the investigation, but his reputation as a shrewd political manoeuvrer was never higher.

German Defence Minister Karl-Theodor zu Guttenberg could have used some of his *sangfroid*. When it was discovered he had plagiarized his doctoral thesis, he initially fought on, then capitulated on 28 February 2011 with the Andy Coulson-meets-Monty Python cry, 'I'm supposed to be the minister for defence, not minister for self-defence.' For an investigation that had not yet had its 'viral moment', this was a gift – and an instant-classic quote that ensured his scandal would outlive him.

Then, in July 2011, came the motherlode: a wave of swansongs from the beleaguered News Corporation. As a long-simmering phone-hacking investigation gathered momentum, amid an atmosphere of scepticism towards the tabloid press in general, Rupert Murdoch's company grew anxious to stamp out the flames that were licking up the elevator shaft towards its Chief Executive's office. Having tried bluff, denial, counter-attack, and offering up a few pawns as sacrifice, News Corp's hand was forced. The big names started falling.

Rebekah Brooks was now Chief Executive of News International, the conglomerate's newspaper arm. But for the period on which many of the phone-hacking accusations were centred, she had been editor of its flagship tabloids, the *News of the World* and the *Sun*. As more and more hacking claims emerged, there were repeated intimations of full support for her from the Murdoch camp. The CEO himself flew into London, and Brooks's welfare was his stated priority. Then, just hours later, Brooks – who many called 'the fire curtain' between the investigation and Rupert Murdoch himself – released this memo to staff.

At News International we pride ourselves on setting the news agenda for the right reasons. Today we are leading the news for the wrong ones.

The reputation of the company we love so much, as well as the press freedoms we value so highly, are all at risk.

As Chief Executive of the company, I feel a deep sense of responsibility for the people we have hurt and I want to reiterate how sorry I am for what we now know to have taken place.

I have believed that the right and responsible action has been to lead us through the heat of the crisis. However my desire to remain on the bridge has made me a focal point of the debate.

This is now detracting attention from all our honest endeavours to fix the problems of the past.

Therefore I have given Rupert and James Murdoch my resignation. While it has been a subject of discussion, this time my resignation has been accepted.

Rupert's wisdom, kindness and incisive advice has guided me throughout my career and James is an inspirational leader who has shown me great loyalty and friendship. I would like to thank them both for their support.

I have worked here for 22 years and I know it to be part of the finest media company in the world.

News International is full of talented, professional and honourable people. I am proud to have been part of the team and lucky to know so many brilliant journalists and media executives.

I leave with the happiest of memories and an abundance of friends.

As you can imagine recent times have been tough. I now need to concentrate on correcting the distortions and rebutting the allegations about my record as a journalist, an editor and executive.

My resignation makes it possible for me to have the freedom and the time to give my full cooperation to all the current and future inquiries, the police investigations and the CMS appearance.

I am so grateful for all the messages of support. I have nothing but overwhelming respect for you and our millions of readers.

I wish every one of you all the best.

You can almost feel the language itself coming apart as it's stretched in all directions at once. It wants to do so many things: to rally patriotic support for our 'freedoms' and the fight against the 'threat' of impending investigation; to protest innocence (personal and corporate) of any wrongdoing; to add a bit of CV-mongering; and to quell staff unrest (Brooks was being well enough looked after, but disgruntled whistleblowers could be bad news, and staff were reportedly deeply unimpressed with the way the company had handled things so far). The resignation becomes a snowscreen of non-sequiturs, relative clauses and clichés. Among those clichés is one that calls Andy Coulson to mind, and perhaps grey cardinals like Donald Rumsfeld too: We decide the news. We don't want to be the news.

With ex-*News of the World* editor Coulson having resigned from Downing Street to face charges relating to the same investigation, and Brooks herself no longer standing between Murdoch and his own summons, events were suddenly moving with a speed that echoed the last, panicked days of Enron and seemed to catch even the twenty-four-hour rolling news operation on the hop. But there were elements that appeared orchestrated. On the same day Brooks (who was later found innocent of charges relating to phone hacking) resigned in London, *Wall Street Journal* publisher Les Hinton resigned from

News Corporation, News International's parent company in New York, with his own virtuoso letter claiming that although his ignorance is 'of what apparently happened is irrelevant . . . in the circumstances I feel it is proper for me to resign from News Corp, and apologize to those hurt by the actions of the *News of the World*. When I left News International in December 2007, I believed that the rotten element at the *News of the World* had been eliminated; that important lessons had been learned; and that journalistic integrity was restored.'

Bad apples; personal and corporate ignorance; a good organization; integrity and freedom of the press – it's tempting to imagine the same set of eyes looking over each of these letters before it was released to the press, approving them with a nod over the spectacles, just as Rupert Murdoch himself had loved to do with his editors' front pages.

If these resignations were meant to stamp out the flames leading to his air-conditioned office, and to No. 10, they were unsuccessful. The scandal still hadn't claimed its biggest scalp.

In the meantime, another iconic but divisive leader was under siege, and attempting to ease the pressure with his own statement. As a bloody revolution against his rule escalated, Libyan dictator Colonel Gaddafi issued a rambling would-be resignation on 2 March 2011 explaining how he would like to bow to international pressure and resign, but couldn't, because . . . well, that's where it gets complicated.

America and its allies are calling on me to resign as president.

If I were president, I would have resigned, but as I am not, I have no position from which to resign. Muammar Gaddafi is the leader of the revolution, I am not a president to step down.

This is my country. Muammar is not a president to leave his post, he does not even have a parliament to dissolve. Attacks on me are seen by Libyan people as attacks on their symbol and dignity.

The foreigners want Gaddafi to step down, to step down from what? Gaddafi is just a symbol for the Libyan people . . . This is how the Libyan people understood it. The people are free to choose the authority they see fit.

We put our fingers in the eyes of those who doubt that Libya is ruled by anyone other than its people. I have always said that the Libyan people are free.

You men and women who love Gaddafi . . . get out of your homes and fill the streets. Leave your homes and attack them in their lairs . . . Starting tomorrow, the cordons will be lifted, go out and fight them. Peaceful protests are one thing, but armed rebellion is another. The Libyan people and the popular revolution will control Libya.

If Rebekah Brooks's resignation pulled language in directions it didn't want to go, Gaddafi's took it to another level entirely. His claim that he would step down, if only he had a position to step down from, but as a concept and embodiment of his country that was impossible, is at once scary, absurd and impressive.

Then again, it's not only dictators in exotic countries who use this sort of shadow-sense to get their point across. The dance of resignation between minister and prime minister in our own government is full of feints, implied courses of action and hidden messages.

Read between the lines, and the resignation exchange on Friday, 14 October 2011 between Defence Secretary Liam Fox and PM David Cameron is a case study in political power-trading. Fox had broken the ministerial code, allowing friends access to classified meetings. This is not so much a parting shot as an oath of continued loyalty and a CV for future reappointment.

As you know, I have always placed a great deal of importance on accountability and responsibility. As I said in the House of Commons on Monday, I mistakenly allowed the distinction between my personal interest and my government activities to become blurred. The consequences of this have become clearer in recent days . . .

I am particularly proud to have overseen the long overdue reforms to the Ministry of Defence and to our armed forces, which will shape them to meet the challenges of the future and keep this country safe.

I am proud also to have played a part in helping to liberate the people of Libya, and I regret that I will not see through to its conclusion Britain's role in Afghanistan, where so much progress has been made . . .

I appreciate all the support you have given me – and will continue to support the vital work of this government, above all in controlling the enormous budget deficit we inherited, which is a threat not just to this country's economic prosperity but also to its national security.

This is the polar opposite of the resignation by

Donald Rumsfeld, Fox's erstwhile opposite number. Fox is absolutely everywhere in his own statement, with a breathtaking twenty-one 'I's and 'my's. It's almost if you're reading the 'Personal Testimony' part of someone's Duke of Edinburgh Award entry, or hearing an anecdote told by someone who wants to put himself at the centre of it.

On one hand, Fox's letter is extraordinarily deftly written. It manages to pull the resigning parliamentarian's time-honoured trick of turning something rather sleazy – having old chums pose as advisers on junkets to attend high-level meetings and court secretive right-wing lobbyists – into an opportunity for the display of moral rectitude, even scoring a party political point at the end.

On the other, it is surely overplayed. It's unlikely that history will remember him as a liberator of Libya, if at all. But he was an ambitious, short-lived Minister; and this may have looked like the closest he'd now get to penning a political memoir. One is left with the nagging sense that there's something overreaching about it; something too quick by half, which reminds us why he's resigning in the first place.

Nevertheless, it's a reassuring letter to receive. The Prime Minister will have been calmed by Fox's expressions of thanks for his support. Nothing worse than a loose cannon.

David Cameron's response reveals even more. The PM's point-by-point reiteration of Fox's claims shows he understands the letter's coded appeal. It's hard not to hear the implied menace in the last paragraph as Cameron takes his pound of flesh: a return could indeed be yours . . . if you're careful who you back in key votes.

I understand your reasons for deciding to resign as defence secretary, although I am very sorry to see you go . . . On Libya, you played a key role in the campaign to stop people being massacred by the Gaddafi regime and instead win their freedom.

You can be proud of the difference you have made in your time in office, and in helping our party to return to government.

I appreciate your commitment to the work of this government, particularly highlighting the need to tackle the deficit, and the relationship between Britain's economic strength and our national security.

You and Jesme have always been good friends, and I have truly valued your support over the years. I will continue to do so in the future.

It's a wonderfully balanced letter. And while we should never forget the extent to which these things are templated, or at least adapted from previous letters – a wet afternoon spent looking through PMs' replies to resigning ministers is one of life's obscure pleasures – Cameron clearly feels the loss of a key ally, and repeatedly invokes personal bonds even as professional ones are severed.

But if we keep our colleagues close and our ex-colleagues closer, what to do with our families?

If Rupert Murdoch hoped the resignations of Les Hinton and Rebekah Brooks would seal the wound, he was mistaken. The phone-hacking inquiry and its vortex continued to widen. In November 2011, his son and heir James Murdoch had resigned from the boards of the *Sun* and *The Times*. By 29 February 2012, he was forced to resign from News International – not that you'd know why from his statement:

> I deeply appreciate the dedication of my many talented colleagues at News International who work tirelessly to inform the public and am confident about the tremendous momentum we have achieved under the leadership of my father and Tom Mockridge. With the successful launch of *The Sun on Sunday* and new business practices in place across all titles, News International is now in a strong position to build on its successes in the future. As Deputy Chief Operating Officer, I look forward to expanding my commitment to News Corporation's international television businesses and other key initiatives across the Company.

By 3 April 2012, it was clear he would have to resign his position at BSkyB too. Just weeks apart, the difference in tone between the 'corporatese' of the first statement and the shrill urgency of the second is striking.

3rd April 2012

[. . .] As attention continues to be paid to past events at News International, I am determined that the interests of BSkyB should not be undermined by matters outside the scope of this Company.

I have been transparent in my evidence and have behaved ethically at all times. However, there continues to be extensive and voluminous commentary around these matters. I am aware that my role as Chairman could become a lightning rod for BSkyB and I believe that my resignation will help to ensure that there is no false conflation with events at a separate organisation.

BSkyB is a great success story and its positive contribution to British broadcasting, and to the country more broadly, should not be questioned. With a strong Board and outstanding management team, I am confident that the Company will achieve even more in the future. I look forward to making a continued contribution in my role as a Non-Executive Director.

Murdoch is still insisting here that it is he who is directing events ('I have now decided . . . I am determined . . .'), and trying to control the unfolding story ('No false conflation with events at a separate company . . . BSkyB is a success story . . . BSkyB's positive contribution to British broadcasting, and to the country more broadly, should not be questioned').

There are echoes of Coulson. I'm the editor here. This is my story. All the rest is just rumour. The whole thing sounds weirdly control-freakish for someone supposedly relinquishing control. The mindset of someone used to owning the news, you might say. Or perhaps that of the boss's son, who's still pretty sure of his influence round here – resignation on paper or not.

With the firewalls between Murdoch and the Conservative Party falling, the blaze now threatened to engulf David Cameron's government. After culture secretary and Murdoch cheerleader Jeremy Hunt was grilled at the Leveson Inquiry on 25 April 2012 over emails between his special adviser Adam Smith and Murdoch's man Fred Michel (who also enjoyed a personal friendship with Hunt), he told Smith:

'Everyone says you've got to go.' Smith's press statement, when it was released, could almost have been drafted for the ambitious young adviser by his erstwhile boss.

> While it was part of my role to keep News Corporation informed throughout the BSkyB bid process, the content and extent of my contact was done without authorisation from the Secretary of State [Jeremy Hunt] . . . I appreciate that my activities at times went too far and have, taken together, created the perception that News Corporation had too close a relationship with the department, contrary to the clear requirements set out by Jeremy Hunt and the permanent secretary that this needed to be a fair and scrupulous process . . .

With Smith's body thrown from the train, the minister hung on. Both Smith and Fox resigned hoping for a comeback. Their resignations are reassurances. They get it. They will take their medicine. Be a good boy and don't sing, and there might well be a way back.

When it becomes clear that there is no way back, the tone of the resignation changes. The Republican Party's Michigan representative Thaddeus McCotter was righteously indignant after being rejected by his party for a presidential nomination. He was so incandescent that on 7 June 2012, he emailed this bitter, bizarrely worded resignation letter quoting Bob Dylan and calling Neo-Con policy God's will.

> After nearly 26 years in elected office, this past nightmarish month and a half have, for the first time, severed the

necessary harmony between the needs of my constituency and of my family. As this harmony is required to serve, its absence requires I leave.

The recent events' totality of calumnies, indignities and deceits have weighed most heavily upon my family. Thus, acutely aware one cannot rebuild their hearth of home amongst the ruins of their US House office, for the sake of my loved ones I must 'strike another match, go start anew' by embracing the promotion back from public servant to sovereign citizen.

I do not leave for an existing job and face diminishing prospects (and am both unwilling and ill-suited to lobby), my priorities are twofold: find gainful employment to help provide for my family; and continue to assist, in any way they see fit, the Michigan Attorney General's earnest and thorough investigation, which I requested, into the 2012 petition filing.

While our family takes this step into the rest of our lives, we do so with the ultimate confidence in our country's future. True, as at other times in the life of our nation, we live in an Age of Extremes that prizes intensity over sanity; rhetoric over reality; and destruction over creation. But this too shall pass, thanks to the infinite, inspired wisdom of the sovereign people who, with God's continued blessings, will again affirm for the generations American Exceptionalism. Truly, it is a challenging and fortunate time to live in our blessed sanctuary of liberty.

Even as he talks about assisting an investigation ('which I requested'), he fails to mention that his nomination was rejected after it was found that 85 per cent of votes for McCotter showed signs of fraudulence. When the State Attorney's investigation reported back in August 2012, they revealed that McCotter's campaign staff had been adding fake signatures to petitions on his behalf in 'a cut and paste job that would make a fourth grade art teacher cringe'. They'd done the same in at least three previous elections. McCotter was not directly implicated, but had, said Michigan Attorney General Schuette, been 'asleep at the wheel'. Like Gullit, McCotter's saying none of this matters, this is just a job; I'm part of something bigger and better; I'm with all the *real* American heroes. So long, losers. So McCotter's statement tried to channel those heroes – flitting between Dylan lyrics and a bizarre, nineteenth-century American English. This is not him, but a slippery shoal of bulletproof, shame-deflecting personae. We put on voices to cover our embarrassment. We split apart when we cannot reconcile ourselves with what we have done. We hide behind those who are beyond reproach.

These strange voices erupt into the best-panned resignations. When his reckoning came in 2003, Liberian President Charles Taylor resigned in a succession of accents and personae. From the butcher of West Africa to comedically OTT Nigerian to a Baptist preacher, Jesus, and little boy.

Just as often, resigners feel as if their public voice has become so twisted by what James Murdoch indignantly refers to as 'the ongoing commentary' that even in resigning, they must frantically search for another, less compromised persona. McCotter is a downtrodden but unbeaten working man. Brooks is the light of press freedom in Britain's darkest, most Orwellian hour. One is reminded of Mike Tyson's explanation for biting off an opponent's ear. We're all just trying to protect our families.

These accounts seldom survive scrutiny – and when scrutiny comes with a point-by-point dismantling of your resignation by the company you leave, the results can be wincingly funny. With one of Ghana's biggest football teams, Accra Hearts of Oak, languishing on the edge of the relegation zone, the club's physical trainer Warrant Officer (1st Class) Tandoh – alias WO1 – went AWOL. While the club debated his fate, Tandoh made a very public resignation. He got more than he bargained for in return.

> 25 October 2012
>
> With great delight, I am glad to inform you of my resignation from our famous club as a physical trainer. This decision has become very necessary on personal grounds. I wish to thank board, management, supporters and all who loved our dear club for the opportunity given me to work. For any reason, if I stepped on a toe while working, it was for the good of all. God bless,
>
> Warrant Officer (1st Class) Tandoh, Physical Trainer

If Tandoh hoped his resignation letter would tie his legacy up nicely, he was wrong. His note drew a withering response from his bosses at the club, invoking the military term 'French leave'. The phrase is thought to originate in the French and Indian War in 1750s America, from an incident when scores of French soldiers held POW on a supposedly secure island by the British, escaped by wading to the far bank while their guards slept. In World War II, it became semi-official parlance for desertion. As a euphemism for the disappearance of a squad coach who habitually referred to himself by his military rank, it is superbly catty.

> Accra Hearts of Oak asked physical trainer WO1 Tandoh, who had deserted camp on 18th October 2012, to vacate camp till the club takes a final decision on his fate. After the said desertion . . . WO1 Tandoh proceeded to take a 'French leave', avoiding contact with management till . . . the General Manager, on a visit to the team's hotel camp, saw him and asked him to go away to continue his French leave. This explains his absence from Berekum when Hearts played Chelsea on Sunday 28th October 2012. WO1 Tandoh's purported resignation on some concocted or flimsy grounds is therefore only a smart move by the departing Physical Trainer to escape sanctions, and must be dismissed as such.

If only more major clubs issued statements calling players and other high-profile club employees out for any flimsy, concocted and self-serving statements they make when they leave. Then again, the sports section is only so thick.

This tendency towards self-dramatization and role-playing is heightened as our lives become public. Putting the record straight implies that someone is recording. And when people who should know better play fast and loose with that public record, all hell breaks loose.

As New York was shaken by Hurricane Sandy on 30 October 2012, Twitter users noted that many of the scarier rumours of chaos, damage and collapse originated from the @ComfortablySmug account of Shashank Tripathi, hedge-fund boss and Republican Party campaign manager. Tripathi spent the night of greatest destruction doing the social media equivalent of shouting 'Fire!' in a crowded theatre.

First, he tweeted: 'BREAKING: Con Edison has begun shutting down ALL power in Manhattan.' He then tweeted that waters had risen to cover the New York Stock Exchange; that the Governor (whom he opposed) had fled to a secure shelter; and that the subway network had been flooded and shut down. As some began to rumble him, Tripathi went on the offensive, demanding apologies from anyone who 'smeared' him. Then, as the news organizations he had fooled rounded on him, he tweeted a link to this letter, a perfect storm of line-drawing, self-erasure and diversionary tactics itself.

I wish to offer the people of New York a sincere, humble and unconditional apology.

During a natural disaster that threatened the entire city, I made a series of irresponsible and inaccurate tweets.

While some would use the anonymity and instant feedback of social media as an excuse, I take full responsibility for my actions. I deeply regret any distress or harm they may have caused.

I have resigned from the congressional campaign of Christopher Wight, effective immediately. Wight is a candidate with the ideas, philosophy and leadership skills to make New York a better place and who will be an outstanding advocate for the people of the 12th Congressional District. It is my sincere hope that the voters of New York will see him based on his merits alone, and not for my actions of the last 24 hours.

Again, I offer my sincere apologies.

It's a consummate conversation killer – Tripathi clearly wants to apologize and move on, to avoid damaging the campaign any more – but for that third paragraph. 'Some' would say there was an excuse – the anonymity and instant feedback? Certainly, those things *enabled* his behaviour, but it's hard to see how they might logically, let alone morally, qualify as excuses. The instinct to duck, dive, deflect and play games is still too strong for Tripathi to create the resignation he wants to. Even caught out, even now, he simply can't bear to say it straight.

There were those who defended Tripathi, claiming that he was known for his wind-ups and that nobody paid him any mind until news channels began reposting his claims as fact, without running any checks. But if you dance with the media like Tandoh and Tripathi, you had better make sure you know the dance well enough not to end up on your back. Even the best string-pullers can only stay out of shot for so long. Which brings us to what may be the final master stroke in a long and infamous career.

On 12 November 2012, seven-time Tour de France winner Lance Armstrong resigned as chairman of the Lance Armstrong Foundation, aka Livestrong. Armstrong had been found guilty of coordinating a doping regime so long-running, and so deeply entwined with coaches, trainers, physiotherapists and other cyclists, that it had hijacked the sport.

He had originally sought to brazen out the controversy, posting photos of himself relaxing on his couch in response to calls for him to apologize, and hosting a glittering gala bash in Austin, Texas, for the cancer charity he founded in 1997, even after he had been stripped of his titles and banned from sport for life by the US Anti-Doping Agency.

The forty-one year-old had underestimated the collateral damage his drug-taking and lying had done to Livestrong. The USADA released a gigantic file of witness and forensic evidence against him; confessionals implicating him further began to pile up; high-profile sponsors and his union deserted him; bookshops and public libraries even refiled his autobiography as 'Fiction'. Armstrong finally drafted a rather odd resignation.

> I have had the great honor of serving as this foundation's chairman for the last five years and its mission and success are my top priorities. Today therefore, to spare the foundation any negative effects as a result of controversy surrounding my cycling career, I will conclude my chairmanship . . . My family and I have devoted our lives to the work of the foundation and that will not change. We plan to continue our service to the foundation and the cancer community. We will remain active advocates for cancer survivors and engaged supporters of the fight against cancer. And we look forward to an exciting weekend of activities marking the 15th anniversary of the foundation's creation.

Armstrong's announcement is almost spectral in the lightness and vagueness with which it touches on anything its recipients would recognize. There is a hole where regret might ordinarily be found. Or disclosure. Or anything like discussion of the reason he's resigning beyond passing reference to 'controversy'. But resignations that look like conversation killers may not be what they seem. And Armstrong may just have been a smarter operator than anyone realized. Even as press and public scratched their heads over his resignation and asked where was the admission of guilt, where was the apology, where was the regret, Lance Armstrong was negotiating with Oprah Winfrey.

Her show, broadcast to millions, would include the things his resignation left out. He would have his moment, speak his testimony, perhaps make his apology. But it would be subject to his input and set direction; his sign-off on questions. He would be in control. This statement? It was a holding operation. It would be 2013 before the other foot landed. Armstrong turned evidence against those who had allegedly supplied him with doping products. More names are expected. The spotlight falls on more and more people. The real statement was yet to come

Armstrong's resignation didn't protect him, but it might yet turn him from headline to footnote – a smaller player in a far, far bigger story.

3:

The Insider Hit

'Life being what it is, one dreams of revenge.'

– Paul Gauguin

'These people fucked me over.'

– Former Yahoo! CEO Carol Bartz

'We regret to inform you that a Duel took place yesterday morning, between Lord Castlereagh and Mr Canning, in which the latter received a wound in his left thigh, but happily it is not dangerous, being merely a flesh wound. The meeting took place at Putney Heath . . . Lord Castlereagh resigned the Seals of his office as Secretary of State last week; and Mr Canning having also tendered his resignation, remain in place only until a successor is appointed. Some misunderstanding has since arisen between them, the nature of which has not been publicly stated, but we understand it to be more of a private and personal, than an official or public character . . . Beyond this, we deem it prudent, not to venture any statement.'

The Morning Post, 22nd September 1809.

Until 1990, Lord Castlereagh, George III's Secretary of State for War and the Colonies – for whose removal fellow minister and rival George Canning had been briefing in secret – was synonymous with the idea of the humiliated parliamentarian as Nemesis, exacting terrible public revenge over differences in policy and personality.

But the man whose name has become a byword for the parliamentary hit-job was in many ways the opposite of the arrogant, flamboyant and irascible Castlereagh. He was also known as something of a gentle giant. While Castlereagh shot his colleague on Putney Heath, his modern counterpart simply stood up in Parliament and read out a letter in the face of his boss and chosen victim, watched and cheered on by hundreds of MPs and spectators. Its destructive power was no less for that. These days, the practice is called 'doing a Geoffrey Howe'.

Sir Geoffrey himself had not only been Prime Minister Margaret Thatcher's longest-serving and most loyal cabinet minister; he was also famously diplomatic, mild and polite. Labour Chancellor Denis Healey once joked that being on the receiving end of an attack from Howe was 'like being savaged by a dead sheep'.

Serving first as Chancellor of the Exchequer, then as Foreign Secretary, then as Leader of the House of Commons and Deputy Prime Minister, Sir Geoffrey was regarded as Thatcher's secret better conscience. From poll tax riots to clashes with the other member states of the nascent European Union, for more than a decade he had counselled diplomacy over fire-breathing rhetoric, and consensus over confrontation. Yet he did so quietly and in private, always careful to present a united front to cabinet, press and public alike.

This letter, penned and delivered on Thursday, 1 November 1990, came not just as a shock to the Prime Minister, but as a deadly blow. Written amid the fall-out of Thatcher's declaration that Britain would 'never' accept monetary union with Europe, he criticized her openly – albeit in personal correspondence – for the first time.

> I am deeply anxious that the mood you have struck will make it more difficult for Britain to hold and retain a position of influence in this vital debate . . . We should be in the business, not of isolating ourselves unduly, but of offering positive alternatives that can enable us to be seriously engaged . . . In all honesty I now find myself unable to share your view of the right approach to this question. On that basis, I do not believe that I can any longer serve with honour as a member of your Government.

It's a fascinating moment, not least for the light it sheds on their relationship, and on their very different personalities. Even in resigning, Howe's tone is almost indulgent – that of an exasperated older friend, teacher or parent. It's almost as if he's trying to help her *get along with people* better. Howe was always a diplomat. Stationed in East Africa after World War Two, his sense for 'Plain speaking . . . matched always by mutual respect and restraint' saw him become the point of contact between his regiment and local pro-communist warlords. But this time, though his tone is regretful and emollient, his frustration at being undermined is palpable.

Thatcher – never quite as adept at finding common ground – was reportedly 'irate' when she received the letter. Yet if she felt betrayed and isolated by his first resignation letter, she could never have predicted his second, public parting shot twelve days later. On 13 November, Howe delivered another, and far less circumspect, missive. He addressed his resignation to the House of Commons. This time, he compared trying to serve under Thatcher and represent the government's policies abroad to being wilfully sabotaged.

[Serving the Prime Minister's government in Europe] is rather like sending your opening batsmen to the crease only for them to find, the moment the first balls are bowled, that their bats have been broken before the game by the team captain.

The point was perhaps more sharply put by a British businessman, trading in Brussels and elsewhere, who wrote to me last week, stating : 'People throughout Europe see our Prime Minister's finger-wagging and hear her passionate, No, No, No, much more clearly than the content of the carefully worded formal texts.' He went on: 'It is too easy for them to believe that we all share her attitudes; for why else has she been our Prime Minister for so long?'

My correspondent concluded: 'This is a desperately serious situation for our country.'

And sadly, I have to agree.

The tragedy is – and it is for me personally, for my party, for our whole people and for my Right Hon. Friend herself, a very real tragedy – that the Prime Minister's perceived attitude towards Europe is running increasingly serious risks for the future of our nation. It risks minimising our influence and maximising our chances of being once again shut out. We have paid heavily in the past for late starts and squandered opportunities in Europe. We dare not let that happen again. If we detach ourselves completely, as a party or a nation, from the middle ground of Europe, the effects will be incalculable and very hard ever to correct.

In my letter of resignation, which I tendered with the utmost sadness and dismay, I said: 'Cabinet Government is all about trying to persuade one another from within'.

That was my commitment to Government by persuasion – persuading colleagues and the nation. I have tried to do that as Foreign Secretary and since, but I realise now that the task has become futile: trying to stretch the meaning of words beyond what was credible, and trying to pretend that there was a common policy when every step forward risked being subverted by some casual comment or impulsive answer.

The conflict of loyalty, of loyalty to my Right Hon. Friend the Prime Minister – and, after all, in two decades together that instinct of loyalty is still very real – and of loyalty to what I perceive to be the true interests of the nation, has become all too great. I no longer believe it possible to resolve that conflict from within this Government. That is why I have resigned. In doing so, I have done what I believe to be right for my party and my country. The time has come for others to consider their own response to the tragic conflict of loyalties with which I have myself wrestled for perhaps too long.

Howe's feelings have clearly hardened here, post-break-up. Days later, the deed done, it's as if he's no longer stumped at what to do for the best, but at what took him so long to do it in the first place. He quotes his last letter to

Thatcher, holding it up like a relic of what their relationship could have been. He talks of the realization that he was fooling himself, if nobody else, in trying to remain with Thatcher. He ends by urging others to get wise, as he has. Together, his resignations would precipitate a rash of leadership challenges that would doom Mrs Thatcher's premiership. By 22 November, she was gone. A mauling at the hands of a dead farm animal suddenly sounded a lot less funny.

But while politicians have long had the forum in which to inflict public damage on their enemies as they resign, to the regular Joe this power is fairly new. The rise of the popular hit-job is the result of both the emergence of a workplace culture that allows people access to their dress-down-casual bosses – where only years ago they would have been isolated by layers of hierarchy – and the simultaneous emergence of desktop communications technology.

As we've seen, fast new communication channels have always corresponded with flowerings in public resignations, as the technology challenges us to work at new levels of speed and transparency, and we in turn test the possibilities of the technology.

Through the twentieth century the press, then radio, then television, had continued to offer public platforms, if the resignations were juicy enough. Then, during a climate of reduced employment protection and weakening union strength, fax, email, the office network, the internet and social media all came to work desktops. Employees now had something that could equalize the losses they'd made in terms of employment protection and union power over the past two decades: for the first time in history, the nine-to-fiver could communicate instantly and directly to a mass audience.

Introducing cheap desktop email to the early 90s spirit of employee disenfranchisement was the equivalent of repealing all the cool-off laws around gun ownership and then winding up a Texas bar full of drunk truckers.

So began a precarious game of cat and mouse between employees and employers. Understandably, employers sought to limit the opportunity for workers to let loose while giving them the communication tools to do their job. For their part, employees needed a weapon. If their grievances weren't being heard, what would make people listen? The 'open letter' was no longer the preserve of those who could buy advertising space in *The Times*. Sometimes, there was reputational risk to the company. Sometimes, the stakes were higher still. On 1 July 2003, with the War in Iraq raging and US presidential candidacy campaigning about to kick off, former US Air Force Lieutenant Colonel and Pentagon official Karen Kwiatkowski resigned with an email torpedo aimed squarely at her boss. Kwiatkowski was not a name anybody would have recognized, but her boss's, Secretary of Defense Donald Rumsfeld, was.

While working from May 2002 through February 2003 in the office of the Undersecretary of Defense for Policy, Near East South Asian and Special Plans in the Pentagon, I observed the environment in which decisions about post war Iraq were made.

What I saw was aberrant, pervasive, and contrary to good order and discipline. If one is seeking the answers to why peculiar bits of 'intelligence' found sanctity in a presidential speech, or why the post-Hussein occupation has been distinguished by confusion and false steps, one need look no further than the process inside the office of the Secretary of Defense.

With the battle lines for the forthcoming campaign already drawn around Iraq, it was explosive stuff. It was also fine marksmanship: nobody could deny that the Iraq occupation had been messier than they imagined; George W Bush's intelligence missteps were legion. This didn't expose, so much as provide the missing explanation for what America already saw.

Kwiatkowski, a remarkable woman whose skillset included two books on foreign policy and work as a speech-writer for the National Security Administration, was using a time-honoured political speechwriting and propaganda technique against the Pentagon.

Before, such communications in the heat of betrayal and despair would have to go through a number of gate-keepers and checks to get 'out there'. Now, for each poor annual appraisal meeting or insensitive management announcement, instant gratification was now just an itchy 'send' button away.

Comparative nobodies are now capable of commanding national headlines on the strength of a cc-everyone resignation. In 2012's biggest viral hit, an employee resigned from the London office of a giant advertising agency with a catalogue of allegations aimed squarely at his manager, with whom he had clearly become disgruntled. With the words, 'I am writing this message in order to expose these failings and protect others in future,' he finished his scree, and emailed it around the company at eleven minutes past eight that bright September morning. Anyone hoping his allegations would stay within the building – or within the jurisdiction of HR – was in for a nasty shock. The email left the company before Tech Support could delete it from the servers; it was uploaded to code-sharing service Pastebin within an hour; it made online magazines that same morning. By the evening, it was in the newspapers and across network TV stations.

By the following day, national and international papers had picked up the story, and the employee, his former company, his line manager and even a job applicant who'd supposedly become part of a sexual intrigue at the company were all fair game for the tabloids. The manager denied all the allegations. The company is still conducting its investigations, and refusing to comment further.

There's something quite spooky in the way the email took on its own life once it went beyond the company. Nobody knew the resigner, his colleagues or his manager. Few outside his sector had ever heard of the company. Yet within hours, they had become fixtures of the public imagination from Shanghai to San Francisco. Like the perpetrators and victims of crimes caught on camera, they had no currency, except what one sudden and terrifying moment fixed in the public eye had given them. Many spend the rest of their careers trying to conquer that moment: during the preparation of this book, Google has begun expunging links relating to the incident under EU 'Right to be forgotten' laws.

Gordon Brown's Work and Pensions Secretary James Purnell had the same deadly cocktail ready when he resigned to then-PM Gordon Brown on 4 June 2009: nothing to lose and an instant platform.

His progress stalled by exposure, however minor, to the MPs' expenses scandal, he claims (in a common thread running through these letters) to have felt he was 'no longer being true to myself'. So he walked in the park, then 'ducked into an office and wrote my letter in five minutes'.

We both love the Labour Party. I have worked for it for 20 years and you for far longer. We know we owe it everything and it owes us nothing.

I owe it to our party to say what I believe no matter how hard that may be. I now believe your continued leadership makes a Conservative victory more, not less likely.

That would be disastrous for our country. This moment calls for stronger regulation, an active state, better public services, an open democracy.

It calls for a government that measures itself by how it treats the poorest in society.

Those are our values, not David Cameron's.

We therefore owe it to our country to give it a real choice. We need to show that we are prepared to fight to be a credible government and have the courage to offer an alternative future.

I am therefore calling on you to stand aside to give our party a fighting chance of winning. As such I am resigning from government.

The party was here long before us, and we want it to be here long after we have gone. We must do the right thing by it.

I am not seeking the leadership, nor acting with anyone

else. My actions are my own considered view, nothing more.

If the consensus is that you should continue, then I will support the government loyally from the backbenches. But I do believe that this question now needs to be put.

Thank you for giving me the privilege of serving.

Yours,

Rt Hon. James Purnell MP

What happened next – once Purnell's email pinged into accounts across the party – offers a key to understanding the darker side of the revenge resignation . . . and the change that comes over resigner and company alike the moment they press 'detonate'.

In an interview shortly after his hit on Gordon Brown, Purnell remembered meeting some of his former colleagues, including one with whom he had been close, around Westminster. They treated him as if he were 'a ghost'. They were, he recalled, 'distressed, agitated, uncomfortable, even confrontational . . . I raised a question for [former close colleague David Miliband, too] . . . People asked why, given I resigned, he didn't resign.'

This is as close as the insiders, the bosses, the successful joiners – get to the chill and shadow of the *memento mori* – the skeleton at the feast. Career suicide had been committed, but the suicide still walked among them.

Membership and service to your position means certain guarantees and responsibilities. Rejecting those guarantees makes you unpredictable, potentially dangerous. This is a phenomenon as old as civilization, and its roots help explain the terror the revenge resignation still packs today. To the ancient Greeks, those who renounced (or forfeited) their citizenship of the walled cities were *apolis*: unknown quantities, beyond the reach of law or custom; outcasts or madmen who were not to be trusted and to be shunned by travellers.

There is a certain superstitious thoroughness about those rituals in which the ex-employee is erased. Their email accounts are deleted, their desks cleaned, their codes changed and their cards destroyed. Once exorcised, their names are muttered, not spoken. They are dead to us, having fallen on their swords (an expression Shakespeare took from Plutarch, who meant it literally). Mix with them at your peril. And if you see them here, for God's sake tell security.

The idea that, once somebody knows they are off, they have nothing left to lose, is uncomfortable for most bosses. Such a divisive figure can do huge damage running around, and they can prove to be contagious. Others have a habit of joining them.

Sure enough, just twenty-four hours after James Purnell's blast to Gordon Brown, something snapped inside Minister for Europe Caroline Flint. She resigned from the government, with this blast at the Prime Minister.

> You have a two-tier Government. Your inner circle and then the remainder of Cabinet.
>
> I have the greatest respect for the women who have served as full members of Cabinet and for those who attend as and when required. However, few are allowed into your inner circle. Several of the women attending Cabinet – myself included – have been treated by you as little more than female window dressing. I am not willing to attend Cabinet in a peripheral capacity any longer.

In my current role, you advised that I would attend Cabinet when Europe was on the agenda. I have only been invited once since October and not to a single political Cabinet – not even the one held a few weeks before the European elections.

Having worked hard during this campaign, I would not have been party to any plan to undermine you or the Labour Party in the run up to 4 June. So I was extremely angry and disappointed to see newspapers briefed with invented stories of my involvement in a 'Pugin Room plot'.

Time and time again I have stepped before the cameras to sincerely defend your reputation in the interests of the Labour Party and the Government as a whole. I am a natural party loyalist. Yet you have strained every sinew of that loyalty.

It has been apparent for some time that you do not see me playing a more influential role in the Government. Therefore, I have respectfully declined your offer to continue in the Government as Minister for attending Cabinet.

There are echoes of Geoffrey Howe in the way Flint talks about natural loyalties being stretched to breaking point by an immovable Prime Minister. Flint followed this up with an interview in which she accused Brown of 'negative bullying'. The charge, and the persistent characterization of Brown as a paranoid and overbearing modern-day Nixon, would dog the rest of his leadership and help sink him, and Labour, at the 2010 general election.

These blasts, as much as Castlereagh's trigger-happiness, underline just why vengeful ex-employees and business associates are called 'loose cannons'.

The image of the loose cannon rolling about, firing shots at its own operators, said to have originated on wooden warships, is first traceable in Victor Hugo's 1874 novel *Ninety Three*, in which 'The enormous cannon was left alone. . . . She was her own mistress, and mistress of the vessel. She could do what she willed with both.' Its first use to describe people came from a December 1889 edition of the *Galveston Daily News*, with reference to enfranchised African-Americans in the Southern states: 'The Negro vote in the South is a unit, mainly because it is opposed by the combined white vote. It would in no event become, as Mr Grady once said, "a loose cannon on a storm tossed ship".'

The language of resignation is shot through with intimations of violence and mortality. We are dead men walking. We deliver parting shots. As our moment approaches, we become loose cannons. There is blood on the boardroom carpet. We terminate, or we are terminated. In fact, the career crossroads can start to look very much like the haunted crossroads: the departed becomes a spectre, a cautionary tale, or a tormentor to the people behind his or her demise.

This visceral urge to spook our employers with ominous tales of revenge for maltreatment or lack of regard has always been strong. So strong, in fact, that in times, places and positions of least personal empowerment, culture itself begins to conjure up the revenge blasts. One of the more curious strands of resignation culture lies in the folklore of resignation and employee vengeance – the tales, shared delusions and phantom incidents – that grew as employment in the West shifted from heavy industry to service sector.

There is a strong tradition of employee revenge fantasy in folk tales and lyrics. The 1800s American frontier song 'The Buffalo Skinners' relates the grisly revenge of a crew of hired hands in Texas on their boss. Things start out well enough, with the promise of work.

> It happened in Jacksboro in the spring of seventy-three,
> A man by the name of Crego came stepping up to me,
> Saying, 'How do you do, young fellow, and how would you
>   like to go
> And spend one summer pleasantly on the range of the
>   buffalo?'

But when the employer makes a shifty attempt to renege on wages, saying that the crew's expenses have left them owing *him* money, they turn on him and skin him too.

> The season being near over, old Crego he did say
> The crowd had been extravagant, was in debt to him that
>   day,—
> We coaxed him and we begged him and still it was no go,—
> We left old Crego's bones to bleach on the range of the
>   buffalo.

There's something primally chilling about the vengeful ex-employee or wronged business associate that makes them ideal ghosts. Charles Dickens' *A Christmas Carol* (1843) sees Ebenezer Scrooge – a satire on the boom-era bosses of the 1830s and 1840s – haunted by spirits for his treatment of workers; Rudyard Kipling's ghost stories and Edith Wharton's whole oeuvre seem to place the writers in horrified thrall to the idea of the shafted ex-employee, whose judgement exacts terrible vengeance from beyond the grave. Wharton's great supernatural story 'Afterward' (1909) dramatizes common disquiet about business owners' freewheeling ethics and the gnawing angst of meeting a wronged former business associate again, to genuinely terrifying effect; her last tale, 'All Souls' (1937), written as Roosevelt's New Deal aimed to redress simmering Depression-era imbalances between haves and have-nots, never makes it quite clear whether we are witnessing legitimately supernatural horrors, or an elaborately staged ordeal masterminded by an embittered and vengeful employee. Ambrose Bierce's put-upon conscripts return to shoot their tormentors dead. Appalachian mining towns are full of stories of mineworkers returning to the surface after dying in collapsed shafts, to take greedy works-owners back down with them. Even the famous Windsor ghost Herne the Hunter, mentioned in Shakespeare's *The Merry Wives of Windsor*, was according to a 1792 account a 'keeper in the forest in the time of Elizabeth [who] committed some great offence, for which he feared to lose his situation', and hanged himself on a tree in desperation. He now haunts the park, driving mad those he encounters.

From Scrooge's roaring 1830s, to the 1880s, when it rode in tandem with social reform, the 1920s, when it accompanied the birth of muck-raking investigatory journalism, and the New Deal 1930s, this folklore of employee revenge seems to burst forth in popular culture, from whodunnits to horror, whenever issues of wealth and employer power became pressing. Like the resignation letters themselves, it tells the side of the employee-employer relationship that the official histories leave out.

Now, on the crest of the longest bull market in Western economic history, it was as if these – and older folk tales of ghostly miners, nuns, sailors, riders, maids and servants, all exercising the special powers granted them by their demise to wreak revenge on those who'd abused them – had made the transition to the service sector and desktop PCs with the rest of us.

As email generalized, a vogue for circular emails spread. Each one attested that a friend had witnessed such-and-such, or claimed to contain a genuine reply to a boss. Some of the very first social memes to ping from office to office, attaining early viral status along with jokes, chain letters making spurious claims about non-existent sick children and the Cookie Recipe hoax, were resignation letters.

In 'The world's shortest resignation letter', the supposed employee announced simply, 'Sir, I love your wife.' In another, the writer used the last resort of those with no threat to offer – the hanging prophecy. He gave his boss vague clues that he had done terrible things to the company which would not become clear to the board for days, perhaps weeks, yet. Raw liver secreted in a rarely used filing cabinet, and so on.

Like fairy stories in which the poor woodcutter gets to cheat the cruel lord and win the princess's hand in marriage, most were variations on these classic power-plays and fantasies of the powerless and dispossessed. They are Havel's plays, given a redemptive Hollywood ending.

And for a few heady years, every emailed resignation

meme carried such seeds of possibility in it. They were called memes with good reason: the term (coined by scientist Richard Dawkins in his 1976 book *The Selfish Gene* as part of a discussion on factors outside of genetics that affect evolution) is from the Greek *mimem*, or 'imitated thing'; 'an idea, behaviour or style that spreads from person to person within a culture'. This is exactly what began to happen: their content jumped from fictional resignations to real office situations; the idea took on new forms, mutating as it flitted between urban myth and real office. Life imitating art.

A real-life resignation that reads like one of those fantasy letters was penned by Virginia Grover as she quit as secretary to the town of Kittery, Maine, on 28 August 2007. An exemplary employee of eleven years, she wrote an articulate takedown of her police chief boss's 'moods', before declaring that 'I refuse to be stuck in my own version of *Groundhog Day*, where the same scenario is repeated again and again.' She signed off with a rather wonderful piece of reassurance-turned-warning: 'You can rest assured that, while I have been privy to a number of things that I am sure the Chief would not be proud of, I understand the sensitive nature of my former position.'

But drama and reality never make easy bedfellows.

In those great, grandstanding fantasy resignation letters, the resigner walks away into the sunset as the film ends. There is no next act, no heckling, no comeback. Real life is more complicated. Virginia Grover's colleagues, superiors and former bosses soon began to cast doubt upon her claims, suggesting she was more than capable of dishing out unreasonable behaviour, and backing Chief Strong's version of events with a collective letter of their own. The democratization of the big moment put the secretary from Maine in the same shoes as Blair, Gorbachev and Nixon. The spotlight that we crave can be a harsh and unforgiving thing.

Elsewhere, the rash of fictitious resignations occasionally came true, as real-life workers were not just inspired by the canon of email fantasy quitters, but took these form letters as their own, and duly resigned using them. In Dublin, one employee served notice to his colleagues at the HQ of a multinational accountancy firm in 2007 with a quite jaw-dropping collection of potshots at the culture, his bosses, and individual colleagues. Here are a few choice lines.

> I wanted to take this opportunity to let you know what a great and distinct pleasure it has been to type, 'Tomorrow is my last day' . . . Your demands were high and your patience short, but I take great solace knowing that my work was, as stated on my annual review, 'mostly satisfactory' . . . A job opportunity like this comes along only once in a lifetime. Meaning: if I had to work here again in this lifetime, I would sooner kill myself.

Amid the inevitable fallout, media coverage and reputational damage all round, the employee claimed that he had copied his text in large part from a template online, suggesting resigners use it 'for a rainy day . . . of vengeance'. Sure enough, company investigators found the template – created by LA-based comedy writer Chris Kula, it was placed on his website for others to use, with the instruction

'Feel free to copy and paste' to anyone who wanted to adapt it for themselves.

> Last Thursday I sent out a going away email . . . The text was something I pulled off the Internet.
>
> I apologise for any offence that I have caused. I regret that the email could adversely impact on the reputation/ good name of [company name redacted] and my former colleagues. I wish to emphasise that none of the comments were meant to be taken seriously. I hold [company name redacted] and my former colleagues in the highest regard.
>
> If you have passed on the original email or shown it to anyone outside of the recipient list can you please also pass on this apology and refrain from further forwarding of the mail.

In a way, perhaps what's most curious about the resignation of vengeance is its rarity. Protests, truth attacks, big fuck-yous and corporate conversation-killers have become a staple of professional and public life. But these concentrated, premeditated nuggets of darkness are very rare. Perhaps there's even something comforting in knowing that all the enmity, the rivalry, poor management, frustration and thwarted ambition out there can only manage a real-hit job once in a blue moon. The rest of the time, they remain in the realm of the drive-in slasher movie, the spine-chilling ghost story, the Grimm folktale in which the despot winds up in the stew. We scare ourselves just a little with the fantasy hit it's not real. Mostly

Still, somewhere out there, perhaps, someone is sitting at a keyboard: a dead sheep bent on savagery or a Dead

Man Walking – sidelined, alienated, embittered and all out of options. They are about to rise up in a brief but dazzling blaze of rage. All they want is to take someone down with them. It could be you.

4:

The Kamikaze Protest

'There is no more neutrality in the world. You either have to be part of the solution, or you're going to be part of the problem.'
— Eldridge Cleaver

'Leaving my sweet town and dear people all behind,
Now I am to go
To rescue my country
From its national crisis.'
— Kamikaze pilot Junior Lt. Jou Ogata, 21st March 1943

The almost complete absence of protest as an activity in the late 1990s and early 2000s cut right across Western culture. It seems incredible now, but American political scientist Francis Fukuyama's contention in his book *The End of History and The Last Man* (1992) that the end of the Cold War had more or less settled things, and that we were witnessing the end of any conflict of ideologies as liberal democracy conquered all, seemed quite plausible for most.

Even the anti-globalization protests sporadically held in Seattle and London were small, marginal and diffuse in their concerns. The economy was booming, and there wasn't a figure as polarizing as Margaret Thatcher to protest against. The art world played self-referential games. Traditionally a sanctuary for outsiders and refuseniks, it seemed for a while that art was cosying up to corporatism, with Damien Hirst professing that his ambition was to 'become a brand'. Free market triumphalism and money for all was something on which it seemed we could all agree. Britpop and gangsta rap revelled in the feeling that these were fat times. These were the years of Tony Blair's overwhelming majority and Cool Britannia hip-vicar grooviness. It was like Mrs Thatcher had said: there was no alternative. Grumpiness was passé, disobedience marginalized. And while resignations were plenty, resignations in protest were suddenly rather few.

Even the opposition spin missed the point. If the Blair premiership seemed increasingly presidential, it also seemed more Chief Exec-like – more Branson than Clinton. Still, special advisers and spin doctors on both sides kept those awkward and rather quaint party members prone to muttering about democracy on-message.

Then the spell broke. The PM's commitment to the invasion of Iraq in 2003 began to look horribly like one of Thatcher's grandstanding 'not for turning' moments. Cabinet ministers started to become twitchy as being 'on-message' meant being 'pro-war' and being anti-war meant resigning.

In the States, a long tradition of powerful resignations of conscience hung over the build-up to Iraq. In a country more acutely conscious of its own internal divisions, and one formed by revolution against its own colonial boss, the tradition of declaring 'Count me out' is far stronger.

It is also a game with far higher stakes. In its way, the tension between the country's two behavioural archetypes – circle the wagons, be true to your school, swear allegiance on the one hand; strike out alone, trust no one, revolt against your masters and proclaim independence on the other – has never been resolved, and bubbles up daily. And the point at which half the country resigned in protest at the government remains its primal wound.

Before it saw a single casualty, the American Civil War – effectively, the south's resignation from the Union – saw a wave of personal resignations of conscience. Those hastily telegraphed resignations from southern soldiers during the American Civil War were part of the phenomenon called 'Going South' that caused chaos and fear in the Union Army.

Southern officers and men of the US Navy watched with mounting unease as their home state and their country set against each other. Faced with the possibility of being ordered to attack their own town, many either injured themselves, deserted *en masse*, or penned hurried letters of resignation which they hoped would reach their superiors in time to pre-empt orders.

One of these men was General Robert E. Lee. Although he deplored the idea that the Union was breaking up, he could not attack his own people. In what is perhaps the ultimate coded resignation, his phrase 'save in the defense of my native State' meant that he was leaving to joining the Confederate Army and fight against his former colleagues.

The Kamikaze Protest

Arlington, Washington City P.O.
20th April 1861

General:

Since my interview with you on the 18th instant I have felt that I ought not longer to retain my commission in the Army. I therefore tender my resignation, which I request you will recommend for acceptance.

It would have been presented at once, but for the struggle it has cost me to separate myself from a service to which I have devoted all the best years of my life & all the ability I possessed.

During the whole of that time, more than 30 years, I have experienced nothing but kindness from my superiors, & the most cordial friendship from my companions. To no one Genl. have I been as much indebted as to yourself for uniform kindness & consideration, & it has always been my ardent desire to merit your approbation.

I shall carry with me to the grave the most grateful recollections of your kind consideration, & your name & fame will always be dear to me. Save in the defense of my native State, I never desire again to draw my sword.

Be pleased to accept my most earnest wishes for the continuance of your happiness & prosperity & believe me most truly yours

R. E. Lee

Others were more overt in their protest. Commodore Isaac Mayo of the US Navy, a well-regarded veteran of the Mexican war, the war of 1812 and the Seminole war, is credited with locating the US Naval Academy at

Annapolis, Maryland. He was of distinguished naval stock. Nevertheless, on hearing that hostilities had broken out between the Confederacy and the Union, Mayo – alongside 300 other enlisted men – felt he could not remain in the Union navy. He resigned on 1 May 1861 with this message, addressed personally to President Abraham Lincoln.

Sir,

For more than *half a century* it has been the pride of my life to hold office under the Government of the United States. For *twenty-five*, I have engaged in active sea-service and have never seen my flag dishonored, or the American arms disgraced by defeat. It was the hope of my old age that I might die, as I had lived, an officer in the Navy of a free Government. This hope has been taken from me. In adopting the policy of coercion, you have denied to millions of freemen the rights of the Constitution and in its stead you have placed the will of a sectional Party. As one of the oldest soldiers of America, I protest – in the name of humanity – against this 'war against brethren!' I cannot fight against the Constitution while pretending to fight for it. You will therefore oblige me by accepting my resignation.

Lincoln granted many of his requests. But Mayo's resignation went further than most. The President dismissed Mayo from service altogether on 18 May. It made no odds: Mayo killed himself the day his notice of dismissal arrived. It is unknown whether he read the acceptance of his resignation before he delivered the fatal shot.

Over the coming days and weeks, such resignations – dubbed 'Going South' in the press – became first common, then a craze, spreading along the country's newly opened telegraph wires and into its newspapers as fast as they could be copied and sent.

Indeed, it's possible that, as with email and radio in the twentieth century, the first transcontinental US telegraph network (built between 1851 and 1861) actually swelled the first formally recorded popular wave of resignations, helping to turn isolated pockets of sentiment into an exciting, volatile sensation. The telegraph was sexy; it was exciting and ultra-high tech. As with Twitter today, if something happened by telegraph, the story came with a ready angle for reporters. Some of these telegraphed resignation letters seemed to sense that they would be talked about, in a way that a closed packet going by steam boat or pony never would. Perhaps, for some, that spectacle was part of the protest. First Lee, then Mayo were soon joined by a flood of southern-born Union army and navy servicemen unwilling to attack their home states.

The phenomenon – or at least, the widespread fear of it, and speculation about where it would end – was popular enough to have worked its way into the popular art, music and stories of the day, much as popular fear of one's neighbours 'turning Commie' fuelled stories of mind-controlling aliens in 1950s B-movies. It is a recurring theme in American Gothic literature of the era and the years following: Ambrose Bierce's supernatural tales are full of Civil War soldiers who, having left the ranks, return from some inexplicable, irreducible 'other side' to do us harm; or who send messages through the ether, warning us against that rendezvous, or that fork in the road. How many of the stories we hear today of Civil War ghosts turning up at their homes many years after going 'missing, presumed dead' can be attributed to these comrades who resigned and crossed over to the Other Side, we will never know.

These were resignations of conscience, but they were also a threat familiar to anyone who's resigned under a cloud. They represent the former colleague as rogue element, confidante turned fifth columnist; friend as would-be vampire.

No aggrieved resignation, whistleblower's report or boss's defensive statement about disgruntled ex-employees, from Robert E. Lee to Geoffrey Howe to Edward Snowden, can be properly understood unless we reckon with the almost tribalistic fear of receiving a resignation letter from a comrade that means he or she may do his or her best to kill you when your paths next cross.

Just over a year after resigning as Deputy Sheriff of Pima County in Arizona, reformed criminal and gunfighter-lawman Wyatt Earp had already used up local reserves of goodwill in his new job as a US Deputy Marshal based in Tombstone, along with his brother Virgil.

His activities around town – including catching criminals, but also high living and selling gambling concessions – caused public uproar around Tombstone. Under their reign, robberies on the edge of town had become commonplace; whispers persisted of their involvement in a stagecoach heist; and by January, it was widely believed that the Earps themselves were behind many of the crimes they claimed to be trying to solve. On February 1, they handed in their joint resignation to United States Marshal Major Cawley P. Dake at the Grand Hotel, Tombstone, on the grounds that they weren't left well enough alone, and honest gunfighting work in the face of such hostile public opinion was impossible. Their statement (spellings left intact) was reprinted in the wonderfully named local newspaper the *Tombstone Epitaph,* under the bold-caps headline: 'DRAW YOUR OWN INFERENCE. Resignation of Virgil W. Earp and Wyatt S. Earp as Deputy Marshals.'

Dear Sir:

In excerising out official functions as deputy United States marshals in this territory, we have endeavored always unflinchingly to perform the duties entrusted to us. These duties have been exacting and perilous in their character, having to be performed in a community where turbulence and violence could almost any moment be organized to thwart and risist the enforcement of the process of the court issued to bring criminals to justice. And while we have a dep sense of obligation to many of the citizens for their hearty cooperation in aiding us to suppress lawlessness, and their faith in our honesty of purpose, we realize that, notwithstanding our best efforts and judgement in everything which we have been required to perform, ther has arisen so much harsh criticism in relation to our operations, and such a persistent effort having been made to misepresent and misinterpret out acts, we are led to the conclusion that, in order to convince the public that it is our sincere purpose to promote the public welfare, independent of any personal emolument or advantages to ourselves, it is our duty to place our resignations as deputy United States marshals in your hands, which we now do, thanking you for your continued courtesy and confidence in our integrity, and shall remain subject to your orders in the performance of any duties which may be assigned to us, only until our successors are appointed.

Very respectfully yours,

Virgil W. Earp

Wyatt S. Earp

To public outcry, Dake initially refused the brothers' resignation – only, it seems, because they had outstanding debts to pay off. In the meantime, their ongoing battles (including an assassination attempt on Wyatt) made it impossible for them to operate as US Government employees. By the end of the month, resignation or not, the Earps had decided to go freelance – and to pursue their own, for-profit strategy for dealing with murderers. The brothers' careers were spent crossing and re-crossing the line between lawman and businessman, peacekeeper and gunfighter. Their employers and alliances were always temporary; their work was chillingly consistent.

In a federal country that only exists as an agreement between states and citizens to cooperate, and where resignations had come so close to splitting it in two, President George W. Bush's assertion in his address to Congress on 20 September 2001 that 'You're either with us or you're with the terrorists' begins to make sense. The Confederacy and Wild West lawlessness, Waco and bunker survivalists, States' Rights and the circumstances of its own Revolution loom large in the American psyche. That those around you may cross over, becoming Other, is not just a threat, but an existential one. Are you one of Us – write it out U.S. – or one of them? From the one-time US capital of

Annapolis, Maryland to *apolis* itself is just a short step over the line, and into the shadows.

Viewed from the other side, resignations of this nature are the sound of something stretching to breaking point: the chains of loyalty, the credibility of the organization's plan.

These are resignations *in extremis* – often desperate, self-immolating cries whose purpose is not to resign from a position at all (that is a side effect), but to be heard. Often, they also feel oddly panicked. In every case, they are written in the full consciousness of being the weaker side in a dialogue. There is no time to lose. Send the telegram, grab your gun and jump on your horse. The enemy has struck first and is already winning.

Revolutionary thinking is the United States' origin, and its great internal engine of change. And for much of its history – until the Cold War established America as Team Capitalism – left-wing revolutionary thinking was a large part of that.

Faulkner's brief kiss-off to the University of Mississippi invoked the possibility of choosing another way. On the other side, America's socialist organizations were struggling to define themselves. Just eight years before Faulkner's note, in 1916, just a few months before his death of gastro-intestinal uraemia caused by alcoholism, fellow American author Jack London resigned from the US Socialist Party in protest at its move towards the moderate centre. His health failing, knowing he was on his way out anyway, his resignation became London's way to make his demise count. Written pre-Russian revolution when the very idea of revolutionary socialism was still quite fluid, it's quite a shocking letter, in lots of ways.

Dear Comrades,

I have just finished reading Comrade Edward B. Payne's resignation from the Local, of recent date, undated.

I am herewith tendering my own resignation from Local Glen Ellen, and for the diametrically opposite reason from the one instanced by Comrade Payne. I am resigning from the Socialist Party because of its lack of fire and fight, and its loss of emphasis on the class struggle.

I was originally a member of the old, revolutionary, up-on-its-hind-legs, fighting, Socialist Labor Party. Since then, and to the present time, I have been a fighting member of the Socialist Party. My fighting record for the Cause is not, even at this late date, already entirely forgotten.

Trained in the class struggle, as taught and practised by the Socialist Labor Party, my own highest judgement concurring, I believe that the working class, by fighting, by never fusing, by never making terms with the enemy, could emancipate itself.

Since the whole trend of socialism in the United States of recent years has been one of peaceableness and compromise, I find that my mind refuses further sanction of my remaining a party member. Hence my resignation. Please include my comrade wife, Charmain K. London's resignation with mine.

My final word is that liberty, freedom and independence, are royal things that cannot be presented to, nor thrust upon, races or classes. If races and classes cannot rise up and by their own strength of brain and brawn wrest from the world liberty, freedom and independence, they never, in time, can come to these royal possessions – and if such royal things are kindly presented to them by superior individuals on silver platters, they will not know what to do with them, will fail to make use of them, and will be what they have always been in the past – inferior races and classes.

Yours for the Revolution

Jack London

It's strange to think how far from what we now accept as socialist rhetoric are London's thoughts on liberty, revolution and whether it should be shared. But even in post-revolutionary Russia, ideas of what that revolution should represent could be perilously fluid. It's one thing to ask whether you're with us or against us; another entirely to ask what 'us' means at all. And if you didn't know, or your definition was different from someone else's, it was time to watch your back.

For Bolshevik commander Marshal Mikhail Tukhachevsky, the 1923 campaign against Poland was not going well. It was marked by disagreements with Stalin, jockeying for influence between Army and Kremlin, and failure to capture key objectives. Tukhachevsky, a brilliant strategic thinker whose bravery nevertheless often bordered on foolhardiness and bloodlust (his infamy as the commander behind village massacres seems to be the inspiration for the paranoid, dandy 'butcher of the Crimea' in Mikhail Bulgavov's *Flight*), was in a fit of exasperated pique when he sent his resignation to Trotsky from the field. Robert E. Lee's letter to his commanding officers is one thing; to announce to your revolutionary commander from the field that you're going it alone is to become a terrifying loose cannon indeed.

Russian Soviet Federation Socialist Republic
Commander, Western Front Troops
21st November 1923
To: Comrade Trotsky, Chairman of the USSR Revolutionary
Military Council,

Comrade Antonov Ovseenko told me that you're floating, yet again, the idea of re-establishing the Revolutionary Council under my command.

Never mind the fact that I will not be able to work productively if that happens; for me, holding such a position is absolutely out of the question.

This is partly because, as I'm sure you know, this new Revolutionary Council thing will drag up all those old bizarre and unproven rumours. You know the ones, the reports about my documents being lost by my stenographer, and so on.

No documents have ever been lost by my stenographer.

This is because I have never had a stenographer.

Anyway, I can't see how restoring this Revolutionary Council idea is anything other than an open show of distrust, and I have to tell you that the chances of my working under such conditions – not to mention such work being acceptable to me – are zero.

I therefore ask that you relieve me from my post. If this is what you're going ahead with, I'd rather do all my operational training at the Front without holding any position at all.

Signed,
Marshal of the Soviet Union Tukhachevsky

It's a delightfully flouncy letter, full of ego and intrigue: when he talks about his non-existent stenographer, Tukhachevsky's tone is so withering as to be almost Blackadderish.

But he would regret making himself so difficult with a colleague. The unspoken presence that pervades this letter – and likely source of the rumours to which Tukhachevsky is referring – is Stalin himself. Uncle Joe had long seen Tukhachevsky as a rival and potential challenger, and blamed him for the failure of Russia's plan to capture Warsaw in 1920–21. This letter would come back to haunt its writer. By 1935, Stalin was looking for 'evidence' that Tukhachevsky (whom he called *Napoleonchik*, or 'Little Napoleon') was looking to overthrow the Politburo. After a secret trial in 1937, Tukhachevsky would become one of the most famous victims of Uncle Joe's bloody purges. With this in mind, Bulgakov's own letter to Stalin, written nearly six years after Tukhachevsky's – in whose society circles the writer occasionally mixed – feels even more desperate.

Tukhachevsky's resignation letter may have become his death warrant; the leaving party as shooting party. For First World War Tommies called to the Western Front, refusal to report to the front line was grounds for court martial and death by firing squad. When Max Plowman enlisted on Christmas Eve 1914 to fight in the trenches, the poet and writer was already convinced that all war was morally wrong. After being concussed by an exploding shell in 1917 and recovering at the infamous Craiglockart mental hospital (alongside Wilfred Owen and Siegfried Sassoon), he decided to try and resign from the Army altogether in protest.

Sir,

I have the honour to request that you will lay before the Commanding Officer the following grave & personal matter.

For some time past it has been becoming increasingly apparent to me that for reasons of conscientious objection I was unfitted to hold my commission in His Majesty's army & I am now absolutely convinced that I have no alternative but to proffer my resignation. I have always held that (in the Prime Minister's words) war is a 'relic of barbarism', but my opinion has gradually deepened into a fixed conviction that organised warfare of any kind is always organised murder. So wholly do I believe in the doctrine of Incarnation (that God indeed lives in every human body) that I believe that killing men is always killing God.

As I hold this belief with conviction, you will, I think, see that it is impossible for me to continue to be a member of any organisation that has the killing of men for any part of its end, & I therefore beg that you will ask the Commanding Officer to forward this my resignation for acceptance with the least possible delay.

Plowman was arrested and court-martialled, but was dismissed rather than being shot. In a bizarre twist, as he was no longer an enlisted man, he could be called up again. He was called up for civilian war-work just days later, but appealed successfully against that too.

His letter now reads like a key to understanding these resignations. These are not resignations undertaken through difference of opinion, but the result of an irreconcilable diverging of fixed conviction and obligation.

The conviction has been arrived at carefully, and over time, so this is no whim. The circumstances may be local, but the principle is universal. The choice to speak out is therefore not a choice at all. The protest resigner is not rebelling, but simply answering to a higher authority: God, justice, law, fair play, logic or history itself.

Perhaps the most famous example is that of First Lady Eleanor Roosevelt. In January 1939, African-American opera singer Marian Anderson was scheduled to sing at Constitution Hall in Washington, DC. The hall's owners – the Daughters of the American Revolution (DAR) – refused to allow the concert, as it violated their strict policy of racial segregation. The First Lady was a champion of civil rights, and resigned her membership of DAR on 26 February. There's even something curiously martial about her letter that recalls Lee, Mayo and Plowman.

I am afraid that I have never been a very useful member of the Daughters of the American Revolution, so I know it will make very little difference to you whether I resign, or whether I continue to be a member of your organization.

However, I am in complete disagreement with the attitude taken in refusing Constitution Hall to a great artist. You have set an example which seems to me unfortunate, and I feel obliged to send in to you my resignation. You had an opportunity to lead in an enlightened way and it seems to me that your organization has failed.

Not satisfied that her point would be heeded, Mrs Roosevelt decided to use her magazine column to set the media snowball rolling. She followed up her private resignation with an open letter in her 'My Day' column, the following day, writing that DAR 'have taken an action which has been widely talked of in the press. To remain as a member implies approval of that action, and therefore I am resigning.'

Mrs Roosevelt's deliciously disingenuous line that 'it will make very little difference to you whether I resign' is just one of the many joys in her resignation. Tonally, Mrs Roosevelt's note is also a prototype for Geoffrey Howe's letter to Prime Minister Margaret Thatcher. Today, it seems incredible that a First Lady would do something so courageous and potentially divisive on grounds of principle.

To remain would be to approve. To keep silent is to consent.

These words were more loaded in 1939 than we can imagine today. For African-Americans in the worst and lowest-paid stations, Mrs Roosevelt's choice of words cannot have been lost. There too, public resignations were made in protest on a daily basis. In the segregated South, plantation labourers' field songs and blues were frequently none-too-codified resignation notices, endlessly refined and rehearsed in song for their eventual verbal delivery, someday when it finally got too much. Just one year after Roosevelt's protest, plantation worker Gabriel Brown was singing his own resignation – or at least, his refusal to work as his bosses commanded – in a Florida field. As a notice to quit an entire system, it's pretty devastating.

Brown's song struck a chord. It became a local hit, and was pressed as a record, earning him some fame, a little money . . . and an escape.

On the boom of coded resignations disguised as blues, historian Paul Oliver sounds like Václav Havel: 'Lack of incentives, lack of opportunity, lack of hope, could dispirit a man until he no longer wished to live or work, so he might resort to protest.' These resignation speeches were equivocated, disguised as simple songs, communicated among co-workers coded as innocuous tunes until their moment of delivery.

Brown's case illustrates another point resigners must consider. If silence implies consent, the alternative is by no means a simple thing. The sense of the ongoing, pervading pressure and coercion to stay silent – economic, social, emotional, political – only makes protest resignations the more insistent when they do burst forth.

⋆ ⋆ ⋆

One resignation in particular has come to be something of an inspiration to protesters. Jerald F. terHorst was the White House Press Secretary under President Gerald Ford. His resignation letter, written more in sorrow than anger, cast a long shadow across American politics; longer, perhaps, than Geoffrey Howe's slaying of a Prime Minister.

Mr terHorst was the last of the great Watergate-related resignations. Some still call him the last honest man in politics. Unlike most, his resignation came not amid personal scandal, but in protest at the new President's unseemly rush to let Richard Nixon off the hook. On 8 September 1974, President Ford declared his predecessor had 'suffered enough', and signed Nixon's pardon. This was too much for terHorst, who stayed up through the night agonizing over what, by morning, had become his letter of resignation.

In his letter, terHorst (like Howe) starts by establishing just how much he supports Ford, and values both his leadership and friendship. This is essential in any effective letter of conscience: the resigner must first account for the response that they were disaffected, disgruntled or harboured a grudge. That done, he states his reasons for resigning dispassionately.

His note was devastating in its simplicity.

September 8, 1974
The White House
Washington

Dear Mr President,

Without doubt this is the most difficult decision I ever had to make. I cannot find words to adequately express my respect and admiration for you over the many years of our friendship and my belief that you could heal the wounds and serve our country in this most critical time in our nation's story. Words also cannot convey my appreciation for the opportunity to serve on your staff during the transitional days of your Presidency, and for the confidence and faith you placed in me in that regard. The Press Office has been restructured along professional lines. Its staff, from Deputy Press Secretary John W. Hushen down the line, is competent and dedicated and comprises loyal employees who have given unstintingly of their time and talents.

So it is with great regret, after long soul-searching, that I must inform you that I cannot in good conscience support your decision to pardon former President Nixon even before he has been charged with the commission of any crime. As your spokesman, I do not know how I could credibly defend that action in the absence of a like decision to grant absolute pardon to the young men who evaded Vietnam military service as a matter of conscience and the absence of pardons for former aides and associates of Mr Nixon who have been charged with crimes – and imprisoned – stemming from the same Watergate situation. These are also men whose reputations and families have been grievously injured. Try as I can, it is impossible to conclude that the former President is more deserving of mercy than persons of lesser station in life whose offenses have had far less effect on our national wellbeing.

Thus it is with a heavy heart that I hereby tender my resignation as Press Secretary to the President, effective today. My prayers nonetheless remain with you, sir.

Sincerely, Jerald F. terHorst

Whatever else this is, it is not the sound of a man enjoying his platform. terHorst is clearly struggling, from the beginning. He begins on comfortable territory, and speaks with obvious sincerity, before summoning the strength to speak his piece. You can sense the extra push in his voice as he adds small, forceful touches like 'imprisoned' and 'grievously'. The killer line is 'Try as I can . . .' This is Ford's most loyal servant and staunchest ally; his most charitable audience and most forgiving eye. Even for him, it is impossible to agree with what the President has done.

As in all the best resignations, something happens in its midst. These aren't just messages, they are dramas, and terHorst needed every ounce of strength to remain in control to deliver this one cleanly.

This sense of control matters hugely. Unlike truth bombs, revenge attacks or fuck-yous, protests are all about being the *sensible* one. While a little extra emotion can help you emphasize the depth of your loyalty (and conversely the strength of your feelings), getting drunk on the sound of your own righteousness is deadly.

One British politician got this so memorably wrong that his high-camp car-crash of an announcement – that he would be stepping back from politics to clear his name of smears – became his one claim to fame.

Jonathan Aitken was Conservative Minister of Defence when the *Guardian* exposed a number of secret deals he had made with Saudi princes, including weaponry and the procurement of girls. On the day the story was published – 11 April 1995 – he released a spectacular, sabre-rattling letter announcing he was stepping back from the front line of public life in order to clear his name in court. As it turned out, his principled protest against 'falsehood and those who peddle it' was based on lies. If you speak out in protest at 'smears', do check you're not guilty of them first.

> I believe my experience of various walks of life, including the experience of doing honourable business in the Middle East, has strengthened my ability to make such a contribution. And because I do have such a strong commitment to the ideal of public service, I would like to make it clear that I am taking legal action not simply to clear my own name and reputation of the deeply damaging

slurs that have been cast upon me. For there are greater public interest issues at stake here, far more important than my own position.

Here in Britain we have both the best media in the world and the worst media in the world. That small latter element is spreading a cancer in our society today, which I will call the cancer of bent and twisted journalism.

The malignant cells of that bent and twisted journalistic cancer include those who engage in forgeries or other instruments of deceit to obtain information for the purposes of a smear story.

They include those who hold grievances or grudges of their own and are prepared to give or sell false testimony about others to further their own bitter agendas.

Above all they include those who try to abuse media power to destroy or denigrate honourable institutions and individuals who have done nothing seriously wrong.

I have done nothing wrong.

I have certainly made my fair share of mistakes in 30-odd years of life as a writer, businessman, parliamentarian and minister but I am prepared to stand on my record as a decent and honourable one – in Saudi Arabia and elsewhere – and to defend it not only before the jury of the courts but before the wider jury of all fair minded people.

If it falls to me to start a fight to cut out the cancer of bent and twisted journalism in our country with the simple sword of truth and the trusty shield of British fair play, so be it. I am ready for the fight. The fight against falsehood and those who peddle it.

My fight begins today. Thank you and good afternoon.

Fine words – with more than a little of Getúlio Vargas' martyr pose overshadowing the message of conscience and morality. But Aitken's evidence began to unravel at trial. Finally, it was revealed that he had fabricated evidence to support his claims. He was charged with perjury and perverting the course of justice, and was jailed for 18 months in 1999. Aitken, no longer a politician having lost his parliamentary seat, was declared bankrupt.

There were plenty of clues in his statement. When people resign in protest, they speak with their own voices. They are being wronged, and they need to be heard. But Aitkin's voice here is not really his own. There's no theatricality to it. Maybe it's his previous career as a journalist coming out, just as No. 10 spokesman Andy Coulson's tabloid voice came out in his resignation. Lies are 'wicked'; truth and fair play are a 'sword and shield'; enemies are a 'cancer' and he is 'honourable'. It's all very *Julius Caesar* via *The Pirates of Penzance*. He really should have known the journalist's rule-of-thumb for claims like this: whenever any member of a government in power uses the word 'smear', you ask whether they're trying to deflect attention away from the issue. And you get digging.

Contrast Aitken's bluster with former President George Bush senior's blistering resignation from the National Rifle Association just days later, also in protest at statements he felt went far beyond the pale. In the aftermath of the Oklahoma City bombing on 19 April 1995, the authorities had launched the largest criminal investigation in US history. The National Rifle Association pushed back hard.

I was outraged when, even in the wake of the Oklahoma City tragedy, Mr Wayne LaPierre, executive vice president of NRA, defended his attack on federal agents as 'jack-booted thugs'. To attack Secret Service agents or ATF [Bureau of Alcohol, Tobacco, Firearms and Explosives] people or any government law enforcement people as 'wearing Nazi bucket helmets and black storm trooper uniforms' wanting to 'attack law abiding citizens' is a vicious slander on good people.

You can already feel that Bush's thunder is rooted in reality, in a way that Aitken's can't be. But his next move is devastating to the NRA's campaign. He points to real people – administration employees and law enforcement agents of the kind LaPierre had painted as faceless storm troopers.

Al Whicher, who served on my [United States Secret Service] detail when I was Vice President and President, was killed in Oklahoma City. He was no Nazi. He was a kind man, a loving parent, a man dedicated to serving his country – and serve it well he did.

In 1993, I attended the wake for ATF agent Steve Willis, another dedicated officer who did his duty. I can assure you that this honorable man, killed by weird cultists, was no Nazi . . .

The stage is set for the *coup de grâce*. Bush's natural loyalties and affinities, like terHorst's, are declared most vehemently at the very moment they are severed.

I am a gun owner and an avid hunter. Over the years I have agreed with most of NRA's objectives, particularly your educational and training efforts, and your fundamental stance in favor of owning guns.

However, your broadside against Federal agents deeply offends my own sense of decency and honor; and it offends my concept of service to country. It indirectly slanders a wide array of government law enforcement officials, who are out there, day and night, laying their lives on the line for all of us. Please remove my name from your membership list.

You can feel the credibility gap between this and Aitken's resignation. This is the sound of a man who knows exactly what he is saying and is prepared to say it plainly – now, not at some future day in court. Bush refuses to be drawn into the rhetoric; instead, he answers the posturing with real, flesh-and-blood experience, point by point. His natural loyalties and principles are with the NRA; but he knows what he knows. His loyalty doesn't just snap here; it unravels. It is merciless.

The ironic thing is how uncannily the NRA's own over-the-top comments about 'jackbooted thugs' sound like Aitken.

So beware of resignations from protesting ventrilo-quists. And always ask: If they aren't speaking as plainly as George Bush, with their own voices, at a time like this, why might that be?

* * *

When businessman and football investor Ken Bates (for-merly Chelsea, then Leeds United) resigned from the

Wembley Stadium redevelopment project in a fit of pique in 2001, his line, 'Even Jesus Christ suffered only one Pontius Pilate – I had a whole team of them', may have been said in partial jest; but in black-and-white print, it just looked insane.

As Bates, Aitken and our Whole Foods buyer found, the temptation to invoke authority from the history books is fraught with peril. Yet resigners who want to rally support, sincere or otherwise, seem drawn to history for its ready-made sense of mission, seriousness and portent.

Between July 2011 and March 2012, international law enforcement agencies led a clampdown on the hackers' collectives behind a number of high-profile security breaches. One such collective was Lulzsec. In June 2011, its members had hacked the website of Rupert Murdoch's *Sun* newspaper, releasing a huge payload of company-held data onto the web. Two of its leading lights were hackers known as Topiary (real name Jake Davis) and Sabu (later identified as Hector Xavier Monsegur). As law-enforcement moved in, both announced their departure from Lulzsec to followers with cryptic announcements on Twitter.

@ATopiary
7:02 PM – 21 Jul 11
You cannot arrest an idea

Davis's leave-taking was an adaptation of the climactic quote from Alan Moore's *V for Vendetta* graphic novel. In the book, a revolt against Britain's authoritarian government is led by a shadowy figure dressed in a Guy Fawkes mask (of the kind adopted by the Lulzsec-affiliated group Anonymous).

Going dark didn't save Topiary. Davis, who turned out to be an intelligent and photogenic teenager from Shetland, was already behind bars awaiting trial when his erstwhile comrade and commander tweeted his own two-part resignation from the group.

> @AnonymouSabu
> 12:24 PM – 5 Mar 12
> The federal government is run by a bunch of fucking cowards.
> Don't give in to these people. Fight back. Stay strong.

> @AnonymouSabu
> 3:57 PM – 5 Mar 12
> Die Revolution sagt ich bin, ich war, ich werde sein.

The second lifts assassinated German pre-war Marxist Rosa Luxemburg's famous slogan ('The revolution says I am, I was, I will be'). The phrase was also used by the anti-consumerist Baader-Meinhof terror group in seventies West Germany. But something about his invocation brings Monsegur close to the campery of the Whole Foods round robin, with its misattributed 'Edmund Burke' quote. It recalls Jonathan Aitken too, and alarm bells start ringing. It would later emerge that by the time he posted these two farewell tweets, Monsegur had been cooperating with the FBI for some time, working as a government informant to ensnare his former comrades, including Davis.

Its self-conscious high seriousness also conjures up what might be the great, cringeworthy high-water mark of the protest resignation before Britain slipped into its conscience-free 'Cigarettes & Alcohol' decade. On 8 August 1993, BBC Radio 1 DJ Dave Lee Travis (aka 'The Hairy Cornflake') resigned in protest over the station's 'new broom' policy, which he suspected would leave him without a contract renewal that October, with this live announcement over the airwaves.

> I just want to take a short break from the music for a moment to tell you about something which is very, very important to me.
>
> Recently there has been a lot in the press about the BBC and I really wanted to put the record straight at this point.
>
> I think you, the listeners, ought to know first. One point I wish to make clear is that I have the greatest admiration for what the BBC has stood for. But nothing stays the same. Changes are being made here which go against my principles, and I just cannot agree with them. The only option for me is to leave, so that is what I am going to be doing.
>
> But as we DJs say, 'The show must go on'. At least until October.

The language (at least until the wonderfully hammy segue back into showbizland at the end) is almost that of the civil rights struggle or social reform. But where Nye Bevan and Martin Luther King took to the airwaves to fight for equal rights and universal healthcare, this finger-wagging moment is about a breakfast DJ's contract renewal. Like Sky Sports presenter Richard Keys, who – having been fired in 2011 for making a string of sexually offensive remarks during a broadcast when he thought he was off-camera – famously took to the airwaves to proclaim that 'dark forces have been at work' in engineering his ousting, Travis seems to cast himself as something of a cosmic warrior on the side of Right.

It is worth contrasting these thundering strings of hammery, quotation and authority with the sound of real crises of conscience – and very real crises in general.

If the affluent, good-timey late 1990s were a low point for resignations of conscience in the West, the chain of events set in motion on 11 September 2001 would change everything. The double boom of the planes hitting the World Trade Center rippled outwards. And in the brief but spectacular protest renaissance around the build-up to the Iraq War in 2003, you could almost hear party, corporate and national loyalties groaning as they were stretched to breaking point.

The build up to Iraq's intense, public agonizing about right and wrong, responsibility and loyalty, created a sudden wellspring of inspiration for protest resignations to come. Yet reading the Iraq resignations back now, they sound oddly Shakespearean in their register. The language veers between the rhetoric of the barrister – protest resignations often read back like court testimony – and the clear-eyed piety of the holy martyr.

The other thing that shines through is how few genuinely big names were among the protesters. Recalling Jerald terHorst's letter to Ford, US political correspondent Glenn Greenwald noted in 2010, in an article called '10 Things that Would Not Happen Today':

It is interesting that such conscience resignations as Jerald terHorst's occur among mid-level current and former military members, but not among the political class. [Today] anyone who sacrificed a position of political power, and did so based on an announced principle, would be derided by our power-worshiping political media as UnSerious, UnSavvy, and an overly earnest loser.

On 25 February 2003, US diplomat John Brady Kiesling wrote a furious letter of resignation to Secretary of State Colin Powell. Kiesling, who had reportedly been in deep despair over the momentum building towards a US-led invasion, would later recall 'a certain lucidity, a strong, liberating feeling' in writing it. More than any other resignation in this book, it feels like a manifesto for another way, reached in a moment of burning clarity; a blueprint for a possible America that looked like it might still have a chance, or a requiem for its passing.

It is inevitable that during twenty years with the State Department I would become more sophisticated and cynical about the narrow and selfish bureaucratic motives that sometimes shaped our policies. Human nature is what it is, and I was rewarded and promoted for understanding human nature. But until this Administration it had been possible to believe that by upholding the policies of my president I was also upholding the interests of the American people and the world. I believe it no longer.

The policies we are now asked to advance are incompatible not only with American values but also with American interests. Our fervent pursuit of war with Iraq is driving us to squander the international legitimacy that has been America's most potent weapon of both offense and defense since the days of Woodrow Wilson. We have begun to dismantle the largest and most effective web of international relationships the world has ever known. Our current course will bring instability and danger, not security [. . .]

The September 11 tragedy left us stronger than before, rallying around us a vast international coalition to cooperate for the first time in a systematic way against the threat of terrorism. But rather than take credit for those successes and build on them, this Administration has chosen to make terrorism a domestic political tool, enlisting a scattered and largely defeated Al Qaeda as its bureaucratic ally. We spread disproportionate terror and confusion in the public mind, arbitrarily linking the unrelated problems of terrorism and Iraq [. . .]

We should ask ourselves why we have failed to persuade more of the world that a war with Iraq is necessary. We have over the past two years done too much to assert to our world partners that narrow and mercenary US interests override the cherished values of our partners. [. . .]

Halfway through his resignation, something strange happens. Kiesling has outlined his charges against the administration, and he pauses. Then he plays what must be his best card. Perhaps it is his only card. He offers the view from outside America – what he knows as a diplomat stationed in Europe, but neither the President, the Defence Secretary, nor any of the hawks of Washington DC can see. It is a classic eleventh-hour stall; the desperate search for fresh evidence that would mean a stay of execution. Hold off the final order, at least while you read this letter.

We have a coalition still, a good one. The loyalty of many of our friends is impressive, a tribute to American moral capital built up over a century. But our closest allies are persuaded less that war is justified than that it would be perilous to allow the US to drift into complete solipsism. Loyalty should be reciprocal. Why does our President condone the swaggering and contemptuous approach to our friends and allies this Administration is fostering, including among its most senior officials?

I urge you to listen to America's friends around the world. Even here in Greece, purported hotbed of European anti-Americanism, we have more and closer friends than the American newspaper reader can possibly imagine. Even when they complain about American arrogance, Greeks know that the world is a difficult and dangerous place, and they want a strong international system, with the US and EU in close partnership. When our friends are afraid of us rather than for us, it is time to worry.

Kiesling's letter is a constructive approach to protest – a diplomat's approach, you might say. Even as he resigns, he is pitching, and pitching hard, for his alternative vision. It's informed by on-the-ground realities that a diplomat sees – the casual talk of allies about US policy in the Middle East; the vanishing of America's 'moral capital' around the world – and a Secretary of State in Washington does not. It's also informed by a desire to help, and not to hurt. In the face of the single-minded drive for war in the White House, its plea feels deeply and unusually human.

It also feels desperate. The pleading is on so many different fronts – the illogic of war in Iraq, the finite patience of coalition partners, the squandering of worldwide goodwill, the hobbling of American diplomacy and moral authority – that the impression is of someone frantically trying to stop a car when his brake cables have been cut.

Within days, it had gone viral. On 28 February, the letter appeared in the *New York Times*. Other newspapers and websites leaped on it. It made no difference. The invasion date was set for 19 March.

Meanwhile, Iraq was prompting career reassessments in Britain. On the eve of the invasion, pressure was mounting on Elizabeth Wilmshurst, a deputy legal adviser to the government as it geared up for war. Under severe duress from Tony Blair's cabinet to rubber-stamp legal approval for an invasion and legitimize the case for war, on 18 March 2003 she instead delivered a resignation whose first paragraph was so devastating, its last so chilling, and its logic so irrefutable, that the Government immediately censored its key points.

> I regret that I cannot agree that it is lawful to use force against Iraq without a second Security Council resolution to revive the authorisation given in SCR 678. I do not need to set out my reasoning; you are aware of it . . . I cannot in conscience go along with advice – within the Office or to the public or Parliament – which asserts the legitimacy

of military action without such a resolution, particularly since an unlawful use of force on such a scale amounts to the crime of aggression; nor can I agree with such action in circumstances which are so detrimental to the international order and the rule of law . . . I therefore need to leave the Office: my views on the legitimacy of the action in Iraq would not make it possible for me to continue my role as a Deputy Legal Adviser or my work more generally.

For example in the context of the International Criminal Court, negotiations on the crime of aggression begin again this year.

The letter is calculating in its statement of facts. Wilmshurst could not be recast as a disgruntled careerist 'getting back' at anyone by blowing the whistle. The lightly coded warning that her position in an administration bent on war would conflict with her duties at the International Criminal Court in the Hague continues to linger over Tony Blair's legacy.

But an even greater blow to the government landed that same day in the Commons. Labour minister Robin Cook's resignation over Tony Blair's plans to invade – and over the latter's claim that Iraq possessed weapons of mass destruction – was the most spectacular dismantling of a leader in Parliament for over a decade.

Cook was a key ally of the PM's, and their history together was long. A popular figure in the cabinet, he was no disaffected, jaundiced score-settler. Even today, to read his resignation is to gain a fascinating window into the broken heart of a man who knows he must speak out, clearly, urgently and decisively; even if it means going against his closest comrades.

The present Prime Minister is the most successful leader of the Labour party in my lifetime. I hope that he will continue to be the leader of our party, and I hope that he will continue to be successful. I have no sympathy with, and I will give no comfort to, those who want to use this crisis to displace him.

I applaud the heroic efforts that the prime minister has made in trying to secure a second resolution. I do not think that anybody could have done better than the foreign secretary in working to get support for a second resolution within the Security Council.

But the very intensity of those attempts underlines how important it was to succeed. Now that those attempts have failed, we cannot pretend that getting a second resolution was of no importance. [. . .]

The threshold for war should always be high. [. . .]

We cannot base our military strategy on the assumption that Saddam is weak and at the same time justify pre-emptive action on the claim that he is a threat. Iraq probably has no weapons of mass destruction in the commonly understood sense of the term – namely a credible device capable of being delivered against a strategic city target. It probably still has biological toxins and battlefield chemical munitions, but it has had them since the 1980s, when US companies sold Saddam anthrax agents and the then British Government approved chemical and munitions factories.

Why is it now so urgent that we should take military action to disarm a military capacity that has been there for 20 years, and which we helped to create?

Why is it necessary to resort to war this week, while Saddam's ambition to complete his weapons programme is blocked by the presence of UN inspectors?

There is something terrible in the simplicity of these questions, and the note of vexed dismay they strike. This is the sound of a man on the rack. As with so many of the best protest resignations, from terHorst to Bush Senior, there is no posturing, no score-settling. It is the anti-Aitken: a resignation in which there really is nothing to say except the truth as he sees it, and perhaps his regret that he has to be the one to speak it.

Only a couple of weeks ago, Hans Blix told the Security Council that the key remaining disarmament tasks could be completed within months. I have heard it said that Iraq has had not months but 12 years in which to complete disarmament, and that our patience is exhausted.

Yet it is more than 30 years since resolution 242 called on Israel to withdraw from the occupied territories. We do not express the same impatience with the persistent refusal of Israel to comply.

I welcome the strong personal commitment that the prime minister has given to Middle East peace, but Britain's positive role in the Middle East does not redress the strong sense of injustice throughout the Muslim world at what it sees as one rule for the allies of the US and another rule for the rest.

Nor is our credibility helped by the appearance that our partners in Washington are less interested in disarmament than they are in regime change in Iraq.

That explains why any evidence that inspections may be showing progress is greeted in Washington not with satisfaction but with consternation: it reduces the case for war. What has come to trouble me most over past weeks is the suspicion that if the hanging chads in Florida had gone the other way and Al Gore had been elected, we would not now be about to commit British troops.

The longer that I have served in this place, the greater the respect I have for the good sense and collective wisdom of the British people. On Iraq, I believe that the prevailing mood of the British people is sound. They do not doubt that Saddam is a brutal dictator, but they are not persuaded that he is a clear and present danger to Britain.

They want inspections to be given a chance, and they suspect that they are being pushed too quickly into conflict by a US Administration with an agenda of its own.

Above all, they are uneasy at Britain going out on a limb on a military adventure without a broader international coalition and against the hostility of many of our traditional allies.

From the start of the present crisis, I have insisted, as Leader of the House, on the right of this place to vote on whether Britain should go to war.

It has been a favourite theme of commentators that this House no longer occupies a central role in British politics.

Nothing could better demonstrate that they are wrong than for this House to stop the commitment of troops in a war that has neither international agreement nor domestic support.

I intend to join those tomorrow night who will vote against military action now. It is for that reason, and for that reason alone, and with a heavy heart, that I resign from the government.

Cook's greatest trick is to make this about more than his personal qualms. In its final moments, his speech zones in on its target. This is no longer about the logic of war; about hypocrisy; about lives caught in the headlights of History; but about the role of Parliament; the conscience of the individual member. It is personal. To you. Here. Now. Cook becomes the inner voice. Make no mistake: this is a hell of a rhetorical device to spring, especially in a Commons environment that mitigates in favour of performance speechifying. It was the speech of his life, because it had to be.

Yet, like Kiesling and Wilmshurst's resignations, Cook's speech made no difference. Within twenty-four hours, the invasion was under way.

Behind the scenes, more resignations were brewing. International Development Secretary Clare Short had been expected to resign after calling Tony Blair 'reckless' in a radio interview. She later claimed, she had told the Prime Minister of her intention to resign, but stayed silent having received assurances from him that the UN would lead any reconstruction. As the blowback began, she followed Cook in resigning from the cabinet, with a letter to Mr Blair on 12 May.

As you know, I thought the run-up to the conflict in Iraq was mishandled, but I agreed to stay in the government to help support the reconstruction effort for the people of Iraq.

> I am afraid that the assurances you gave me . . . have been breached.
>
> The Security Council resolution that you and Jack [Straw] have so secretly negotiated contradicts the assurances I have given in the House of Commons and elsewhere . . . This makes my position impossible . . .

Much of Short's resignation letter feels eerily familiar. This is an email from someone terrified of being blamed.

We've all recived one. They're the emails CC'd round the office that attempt, even as it all goes wrong, to put on the record things that probably should have been straightened out before: 'As was agreed by you at the last meeting'; 'As you told me in our phone call yesterday', and so on. They bear witness after the event to a wider audience – and one they are afraid will hold them responsible – while challenging the recipient to either speak up or accept their version of events.

Short's brief memo contains no fewer than three of these devices. 'As you know . . .'; 'The reassurances you gave me . . .'; 'You . . . have secretly negotiated . . .'. They served her well. From the Chilcot inquiry into the Iraq dossier to a tumultuous BBC *Question Time* appearance in 2010, Short has often pointed to the record of discussions her note established. Even today, her website functions as an archive of her evidence at Chilcot and her letters to Tony Blair.

As for Blair, while he survived as Prime Minister, he never again enjoyed the uncritical support of the electorate or his party. By the time his own resignation came, he was dogged by the claims he had prosecuted an illegal war and abetted war crimes, torture and rendition.

The irony was too good to miss. Blair's own resignation would not be the glorious leave-taking he had wanted, but a rather back-foot defence of his botched and bloody legacy.

Iraq put history up for grabs. Back in the US, Army Sergeant Matthis Chiroux became the first member of active service personnel to resign in a public letter to the President.

Chiroux took a stronger line than Cook or Kiesling, one that recalled Mrs Roosevelt's letter to the Daughters of the American Revolution. For a soldier refusing to return from active duty, it's also a smart line: the greater crime is not to desert, but to participate. It's a resignation that all but dares the Army to challenge it.

15th May 2008

As an Army journalist whose job it was to collect and filter service member's stories, I heard many stomach-churning testimonies of the horrors and crimes taking place in Iraq. For fear of retaliation from the military, I failed to report these crimes, but never again will I allow fear to silence me. Never again will I fail to stand . . . This occupation is unconstitutional and illegal and I hereby lawfully refuse to participate as I will surely be a party to war crimes . . .

Even as Chiroux wrote, a new threat to global stability had arrived. The summer of 2008 would see the global financial system brought to the brink of collapse. With governments and taxpayers worldwide stepping in to bail out the banks, it was time for the public to call the shots on policy.

There was just one problem. Plenty of those who had done very well out of the bubble didn't share Andrew Lahde's view that the system had failed. They didn't share the prevailing view that they should give up their bonuses either. And some of them were prepared to resign in a public act of highly-principled protest.

Iraq had turned us all, if not into unwitting activists, then at least into citizens fluent enough with the language of protest to use it again. And when erstwhile 'Masters of the Universe' began to use it, it became clear just how badly they had misread the public mood.

Jake DeSantis, executive vice-president of bailed-out insurer AIG's disgraced financial products unit, resigned on 24 March 2009 – in protest at his salary being cut to just $740,000. His open resignation letter, published in the *New York Times*, is widely credited with igniting popular anger in the US. And no wonder: where the likes of terHorst and Cook reached breaking point with a sigh, DeSantis reached his with a whine.

> As most of us have done nothing wrong, guilt is not a motivation to surrender our earnings. We have worked 12 long months under these contracts and now deserve to be paid as promised. None of us should be cheated of our payments any more than a plumber should be cheated after he has fixed the pipes.

This seemed, to many, to be greed speaking the language of morality and high purpose, just as it had through those fat years of organized tax avoidance and occasional, high-profile dollops of vanity philanthropy. He then made what is perhaps the most misjudged attempt to garner sympathy of any resignation: AIG employees, he wrote, 'are now angry about having been misled by AIG's promises and are not inclined to return the money as a favor to you'.

The idea that DeSantis could even consider using the word 'anger' for the way bailed-out AIG bigwigs felt about their bonuses being nixed is beyond mind-boggling. The public were not ready to see the fatcats of bailed-out US corporations as a persecuted minority group.

A less misguided sense of moral indignation came back to the fore on 20 February 2012, when Josh Lapidus, Legislative Director to US politician Sam Arora of Maryland, resigned in protest at Arora's vote against same-sex marriage. Again, his reframing of expediency against history's march recalls the spirit of John Brady Kiesling and Roosevelt.

> It saddens me that you are standing against the tide of history and ending your career over an issue that will no doubt be decided in the affirmative, with or without your vote, over the next couple years . . .
>
> We have a right to be religious. You have a right to disagree with the marital union between not just a man and a woman. But we do not have the right to impose our religious beliefs on the people of Maryland and impede societal progress. You will be on the wrong side of history and I will not have any part in it.

We return to those major resignation themes: I am not your enemy; there's a choice; history will be your judge; to be silent is to consent.

Whether you are a Southern soldier in the Union Army, a politician keen to stay on-message or just a regular Joe in a corrupt world. It's a feeling we all have from time to time. Who knows? It might do us good to listen to that feeling a bit more often.

5:

The Message in a Bottle

'I pray you, in your letters, When you shall these unlucky deeds relate, Speak of me as I am; nothing extenuate, Nor set down aught in malice. Then must you speak Of one that loved not wisely but too well'

– William Shakespeare, *Othello*

'For me they were steps. I have climbed upon them, therefore I had to pass over them. But they thought I wanted to settle down on them.'

– Friedrich Nietzsche, *Twilight of the Idols*

'In soloing – as in other activities – it is far easier to start something than it is to finish it.'

– attributed to Amelia Earhart

Part of the reason for my ongoing fascination with reading old resignation letters is that they represent a frozen moment in time. Yet that moment seems to change every time you go back and look at them.

They are the resigner's chance to fix themselves as they want to be remembered; a soliloquy as they leave the stage. This is what makes the resignations in this section so rewarding to revisit. They are public resignations knowingly addressed, in part, to history. They are speaking for the record; to posterity as well as to line managers.

Done badly, they are appallingly self-aggrandizing – as clumsily delusional as a drunken karaoke stab at 'My Way'. Done well, they are almost shamanic in their theatrical intensity. And as soliloquies go, they can match anything written for the theatre.

The first really masterful effort I witnessed was Mikhail Gorbachev's resignation as leader of the Soviet Union, the day the union itself ended back on Christmas 1991. Gorbachev knew he was giving a funeral oration for the USSR as well as his own resignation address, and that, rightly or wrongly, people blamed him for dissolving the union. He knew he was more popular abroad than he would ever be in his own country, and that his speech would be hailed everywhere, but slammed in his homeland. He also knew that, in terms of the everyday quality of a Russian's life – living standards, job security, crime – he had failed. So what could he do?

He told them a story in which *he had not failed*. It was a story about history – one that stepped back and took in the future as well as the past. It was a future in which no nuclear warheads had been detonated; in which 'the heirs of a great civilization' would see 'its rebirth into a new, modern and dignified life'. It was a story in which democracy was a work in progress, not a cock-up. And it was amazing:

Dear fellow countrymen, compatriots.

In light of the unfolding situation – and the formation of

the Commonwealth of Independent States – I hereby discontinue my activities as President of the USSR.

I am making this decision out of considerations based on principle. I have firmly stood for independence, self-rule of nations, for the sovereignty of the republics, but at the same time for preservation of the union state, the unity of the country.

But events went a different way. The policy chosen was one of dismembering this country, and disuniting the state. It is one with which I cannot agree. After the Alma-Ata meeting and the decisions taken there, my position on this matter has not changed. Besides, it is my conviction that decisions of this calibre should have been made on the basis of popular will. However, I will do all I can to insure that the agreements that were signed there lead toward real concord in society and facilitate the exit out of this crisis and the process of reform.

Addressing you for the last time in the capacity of President of the USSR, I feel I must share with you my view of the road we have travelled since 1985, especially as there are a lot of contradictory, superficial and subjective judgements on that matter.

As fate had it, when I found myself at the head of the state, it was already clear that all was not well in the country. We had a lot of everything – land, oil and gas, other natural resources – and there was intellect and talent in abundance. Yet we lived much worse than developed countries and keep falling behind them more and more. The reason was obvious even then.

This country was suffocating in the shackles of the bureaucratic-command system, doomed to serve ideology and bear the terrible burden of the arms race. It had reached the limit of its possibilities. All attempts at partial reform (and there had been many) had suffered defeat, one after another. We could not go on living like that. Everything had to be changed radically. That is why not once – *not once* – have I regretted that I did not take advantage of the post of general secretary of the Communist Party to rule as czar for several years. I felt that would be irresponsible and amoral. I realized that to start reforms of such a scale in a society such as ours was very difficult, even risky.

But even now, I am convinced that the democratic reform that we launched in the spring of 1985 was historically correct.

The process of renovating this country and radical changes in the world community turned out to be far more complicated than could be expected. However, what has been done ought to be given its due. This society acquired freedom, liberated itself politically and spiritually, and this is the foremost achievement – which we have not yet understood completely, because we have not learned to use freedom. However, work of historic significance has been accomplished. The totalitarian system that deprived the country of an opportunity to become successful and prosperous long ago has been eliminated.

A breakthrough has been achieved on the way to democratic changes. Free elections, freedom of the press, religious freedoms, representative organs of power, a multiparty system became a reality. Human rights are recognized as the supreme principle.

We've started to move towards a multi-tier economy, and the equality of all forms of ownership is being established.

Within the framework of land reform, peasantry began to re-eemerge as a class. Farmers have reappeared; billions of hectares of land are being given to urbanites and rural residents alike. Economic freedom for producers has been legalized, and entrepreneurship, shareholding, privatization are gaining momentum. In turning the economy toward a market, it is important to remember that all this has to be for the sake of the individual. At this difficult time, all should be done for his social protection, especially for senior citizens and children.

We now live in a new world. The Cold War is over. The arms race has stopped, as has the insane militarization that mutilated our economy, public psyche and morals. The threat of world war has been removed. Once again I want to stress that for my part, I did everything I could to keep our nuclear weapons safe and under reliable control during the transition period.

We opened ourselves to the rest of the world, abandoned the practices of interfering in others' internal affairs and using troops outside this country, and we were reciprocated with trust, solidarity and respect. We have become one of the main foundations for the transformation of modern civilization on peaceful democratic grounds.

The different nations and the peoples of this country have gained real freedom of self-determination. The search for a democratic reformation of the multinational state brought us to the threshold of concluding a new union treaty. All these changes demanded immense strain. They were carried out with sharp struggle, with growing resistance from the old, the obsolete forces: the former party-state structures, the economic elite, as well as our habits, ideological superstitions, the psychology of sponging and levelling everyone out. They stumbled on our intolerance, low level of political culture, fear of change. That is why we lost so much time. The old system collapsed before the new one had time to begin working, and the crisis in the society became even more acute. I am aware of the dissatisfaction with the present hard situation, of the sharp criticism of authorities at all levels including my personal activities.

But once again I'd like to stress: radical changes in such a vast country, and a country with such a heritage, cannot pass painlessly without difficulties and shake-up.

The August coup brought the continuing crisis to breaking point. The most dangerous thing about the crisis is the collapse of statehood. And today I am worried by our people's loss of the citizenship of a great country. The consequences may turn out to be very hard for everyone.

To my mind, it is vitally important to preserve the democratic achievements of recent years. They have been paid for by the suffering of our whole history, our tragic experience. They must not be given up under any circumstances or any pretext, otherwise all our hopes for the better will be buried. I am telling you all this honestly and straightforwardly because this is my moral duty.

Today I'd like to express my gratitude to all citizens who supported the policy of renovating the country, got involved in the implementation of the democratic reforms. I am grateful to statesmen, public and political figures, millions of people abroad, those who understood our intentions, gave their support and met us halfway. I thank them for their sincere cooperation with us. I am leaving my post with apprehension, but also with hope, with faith in you, your wisdom and force of spirit.

We are the heirs of a great civilization, and its rebirth into a new, modern and dignified life now depends on one and all.

I wish to thank with all my heart all those who have stood together with me all these years for the fair and good cause. Some mistakes could surely have been avoided. Many things could have been done better. But I am convinced that sooner or later our common efforts will bear fruit, our nations will live in a prosperous and democratic society.

I wish everyone all the best.

And then, even as the speech was typeset and printed, the situation began to change. On his way out of the Kremlin that day, Gorbachev handed the keys of his office to Boris Yeltsin. Within months, Russia was mired in a fresh constitutional crisis; mortality soared; the mafia took over. For the remainder of the 1990s, Gorbachev's speech was lampooned; the civilization he had hymned, like his legacy, looked distinctly less great. His future was a dud. Or so it seemed.

Just after eight o'clock on New Year's Eve 1999 it was Yeltsin's turn to contend with history. He too had let his people down, and he too knew it. Despite the alcohol, the calamitous misjudgements, the corruption, he was still liked because, unlike Gorbachev, he had *dusha* – the Russian quality that roughly translates as 'soul'. But enough was enough. It was his turn to tell a story. And on New Year's Eve, Boris Yeltsin's soul sang like an impaled nightingale. Never mind that he was rumoured to be half-cut. As he read his letter out, his eyes filled with tears.

Dear friends, my dear ones, today I am wishing you New Year greetings for the last time. But that is not all. Today I am addressing you for the last time as Russian president.

I have made the decision. I have contemplated this long and hard. Today, on the last day of the outgoing century, I am resigning.

Many times I have heard it said: Yeltsin will try to hold on to power by any means, he won't hand it over to anyone. That is all lies. That is not the case. I have always said that I would not take a single step away from the constitution, that the Duma elections should take place within the constitutional timescale. This has happened. And likewise, I would have liked the presidential elections to have taken place on schedule in June 2000.

That was very important for Russia – we were creating a vital precedent of a civilized, voluntary handover of power, power from one president of Russia to another, newly elected one. And yet, I have taken a different decision. I am standing down. I am standing down earlier than scheduled. I have realized that I have to do this.

Russia must enter the new millennium with new politicians, new faces, new intelligent, strong and energetic people. As for those of us who have been in power for many years, we must go.

Seeing with what hope and belief people voted during the Duma elections for a new generation of politicians, I understood that I had done the main job of my life. Russia will never return to the past. Russia will now always be moving forward. I must not stand in its way, in the way of the natural progress of history.

So why should I hold on to power for another six months, when the country has a strong person, fit to be president, with whom practically all Russians link their hopes for the future today? Why should I stand in his way? Why wait for another six months? No, this is not me. This is not in my character.

Today, on this incredibly important day for me, I want to say more personal words than I usually do. I want to ask you for forgiveness, because many of our hopes have not come true, because what we thought would be easy turned out to be painfully difficult. I ask to forgive me for not fulfilling some hopes of those people who believed that we would be able to jump from the grey, stagnating, totalitarian past into a bright, rich and civilized future in one go.

I myself believed in this. But it could not be done in one fell swoop. In some respects I was too naive. Some of the problems were too complex. We struggled on through mistakes and failures. At this complex time many people experienced upheavals in their lives. But I want you to know that I never said this would be easy. Today it is important for me to tell you the following. I also experienced the pain which each of you experienced.

I experienced it in my heart, with sleepless nights, agonizing over what needed to be done to ensure that people lived more easily and better, if only a little. I did not have any objective more important than that.

I am leaving. I have done everything I could. I am not leaving because of my health, but because of all the problems taken together. A new generation is taking my place, the generation of those who can do more and do it better.

In accordance with the constitution, as I go into retirement, I have signed a decree entrusting the duties of the president of Russia to the Prime Minister – Vladimir Vladimirovich Putin.

For the next three months, again in accordance with the constitution, he will be head of state. Presidential elections will be held in three months' time. I have always had confidence in the amazing wisdom of Russian citizens. Therefore, I have no doubt what choice you will make at the end of March 2000.

In saying farewell, I wish to say to each of you the following.

Be happy. You deserve happiness. You deserve happiness and peace. Happy new year, happy new century, my dear people.

Yeltsin won back lost hearts and minds that day. His was one of the most shockingly naked confessions of humanity in any resignation letter, or politician's speech for that matter.

Or, it would have been, but for the fact that Yeltsin never even saw his own resignation speech until the moment he stood up and read it out. In fact, the letter was brainstormed up by Yeltsin's two aides: Aleksandr Voloshin and Valentin Yumashev, ventriloquist-ghostwriters to the Kremlin. They penned the letter not on the order of drunk old Boris at all, but to a brief issued by the woman many saw as the real power-holder in Russia: Yeltsin's daughter Tatyana. She'd overseen the Yeltsin administration's communications for years, in a way that made even Peter Mandelson and New Labour's pager army seem positively sloppy. Doctored video, faked foreign trips, ghosted speeches and fantasy quotes all popped up on the nightly news – partially to disguise the President's near-constant leglessness. Russians knew straight away: after all, the President had hardly been able to slur two sentences without falling over for months. *Izvestiya* correspondent Svetlana Babayeva wrote in a carefully coded news report on the address that Mr Yeltsin 'played his part as a great actor'.

Still, this was also a new kind of political resignation speech.

Yeltsin's resignation was the opposite of Gorbachev's. There were no great claims, or talk of hope. Instead, this was a portrayal of a fallible, sentimental, flesh-and-blood man who only ever meant to help. He ended, not by predicting the rise of a great civilization, but as you might after a morose heart-to-heart down the pub with old friends. 'Be happy.'

Across the world, politicians and CEOs took note. Tony Blair, when his turn came in 2007, used the Yeltsin Method to sidestep his critics: melting away before them as a politician, and reappearing as a fallible, flesh-and-blood human. His words, discussed later in this chapter, sometimes even sounded as drunkenly lachrymose as those of Yeltsin: 'I give my thanks to you, the British people, for the times that I have succeeded, and my apologies to you for the times I have fallen short.' . . . I may have been wrong. That is your call. But believe one thing, if nothing else. I did what I thought was right for our country.'

Blair's resignation was one of the few times anyone

had heard him express doubt, or at least uncertainty. And however dramatized, however insincere one might believe it to be, it worked. At least, for a few days.

* * *

For all that it's natural to cast your achievements in a positive light, the sense that resignation letters and statements are works for posterity is relatively new, even among politicians. A hundred years ago, politicians and businesspeople tended to regard their resignations as fairly humble handover notes. At most, they warned their immediate colleagues of what they thought was coming next.

That static quality makes them a kind of fossil record. By reading them closely, we can sometimes spot ourselves, and trace just how we got here. One resignation in particular is quite chilling.

On 23 April 1951, Welsh politician and founder of the National Health Service Aneurin Bevan resigned from the Labour cabinet over the government's plans to fund the Korean War with NHS prescription charges. He used his statement to sound a disturbing prophecy.

Today, it stands out partly for its lack of self-consciousness. It's so unhammy, so unconcerned with his personal legacy, with public opinion or with what biographers would write, that it's almost impossible to believe that it was his farewell. Bevan's moral universe is eerily familiar. The NHS is under siege from carpet-baggers, while we use up precious resources in ill-considered interventions, and private military contractors successfully lobby the government for increased budgets.

The Message in a Bottle

Like all the best prophets, he starts with the auguries his audience can see around them.

The courtesy of being allowed to make a statement in the House of Commons is peculiarly agreeable to me this afternoon, because, up to now, I am the only person who has not been able to give any reasons why I proposed to take this step – although I notice that almost every single newspaper in Great Britain, including a large number of well-informed columnists, already know my reasons [. . .]

It is now perfectly clear to anyone who examines the matter objectively that the lurchings of the American economy, the extravagant and unpredictable behaviour of the production machine, the failure on the part of the American Government to inject the arms programme into the economy slowly enough, have already caused a vast inflation of prices all over the world, have disturbed the economy of the western world to such an extent that if it goes on more damage will be done by this unrestrained behaviour than by the behaviour of the nation the arms are intended to restrain.

His credibility established, he turns to the future. And the future he sketches reads today almost like a history of late twentieth century Britain, from strikes to the darkest days of nuclear stand-off and the fight for diminishing natural resources.

This is a very important matter for Great Britain. We are entirely dependent upon other parts of the world for most of our raw materials. [. . .] It was only last Friday that the

Minister of Supply pointed out in the gravest terms that we would not be able to carry out our programme unless we had molybdenum, zinc, sulphur, copper and a large number of other raw materials and non-ferrous metals which we can only obtain with the consent of the Americans and from other parts of the world [. . .]. The administration responsible for the American defence programme have already announced to the world that America proposes to provide her share of the arms programme not out of reductions in civil consumption, not out of economies in the American economy but out of increased production; and already plans are envisaged that before very long the American economy will be expanded for arms production by a percentage equal to the total British consumption, civil and arms. [. . .]

The fact is that the western world has embarked upon a campaign of arms production upon a scale, so quickly, and of such an extent that the foundations of political liberty and Parliamentary democracy will not be able to sustain the shock. This is a very grave matter indeed. I have always said both in the House of Commons and in speeches in the country – and I think my ex-colleagues in the Government will at least give me credit for this – that the defence programme must always be consistent with the maintenance of the standard of life of the British people and the maintenance of the social services, and that as soon as it became clear we had engaged upon an arms programme inconsistent with those considerations, I could no longer remain a Member of the Government.

I therefore do beg the House and the country, and the world, to think before it is too late. It may be that on such an occasion as this the dramatic nature of a resignation might cause even some of our American friends to think before it is too late. [. . .]

It is no use Hon. Members opposite sneering, because when they come to the end of the road it will not be a sneer which will be upon their faces. There is only one hope for mankind, and that hope still remains in this little island. It is from here that we tell the world where to go and how to go there, but we must not follow behind the anarchy of American competitive capitalism which is unable to restrain itself at all, as is seen in the stockpiling that is now going on, and which denies to the economy of Great Britain even the means of carrying on our civil production.

The insistent realness here is exhilarating. It's impossible to imagine Blair, Cameron, Obama or Merkel saying, 'It is no use them sneering, because when they come to the end of the road it will not be a sneer which will be upon their faces.'

Perhaps even more inspiring is the absence of posturing. At times, it feels like an academic paper is being delivered; or an Old Testament prophet is speaking from the page. Bevan is wholly, vividly present in his speech – he even hopes that the 'dramatic' nature of his resignation will force people to think about his message – but his focus is always the issue. One has to wonder what he would make of the average hustings speech today, with its absurd choreography of glib one-liners and workshopped soundbites.

Yet this resignation was typical of the way the first rank of politicians had seen themselves since the demo-cratic reforms of post-revolutionary Europe and America.

Even future US President George Washington's letter of resignation of his military commission was, by today's standards – see Liam Fox – almost comically humble.

It was also charmingly ad hoc. It went through several drafts, with his scribblings and crossings-out made up to the moment of delivery and still visible on the preserved document. (A strange thought, now that his deification in the States has seen his every utterance treated with the weight of scripture.) Having bade his officers farewell at a tavern in New York City, Washington rode to Maryland. There, on December 23rd 1783, he handed his notice in to Thomas Mifflin, President of the Continental Congress.

Mr President,

The great events on which my resignation depended, having at length taken place, I have now the honor *of offering my sincere congratulations to Congress, and* {&} of presenting myself before {Congress} them, to surrender into their hands the trust committed to me, and to *claim the indulgence of retiring* {request permission to retire} from the service of my country.

Happy in the confirmation of our independence and sovereignty, *and pleased with the opportunity afforded the United States, of becoming a respectable Nation* {as well as in the contemplation of our prospect of National happiness}, I resign with satisfaction the appointment I accepted with diffidence – a diffidence in my abilities to accomplish so arduous a task, which however was superseded by a confidence in the rectitude of our Cause, the support of the supreme Power of the Union, and the patronage of Heaven.

The successful termination of the War has verified the most sanguine expectations – and my gratitude for the interposition of Providence, and the assistance I have received from my Countrymen, increases with every review of the momentous Contest.

While I repeat my obligations to the army in general, I should do injustice to my own feelings not to acknowledge *in this place* the peculiar services and distinguished merits of the Gentlemen who have been attached to my person during the war. – It was impossible the choice of confidential officers to compose my family should have been more fortunate. – Permit me Sir, to recommend in particular those, who have continued in service to the present moment, as worthy of the favorable notice *& patronage* of Congress.

I consider it an indispensable duty {duty} to close this last solemn act of my Official life, by commending the Interests of our dearest Country to the protection of Almighty God, and those who have the *superintendeance* {direction} of them, to his holy keeping.

Having now finished the work assigned me, I retire from the great theatre of action, and bidding an affectionate {a final} farewell to this August body, under whose orders I have so long acted, I here *offer* {today deliver?} my Commission, and take my {ultimate} leave of all the employments of public life.

Best of all, even as he talks about independence and sovereignty, there is absolutely no indication that he dramatizes his own character. This is about something greater than Washington and he, like Bevan, knew it. Washington's presentation was endearingly genuine, too.

He delivered it, all struck through and scribbled on, then reportedly bolted from the room, close to tears; slammed the door; jumped on his horse and fled.

So what happened? When did resignations start to have one eye on the second audience, the people of the future? When did we develop that sense of an audience taking everything down for posterity?

To answer that, we need to look at two very different figures, and how their lives – and our own history – could so easily have taken different paths.

* * *

On 17 January 1961, President Dwight Eisenhower – a former US General who'd swept to power on post-war euphoria after commanding the Allied troops at Normandy and racing the Russians to Berlin – delivered a resignation address that sent a shiver of fear up both sides of the political divide. Dire warnings about the power of a shadowy 'military-industrial complex' have long been the preserve of conspiracy theorists and *X-Files* buffs. But it was Ike – a Republican and former general – who first warned Americans of a takeover by such a complex of interests, with the Cold War in full swing; also taking time to nail the short-circuiting of democratic principles by a tech complex, and the plundering of finite natural resources in the name of quick economic growth.

Eisenhower's was a presidency from the first flush of the Cold War. His famous doctrine made it America's sworn mission 'to secure and protect the territorial integrity and political independence of [nations, requesting] aid against overt armed aggression from any nation controlled by international communism'. Yet even as (or perhaps because) he pushed for this state of permanent war-readiness, and for an aggressive step-up in America's space race, he saw that war-as-business would have its own terrible momentum geared only towards growth. 'Each community in which a manufacturing plant or military installation is located profits from money spent and jobs created in the area,' he noted. He was 'getting awfully sick of the lobbies by the munitions . . . you begin to see this thing isn't wholly the defence of the country, but only more money for some who are already fat.'

But those lobbyists had seized on the paranoia of the times. Any attempt to slow down arms production was met with cries about a (wholly fictitious) 'missile gap' or 'bomber gap' with the Soviets. Eisenhower's hands were tied. For fear of being cast by Democrats as 'soft on the Communist threat', he was effectively gagged. That is, until the moment he quit.

We now stand ten years past the midpoint of a century that has witnessed four major wars among great nations. Three of these involved our own country. Despite these holocausts America is today the strongest, the most influential and most productive nation in the world.

Understandably proud of this pre-eminence, we yet realize that America's leadership and prestige depend, not merely upon our unmatched material progress, riches and military strength, but on how we use our power in the interests of world peace and human betterment . . .

But threats, new in kind or degree, constantly arise.

Of these, I mention two only.

A vital element in keeping the peace is our military establishment. Our arms must be mighty, ready for instant action, so that no potential aggressor may be tempted to risk his own destruction.

Our military organization today bears little relation to that known by any of my predecessors in peacetime, or indeed by the fighting men of World War II or Korea.

Until the latest of our world conflicts, the United States had no armaments industry. American makers of plowshares could, with time and as required, make swords as well. But now we can no longer risk emergency improvisation of national defense; we have been compelled to create a permanent armaments industry of vast proportions. Added to this, three and a half million men and women are directly engaged in the defense establishment. We annually spend on military security more than the net income of all United States corporations.

This conjunction of an immense military establishment and a large arms industry is new in the American experience. The total influence – economic, political, even spiritual – is felt in every city, every Statehouse, every office of the Federal government. We recognize the imperative need for this development. Yet we must not fail to comprehend its grave implications. Our toil, resources and livelihood are all involved; so is the very structure of our society.

In the councils of government, we must guard against the acquisition of unwarranted influence, whether sought or unsought, by the military-industrial complex. The potential for the disastrous rise of misplaced power exists and will persist . . .

Akin to, and largely responsible for the sweeping changes

in our industrial-military posture, has been the technological revolution during recent decades.

In this revolution, research has become central, it also becomes more formalized, complex, and costly. A steadily increasing share is conducted for, by, or at the direction of, the Federal government.

Today, the solitary inventor, tinkering in his shop, has been overshadowed by task forces of scientists in laboratories and testing fields. In the same fashion, the free university, historically the fountainhead of free ideas and scientific discovery, has experienced a revolution in the conduct of research. Partly because of the huge costs involved, a government contract becomes virtually a substitute for intellectual curiosity. For every old blackboard there are now hundreds of new electronic computers.

The prospect of domination of the nation's scholars by Federal employment, project allocations, and the power of money is ever present – and is gravely to be regarded.

Yet, in holding scientific research and discovery in respect, as we should, we must also be alert to the equal and opposite danger that public policy could itself become the captive of a scientific-technological elite . . .

Another factor in maintaining balance involves the element of time. As we peer into society's future, we – you and I, and our government – must avoid the impulse to live only for today, plundering for, for our own ease and convenience, the precious resources of tomorrow. We cannot mortgage the material assets of our grandchildren without asking the loss also of their political and spiritual heritage. We want democracy to survive for all generations to come, not to become the insolvent phantom of tomorrow.

Just try to imagine any President exiting office like that today – it sounds more like a heckling protester, delivering home truths as he's escorted from the arms fair. Its main claim to lasting fame has been its prophetic quality: imagine the impact of Eisenhower, President, General and military hero warning against the military lobby.

But the strangest thing about it is the effortless way Eisenhower consciously adopts the TV news broadcaster's voice – paternalistic, but studiedly neutral. He knew his whole message would be quoted, extracted, and he delivered it as a number of bulletins – each featuring newsreel-style 'colour' ('Today, the solitary inventor . . .'). His wasn't the first televised speech, but it was perhaps the first in which the politician spoke with the voice of the anchorman. He was aware of the world looking on.

And while thanking the networks at the outset ('. . . my gratitude to the radio and television networks for the opportunity they have given me over the years to bring reports and messages to our nation. My special thanks go to them for the opportunity of addressing you this evening') was simply good form, the full speech constantly acknowledges television too ('I wish I could say to you tonight'). At times, he winks at the medium – 'peering into the future'.

His resignation speech saw Eisenhower finding a voice with which to speak. His job had kept him silent. It may have been his finest moment as President. But it wasn't the first resignation he had penned as a public figure. And it so nearly didn't happen.

Seventeen years before, as Allied commander-in-chief during the Normandy landings, Eisenhower wrote his resignation letter to be transmitted in the event of defeat on the beaches.

5 June 1944

Our landings in the Cherbourg-Havre area have failed to gain a satisfactory foothold and the troops have withdrawn.

My decision to attack at this time and place was based on the best information available. The troops, the air and the navy did all that bravery and devotion to duty could do.

If any blame is found attached to the attempt it is mine alone.

The note prises open one of those rare holes in the fabric of history, through which we can get a tantalizing glimpse of another history that might have been.

The note is shorter – though no less impressive – than Eisenhower's 1961 address. But it is very different. There's no sense that anything but the information matters – certainly not the style of delivery. Nothing is being said here with any expectation of lasting fame.

This is what Eisenhower sounded like under pressure. It is also what Eisenhower sounded like when he was not addressing a camera.

Consciousness of the screen – awareness of how one would sound not here and now, but at some point in the future – arrived with Middle America's family set somewhere in the late 1950s and early 1960s. But it would be the career of Eisenhower's one-time Vice-President that would prove the ultimate test case for the changes mass-broadcast television would bring to the way we take our leave. That Vice-President was Richard M. Nixon.

Nixon's career was recorded in unique detail and at unique length – not just by cameras, but by his own secret taping operations. And more than a decade before he was forced to resign as President in the wake of the Watergate affair, Nixon had already once quit politics for good, after losing the 1962 California Governor's race.

> You don't have Nixon to kick around anymore. Because, gentlemen, this is my last press conference. And I hope that what I have said today will at least make television, radio, the press recognize that they have a right and a responsibility, if they're against a candidate, to give him the shaft; but also recognize if they give him the shaft, put one lonely reporter on the campaign who'll report what the candidate says now and then. That's all. Goodbye.

The whole thing was over in seconds. Another of those chasms – peepholes into worlds that never come to pass; in this case, a brief moment during which Watergate, détente and his secret sabotaging of the Vietnam peace process were wiped from our collective future.

His 1962 resignation was the sound of Nixon ranting against the networks who had already undone him in a previous election. His defeat to John F. Kennedy in the 1960 presidential election came partly on the strength of a disastrous performance in the first televised debate, where he came across – visually, at least – as stressed, sweaty and rather sinister.

Nixon wised up quickly to the concept of performance. By the time he took office in 1968 he had turned himself into something of a ham, delivering aphorisms, soundbites and epiphanies to order, with his own standing and career progress a specialism.

His eventual resignation as President – in order to escape impeachment for his role in the Watergate affair – began with a televised announcement at 9.01 p.m. on 8 August 1974. The oddest part of it all was the creeping sense that, the worse things got, the more inclined Nixon was to speak beyond his immediate audience to an imagined, greater audience to come. His words and phrases were so self-dramatizing that they would have sounded quaint even to George Washington.

In all the decisions I have made in my public life, I have always tried to do what was best for the nation. Throughout the long and difficult period of Watergate, I have felt it was my duty to persevere, to make every possible effort to complete the term of office to which you elected me . . .

I have never been a quitter. To leave office before my term is completed is abhorrent to every instinct in my body. But as President, I must put the interest of America first . . . These years have been a momentous time in the history of our nation and the world. They have been a time of achievement in which we can all be proud, achievements that represent the shared efforts of the Administration, the Congress, and the people . . .

We have unlocked the doors that for a quarter of a century stood between the United States and the People's Republic of China.

We must now ensure that the one-quarter of the world's people who live in the People's Republic of China will be and remain not our enemies but our friends. In the Middle

East, 100 million people in the Arab countries, many of whom have considered us their enemy for nearly 20 years, now look on us as their friends. We must continue to build on that friendship so that peace can settle at last over the Middle East and so that the cradle of civilization will not become its grave.

Together with the Soviet Union we have made the crucial breakthroughs that have begun the process of limiting nuclear arms . . . We have opened the new relation with the Soviet Union. We must continue to develop and expand that new relationship so that the two strongest nations of the world will live together in cooperation rather than confrontation . . .

For more than a quarter of a century in public life I have shared in the turbulent history of this era. I have fought for what I believed in. I have tried to the best of my ability to discharge those duties and meet those responsibilities that were entrusted to me.

Sometimes I have succeeded and sometimes I have failed, but always I have taken heart from what Theodore Roosevelt once said about the man in the arena, 'whose face is marred by dust and sweat and blood, who strives valiantly, who errs and comes short again and again because there is not effort without error and shortcoming, but who does actually strive to do the deed, who knows the great enthusiasms, the great devotions, who spends himself in a worthy cause, who at the best knows in the end the triumphs of high achievements and who at the worst, if he fails, at least fails while daring greatly'.

I pledge to you tonight that as long as I have a breath of life in my body, I shall continue in that spirit . . .

It's as if Nixon – the great self-taper, self-conscious statesman, self-taught television performer – is speaking straight to the archive; to history. There are initial references to his reasons for leaving, but within moments, it becomes a pitch – for his place in posterity. There are his global achievements: he makes repeated, chiming reminders that we inhabit not the day-to-day existence of newspaper headlines and court cases and office burglaries and polls, but a broader historical field. Our era. Our children's era, come to that.

When he talks about his personal qualities, he gets genuinely excited. There is breath in his body; he is the fighter, face marred by sweat and dust. He is not a quitter. There's an awesome physicality to it.

This is the resignation as self-portrait. Nixon's medium is the sound and flickering lines of the television screen. Permanent colour. A canny archivist himself, he knew that while his viewers that day, his electorate, his friends and enemies would all fade, his performance for the camera would be forever. In some ways, his resignation was not a resignation at all – that was all done. It was his submission for inclusion in popular posterity's Book of Good Guys. Like James Murdoch, Nixon needed to feel he could still control the narrative. In his private farewell to his staff later on, he seemed preoccupied with the way 'the historical record' would show the party: 'I think the record should show that this is one of those spontaneous things that we always arrange whenever the President comes in to speak, and it will be so reported in the press, and we don't mind because they've got to call it as they see it.'

Then it was over. The next day, Richard Milhous Nixon

left a very different, official resignation letter. With no audience and no cameras, there was no performance; it was just a single, functional line: 'I hereby resign as President of the United States of America.' His signature, once clear and bold, had become a vague cardiogram wave of self-erasure and shame. It was as if, having attempted to fix his memory in the public eye on his terms one last time, there was nothing left to say. Richard Nixon, whoever he was, had already left the stage.

★ ★ ★

Nixon's has become the template for political resignations. The worse a situation gets, the higher the rhetoric, and the keener the pitch towards an imagined future audience.

Sometimes, like Yeltsin, we manage a sense of nobility despite ourselves. Mostly, like Ruud Gullit with his shameless plug for his favourite hotel, we look silly. Occasionally, like criminal Charles Taylor resigning as President of Liberia, we simply unravel.

Under indictment by the International War Crimes Tribunal for a campaign of genocide, amputation, organized rape and child slavery in Sierra Leone, Taylor resigned on 10 August 2003 with a bizarre piece of showbiz that featured jokes, asides, comparisons with Jesus and impersonations in a Nigerian accent.

His speech was a gruelling attempt to pretend for the cameras; resignation as a pitch for prime time and a new life as an international statesman-in-exile. After all, he may have reasoned, he might return one day as President, so it made good sense to leave them with a laugh and a quip.

Indeed, it's an almost hypnotic performance. Only not

for the reasons Taylor imagines. Instead, it is compelling for its pile-up car-crash of delusional fantasies, horribly misjudged humour, humble brags, comparisons with Jesus, weird 'global statesman' posturing . . . and a few tantalizingly brief moments when the mask slips.

As we replay the speech, it's worth remembering that in April 2012, he was found guilty of all eleven charges levied by the United Nations Special Court, ranging from terror to murder and a campaign of mass rape, and sentenced to fifty years in prison.

You know, there are those that may believe that this day . . . should be the end of the war. The stepping down of the President of Liberia, the coming into office of vice president, must all be looked at as the process of beginning the rebirth of this nation.

It is essential, exceptionally *essential*, that the international community accept this challenge today as an opportunity to help the people of Liberia . . . Now, you have no excuses. We beg of you, we plead with you not to make this another press event, where you come with the big pronouncements, you are out of here, elections are held, you are gone; disarmament, partial demobilisation never taking place, reintegration never occurring, thus leading to a renewed war and asking another president to leave . . .

And so I have accepted this role, what I would see as the sacrificial lamb – and you know I'm a Christian, so forgive me. I have seen some journalists report that I sometimes talk like a Baptist preacher. Well, I've never been a preacher before, but I speak very well. But I say I see myself as during the days when Jesus was taken before the High Priest,

Caiphus. And you know, Jesus was without sin. And Caiphus looked at him and said: 'Well, it may be expedient that you should die.' And now, because Jesus died, we are saved today. I want to be the sacrificial lamb. I am the whipping boy.

You know, it's so easy to say, 'because of Taylor'. There will be no more Taylor after a few minutes . . .

I want to thank everyone. I want to thank President Bush, even though we have had some disagreements – and I think I'm entitled to my opinions, just as he is entitled to his. But I believe that he's a Christian and I know he has a good heart even though he has been misled with lies and disinformation . . .

There is one individual that is not last. I can remember that about two or three weeks ago, he flew in here. And I do not know how to speak like the Nigerians, but he said [*adopts Nigerian accent*] 'Ah, my brother, this matter, I would like for you to it and come to me. We are brothers. You are my small brother' – and he tapped me on the thigh. And I said I will come . . . and now he's taking on this responsibility through this invitation. I want to praise God for him, the government and the people of the Federal Republic of Nigeria.

I leave you with these parting words, God willing, *I will be back!*

The full speech is astonishing. In comparing himself to Jesus, chastising the international community, adopting characters with different accents, claiming everyone from George W. Bush to South Africa's President Mbeki and Kofi Annan of the UN are his brothers, and thanking the man who has offered to spirit him away before the mob tears him to pieces, Taylor suddenly seems not only utterly alone in his charade, but also totally oblivious to the fact. His resignation is a masterpiece of denial.

So many of them are. And that is the problem with these resignations addressed to posterity. Tricked by our egos, we forget that the action doesn't end when we leave the stage . . . and nor does the chatter. Sun Microsystems CEO Jonathan Schwartz could resign on Twitter in January 2010 with a haiku ('Financial crisis / Stalled too many customers / CEO no more') casting himself as a victim of cosmic forces; but within seconds, the blogosphere had gone mad and an ivy of witty, vituperative and jaundiced ripostes clung to his post ('Boss blind to failings / Tries to justify himself / Doesn't fool anyone').

The future doesn't stay far off for long, and posterity has a habit of judging us by criteria that are very different to the ones we had in mind when we made our pitch.

★ ★ ★

Tony Blair's resignation on 10 May 2007 was masterfully deliveredt, even as protesters outside called for him to stand trial for war crimes in Iraq. Blair knew what he needed to establish with this resignation: history would judge him on his foreign policy record. So he mounted a defence on that front and to show the breadth of his achievements. He could not have guessed what the coming months would do to his words.

> It is difficult to know how to make this speech today. There is a judgement to be made on my premiership. And in the end that is for you, the people, to make . . .
>
> There is only one Government since 1945 that can say

all of the following: More jobs. Fewer unemployed. Better health and education results. Lower crime. And economic growth in every quarter. This one . . .

Sometimes the decisions are accepted quite quickly. Bank of England independence was one, which gave us our economic stability. Sometimes, as with the completely unexpected, you are alone with your own instinct . . .

Removing Saddam and his sons from power, as with removing the Taliban, was over with relative ease. But the blowback since, from global terrorism and those elements that support it, has been fierce and unrelenting and costly. For many, it simply isn't and can't be worth it. For me, I think we must see it through. They, the terrorists, who threaten us here and round the world, will never give up if we give up. It is a test of will and of belief. And we can't fail it . . .

But I ask you to accept one thing. Hand on heart, I did what I thought was right. I may have been wrong. That's your call. But believe one thing if nothing else. I did what I thought was right for our country . . .

Reading the whole speech back, one is reminded of that maxim about generals always fighting the last war, not the one they now face. Blair was a master strategist, who simply didn't see the real enemy approaching.

Of course, it's a great speech. One could single out so many things: the way it's broken down into soundbites so short and self-contained they are barely more than slogans at times, strung together into something as fuzzily, superficially comforting as a hallway *Desiderata*. Decision-making is hard. Always do your best. Look to the future. Count your blessings.

Or Iraq, where Blair has to defend himself. But he's a lawyer, and he clearly knows how to attack a point on different fronts. This is the defence counsel's opening: It was the right thing to do; and even if it wasn't, I believed it was. The lesser charge must surely apply, your honour.

Read today, with Iraq burning once again, Blair's words ring more hollow than ever. Yet it was not Iraq that ended up making his final soliloquy sound so foolish within a matter of months, but the very triumphs to which he pointed.

'Sometimes the decisions are accepted quite quickly. Bank of England independence was one, which gave us our economic stability,' he said. 'Think about your own living standards then in May 1997 and now. [We have] economic growth in every quarter . . .: Look at our economy. At ease with globalization . . . London the world's financial centre.'

That was May. By September, that stability was gone; the financial centre crumbling. The Government was forced to step in and prevent the collapse of Northern Rock. The economic growth on which Blair had staked his reputation went into terrible and protracted reverse, and the entire British economy teetered perilously close to an abyss of bust banks and social unrest. Blair's most toxic legacy may not have been Iraq after all, but his light-touch love affair with the unregulated financial sector, and a Goldilocks economy that never really was. Britain had begun its lost decade, with the too-perfect timing of theatrical farce.

Slippery things, resignation letters. It often pays to be more modest in your ambitions for them. When Japanese Prime Minister Yukio Hatoyama announced his resignation via Twitter in June 2010, he didn't want history to place him in the pantheon. Rather more endearingly, he just wanted to be normal, and to be liked. On social media.

> I announce my intention to resign as Prime Minister today, in order to make the Democratic Party clean again for the sake of the people. From this point, I will stop being PM, but want to continue to tweet as a normal person. Please keep following me!

Of course, he took his share of criticism too. But without a great, inflated self-written hagiography to aim at, the target seemed less tempting somehow.

* * *

Today, private emails have a habit of circulating beyond their intended recipients, going viral and coming back to haunt and humiliate the sender too.

Yet no parting shot ever ricocheted back on its writer quite as catastrophically as the oh-so-carefully-planned resignation letter of Che Guevara.

As far as the world was concerned, the man the Americans nicknamed 'Castro's Brain' did not resign from the Cuban Revolutionary Communist Party he led with Fidel; after delivering a political speech in Algiers in 1965, he simply vanished. Pressed to reveal what he knew of Guevara's disappearance, Castro just stonewalled: 'When Che wants to let you know where he is, he will.' It did nothing to damp rumours of Che's assassination. Finally, on 3 October 1965, Castro produced a letter of resignation he said Guevara had given him back in April. The letter resigned his positions in the Party, his place in the Cuban revolution, and his honorary Cuban citizenship. It also contained Che's private send-off to his family. The note was to have been released only after Che's death. Released while he was still alive, it must have been excruciating.

I formally resign my positions in the leadership of the party, my post as minister, my rank of commander, and my Cuban citizenship. Nothing legal binds me to Cuba. The only ties are of another nature – those that cannot be broken as can appointments to posts. [. . .]

You should know that I do so with a mixture of joy and sorrow. I leave here the purest of my hopes as a builder and the dearest of those I hold dear. And I leave a people who received me as a son. That wounds a part of my spirit. I carry to new battlefronts the faith that you taught me, the revolutionary spirit of my people, the feeling of fulfilling the most sacred of duties: to fight against imperialism wherever it may be. This is a source of strength, and more than heals the deepest of wounds.

I state once more that I free Cuba from all responsibility, except that which stems from its example. If my final hour finds me under other skies, my last thought will be of this people and especially of you. I am grateful for your teaching and your example, to which I shall try to be faithful up to the final consequences of my acts.

I have always been identified with the foreign policy of our revolution, and I continue to be. Wherever I am, I will feel the responsibility of being a Cuban revolutionary, and I shall behave as such. I am not sorry that I leave nothing material to my wife and children; I am happy it is that way.

I ask nothing for them, as the state will provide them with enough to live on and receive an education.

I would have many things to say to you and to our people, but I feel they are unnecessary. Words cannot express what I would like them to, and there is no point in scribbling pages.

This is stirring stuff – and all the more because Guevara never thought he'd be around when it was read. But it is also calculating, vain and self-dramatizing.

At its most breathless, there are even moments when its shiny-eyed zeal for brighter tomorrows, 'the people' and the revolution (at the expense of fleshier, more tangible and infinitely messier realities like individual people, family and the here-and-now) conjure uncomfortable echoes of the modern jihadist's video. Still, there's no denying Guevara cuts a heck of a figure here. He'd always been a committed letter-writer with a flair for drama, and he knew this was the one that really mattered.

Yet the circumstances of its release quickly descended into farce. In fact, Guevara was in central Africa, trying to help Congolese guerrillas organize their own Marxist revolution. When he found out that his resignation letter had been read out, he panicked. (And well he might, given the music he would undoubtedly have faced on the domestic front.) He refused to return with his men to Cuba, instead taking on a series of disguises and going on the lam. Before long, he was discovered, captured and executed in Bolivia. It was a messy, undignified, botched departure. The best laid plans and all that.

But things can go the other way, too. Resignations

written in the depths of ignominy, received with ridicule, can rise again, bathed in strange new light.

Tory Chief Whip Andrew Mitchell resigned to Prime Minister David Cameron on 19th October 2012 after an incident in which a female police officer guarding Parliament asked him to dismount from his bicycle. In the exchange that followed, an officer alleged that Mitchell had become enraged and sworn at her, calling her a c***, a pleb and a moron, and suggested she remember her place.

> Over the last two days it has become clear to me that whatever the rights and wrongs of the matter I will not be able to fulfil my duties as we both would wish. Nor is it fair to continue to put my family and colleagues through this upsetting and damaging publicity.
>
> I have made clear to you – and I give you my categorical assurance again – that I did not, never have, and never would call a police officer a 'pleb' or a 'moron' or used any of the other pejorative descriptions attributed to me. The offending comment and the reason for my apology to the police was my parting remark 'I thought you guys were supposed to fucking help us'. It was obviously wrong of me to use such bad language and I am very sorry about it and grateful to the police officer for accepting my apology . . .

At the time, Mitchell's resignation was considered run-of-the-mill (bad publicity, impossible to do my job). But look and something unusual is going on in the text. When Mitchell speaks of publicity, he does not use it as a smokescreen to avoid the issue as Coulson or Gullit might have done. Even now that all is lost, he protests his innocence of the main charges – and in a manner that's both consistent and free of posture. There is exasperation here – in tell-take words like 'fair', 'obviously', and 'whatever' – but even at the time, there was an unsettling feeling that it was the *honest* exasperation of someone on the receiving end, and not media-savvy play-acting.

So it proved. The case took a turn in December 2012 with the revelation that some of the police testimony appeared to have been fabricated. With officers now facing disciplinary procedures of their own, Mitchell's letter suddenly read very differently. It was not after all the disingenuous toadying of a man who got found out, but the testimony of the innocent man condemned.

As for the police officers? The case, as they say, continues. But then, they all do. The past is no more fixed than what the future has in store for it. We can resign, but our last words, be they ever so carefully chosen, are never quite ours.

Still, given our moment, it is impossible to resist. And we speak to our audience with a voice we hope will carry, half-conscious of the ear of history. These parting gestures suggest we should be careful what we wish for.

6:

The 'F**k You and Goodbye'

'What we are hearing isn't just one guy losing it; it's the howl of market forces, red in tooth and claw.'

– Andrew Leonard, *Salon*

'You can take the mail and the franking machine and all that other rubbish I have to go about with and shove 'em right up your arse.'

– *Quadrophenia*

Adam had the classic thousand-yard stare. This was his twenty-second day straight on shift duty at Taco Bell. Today was the Fourth of July. He'd had plans, a day's leave booked. He was supposed to be with friends. Yet here he was again. Taco Bell. The onions. The heat. The grease, cheese and chilli. And the manager who'd cancelled his leave.

From high on the roof, Adam looked down into the car park. There was the manager, by the back door. Adam flattened himself against the enormous roadside hoarding until the figure went back inside, then finished rearranging the metre-high letters. Had to work fast, but he'd always been a perfectionist. He added a 'smiley' – one metre-high bracket, a giant colon – and it was done. Perfect.

Adam climbed down. The sign flickered on. There it was, shining out, 40 feet over Highway 78, in all its glory. **I QUIT – ADAM. FUCK YOU.** ☺

And the cars that passed, and the customers who came, and any minute now the manager too, would know what Adam had done. From the neighbouring KFC, Colonel Sanders' face looked down onto the illuminated shame of Taco Bell Depew, NY, and he seemed to get it too.

* * *

Though it's ubiquitous now – and almost universally accepted in Western political thought as the least worst way of organizing social rank – the term 'meritocracy' is a relative newcomer.

In fact, the idea that conquered the free-market world – that an individual's value in society was an aggregate of their initiative, workrate and talent, and that the best and brightest would therefore rise to the top regardless of, say, existing social barriers, institutional failings or inherited advantage – is younger than rock'n'roll.

It was coined by British sociologist Michael Young, aka Baron Young of Dartington, in a 1958 treatise called *The Rise of the Meritocracy, 1877-2033*. But far from being a manifesto, Young's study rivals anything by Orwell for dystopian prophecy.

The book was archly presented as a warning from the future – it was even subtitled, 'Extracts from a Ph.D. thesis, submitted to the London School of Economics in 2033 A.D.' In it, Young foresaw alienation and lack of social cohesion. The capable-but-unrecognized masses would increasingly reject the free-market valuations of those on the inside of existing power structures.

As a reading of post-Cold War free-market dominance, it's unparalleled. As a prophecy of the past seven years or so, it's uncanny.

What we have just been through feels like something of a golden age in terms of resignations, at least for the common man and woman. Prior to the financial crisis, the future seemed to be one of choice and plenty, so the barriers to off-the-cuff resignation, the downsides of walking out, almost disappeared. Resigning was a low-risk lifestyle choice. 'Fuck you, I quit' was our 'Turn on, tune in, drop out.' While the economic data will show you what's happened to our money, the resignations will show you what's happened to our souls.

This chapter, then, is almost wholly dominated by the post-1990 period. It traces the rise of that resistance: the aural graffiti we scrawl when we're told we don't have a say. There is No Alternative. Or is there just one?

These fuck-you resignations were always out there, of course, but there was a shift. Whereas the fuck-you used to come from poor, pill-popping loser Jimmy in *Quadrophenia* who told the boss where to put his franking machine, now it was the MO of TV stars, restaurant critics and World Cup football captains. It was *glamorous*.

Republic of Ireland captain Roy Keane's resignation to Mick McCarthy in the dressing room in Saipan, as their team mounted its assault on the 2002 Japan/Korea World Cup, is the FY movement's Dylanesque clarion call. In the weeks leading up to the showdown, the media had known he was frustrated – he'd voiced resentment at training conditions, at the priorities of the Irish Football Association, and at McCarthy; he'd been on-and-off about playing. There had been days of running battles with the coaching staff.

Yet even his closest colleagues in the team were spellbound when he unleashed his tirade at a clear-the-air team meeting. According to witness and fellow player Niall Quinn, Keane's tirade lasted some ten minutes, and was the '. . . *most surgical slaughtering I've ever heard . . . Spineless . . . Useless . . . Stupid . . . Incompetent . . . Conman . . .*' The crescendo, and most notorious passage, has gone down in history.

> Mick, you are a liar. You are a fucking wanker.
>
> I didn't rate you as a player, I don't rate you as a manager, and I don't rate you as a person. You are a fucking wanker and you can stick your World Cup up your arse.
>
> The only reason I have any dealings with you is that somehow you are the manager of my country. You can stick it up your bollocks.

According to Keane, McCarthy had hinted that he'd faked injury. According to others present, Keane exploded when McCarthy confronted him with interviews he'd given to the Irish press about the team's arrangements. Having resigned in such a way that even he admitted there was no possible way he could ever be allowed back, Keane walked out, heading home from Japan alone.

Like Keane's resignation, the hairdryer-style emails of restaurant critic Giles Coren to his column's hapless editors have found followers way beyond the audience that knows his work. Miniature works of art in their own right, they have, over the past decade, become the stuff of Fleet Street legend.

His fuck-you-I-quit email to *The Times* on 10 August 2002 is perhaps the most famous of all. Outraged that a sub-editor had meddled with his copy, inadvertently destroying the sense of part of his review in the magazine supplement, he expressed 'relief . . . that nobody reads your poxy magazine'. He then went for the home-run demanding *The Times* 'Never ever ask me to write something for you' again, and keep their money for that review because 'I'd rather take 400 quid for assassinating a crack whore's only child in a revenge killing for a busted drug deal – my integrity would be less compromised.'

Like Keane, Coren seems to find an extra gear as he presses the ejector seat; a transgressive energy turns him from wit to witchdoctor. He seems to enjoy a literary ecstasy in his frustration and release.

This sense of almost shamanic ecstasy is one of the deeper mysteries of the fuck-you resignation. Written and delivered more hurriedly, and often with less thought than any other species of resignation, they are nevertheless the most lyrical, most perfectly expressed of all forms. Reading the resignations in this section, you'll notice things that normally crop up only in poetry: refrains; rhythm; meter; and strange rhyme.

Neil Young's 1976 resignation telegram to Stephen Stills was one of his finest lines – and maybe his best performance, too. The pair had formed a band together, but the relationship was strained. After a gig in South Carolina, both stars' buses continued to the next town on the tour. Unknown to Stills and the crew, Young's bus simply turned off the highway without indicating during the night and disappeared. The following morning, as Stills woke to do the next show on 21 July 1976, there was a knock on his hotel room door. The busboy handed him a telegram: 'Funny how things that start spontaneously end spontaneously. Eat a peach. Neil.'

These are resignations that slip the moorings of fact and become art, or something else. Doctors diagnose mental illness and extreme disturbance by a symptom known as rhyming madness: the greater the disturbance and distress, the more likely the patient is to speak words that hold no connection other than that they rhyme, as he or she looks for order in a hostile, chaotic and inscrutable universe,

There is a similar tendency in extremely angry or distressed resigners. It's as if they need all the formal window-dressing, the poetics or musicality they can get, to keep their words from becoming inarticulate screams of rage. When one senior media planner resigned from his Chicago advertising agency in October 2009, he did so with an email that ordered his thoughts and feelings – themselves so extreme they succumbed to near-inarticulacy – into a presentation-friendly, bullet-pointed list. This is someone who knows that his colleagues will only understand his howl if they can visualize it in PowerPoint.

Here are my top 10 reasons why I'm resigning . . .

10) I added it up, and with the hours I log in a given week, I don't even make minimum wage. True story.

9) When you guys were 'right-sizing instead of down-sizing because of the economy', you fired all the cool people.

8) I've put on a solid 15 lbs since I took this job. Nobody commented on my weight gain but you said it with your eyes.

7) I can't drink a gallon of milk in 5 minutes. It's a physical impossibility and I'll never win the $500.

6) Monday. Morning. Meetings.

5) I don't have to ask you how your weekend was – I don't care. It's exhausting listening to you and pretending to care, then sugar-coating my own weekend stories so you don't recoil in horror.

4) Comscore reports. Everyone knows Comscore's data is garbage but we all drink that Kool-Aid every day, don't we?

3) I hate changing the water cooler and I do it every day just b/c I'm the closest to it. Nobody ever thanks me and those things are heavy when I'm hung over.

2) A rep gave me a fancy USB memory stick with their logo on it last year for Christmas. I diligently saved all my work only to have it take a shit on me right when I was thinking about quitting this job.

1) I've gotten 3 job title promotions since I've been here but no raise. I'll bet if I asked to be promoted to Senior Media Planner Ninja-Czar, I'd get it with a pay freeze until 2020.

If you're my friend, you already have my personal contact info. If not, I can be reached through LinkedIn, but don't ask me to refer you because that's just a joke.

I'm out.

Others place those screams of rage under such tight control that they become all but inaudible – the oh-so-British equivalent of smiling politely and nodding at someone while giving them the two-fingered salute from your jacket pocket, or the hero of Kingsley Amis's *Lucky Jim* pulling faces behind his superiors' backs. On 6 January 2001, *Daily Express* journalist Stephen Pollard left the paper, shortly after its takeover by Richard Desmond, to join *The Times*. Pollard delivered his parting shot in the most public way possible – in his final *Express* leader column. Read the first letter of each sentence, and see if you can spot Pollard's coded message.

Farmers are hardly the most popular group in Britain. Up and down the country areas are blighted by intensive farming practices. Couple this with subsidies the like of which no other industry can dream of and you have a recipe for unpopularity.

Knowledge of organic farming has moved on apace. Years ago, organic farmers were regarded as cranks. On most calculations, their methods were regarded as wasteful and inefficient.

Until now. Destroying the received wisdom, Professor Jules Pretty, head of Essex University's Centre for Environment and Society, has worked out that, in fact, organic farming is cheaper, costing £1.8 billion a year less than intensive farming.

Environmentalists are still sometimes caricatured as unworldly. Sainsbury's, which we praised yesterday for introducing biodegradable packaging, shows that it need not be so. More retailers will, if the Sainsbury's scheme is a success, follow.

Organic farmers, however, receive only £20 million of the £3 billion in farm subsidies. Nothing is more stupid – and, as Prof Pretty shows, self-defeating – than this failure to promote organic farming. Despite this short-termism, the future of farming is now clearly organic.

The offer of a job at *The Times* was summarily withdrawn once they became aware of the 'insulting . . . unacceptable' acrostic. Nevertheless, as a calling card for wit and ingenuity, Pollard's resignation acrostic has gone down in Fleet Street folklore. After a rapprochement with Desmond he returned to the *Express* years later.

Pollard's parting shot tried to make itself invisible. It was an in-joke that got out. It's a common tactic. There's the puzzle, like Pollard's. The 'sleeper' is another: you bury your message somewhere, a kind of time-capsule. Saving it on your computer desktop in a file marked 'Private' is a good one – that's the first one IT will open when you're gone and they're sorting through your computer. Something extra is happening in these missives beyond the fuck-you. They need to say something, but they also need to hide what they say. My message is there – but you have to know my secret to be sure you're reading it correctly. I'm long gone, and you'll never catch me.

This next farewell letter does the same thing in another way. It's a tiny piece of genius that's become part of our cultural heritage in its modest way. If it was never really delivered in anger, it needs to be.

F**k You and Goodbye

Sent: Friday, September 14th 2012, 5.23 p.m.
To: [REDACTED]
Subject: Farewell

As today is my last day (at [REDACTED], not on Earth) I wanted to send a personal message to each person on the distro list. For reasons that should be obvious, I'd rather not assign a name to each message, but hopefully each of you is self-aware to the extent that you can figure out which message is for you.

Here we go . . .

Fuck you.
Fuck you.
You're cool.
Fuck you.
Never got to know you, but you seem pleasant.
Fuck you.
Fuck you.
Fuck you.
Fuck you.
Fuck you.
You're cool.
You're cool.
You're awesome.
I always wanted to ask you out, but you seem unapproachable.
Fuck you.
Fuck you.
You're hot.
Fuck you.

The 'F**k You and Goodbye'

You are the worst person in the world.
You're funny.
Fuck you.
Fuck you.
Fuck you.

Take care, and I hope to see eight of you again in the future!

This farewell crops up time and again, with different authors and contexts, and apocryphal origins. It's been a speech, a video kiss-off and it's been quoted in films. It is a message without known sender, without a revealed recipient: a free-floating fuck-you, waiting to attach itself to one of us, or for us to fill in the blanks. Like Chris Kula's, it is resignation and home truth-telling as a standard form. That's what makes it so tantalizing. It's not too hard to imagine your own colleagues trying to figure it out.

An authentic sense of pain and frustration seeps from the email; the writer can no longer trust their articulation to hit their mark, he or she casts the words to the wind, leaving the audience to pick them up and understand them – or not. You can feel the exhilaration. It's a feeling hard to harness, but never to my complete satisfaction. If you try to do it for someone else, you often sound strangely pat.

That 'Fuck you/You're cool' list, the Chicago media planner's bullet points and even the stop-start repetition of Keane's outburst speak of the need to maintain control and order. They even look like poems. The structure of the rabid assault certainly boosts the impact of the blows.

This brings us to another curiosity of the Fuck You letter. The final secret, in a way.

In the end, it is these obscure howls of rage – not the backstabbings of famous politicians or the principled protests of the great and the good – that survive beyond their contexts. Greg Smith leaving Goldman Sachs, the betrayal of Margaret Thatcher and Edward VIII's manoeuvres are fascinating because they form part of our history. But they are relics, clips from our movie of the past.

It is the examples of weird, spontaneous, freeform working men and women's blues that become part of popular folklore. They go viral. They are handed down and passed on. Riffs and adaptations of the letters in this section often appear within the fabric of conversation between friends and colleagues.

It's easy to see why. While other resignations remain tied to specifics of history, situation, identity or the sheer nature of the job, these are words for Everyman (and woman). Roy Keane wasn't bothered with laying out the organizational specifics of the Irish FA's problems. The emotion behind his torrent was universal – *Somehow* you're my boss. You're useless. You don't know what's going on. I've had enough. I'm gone. Fuck you.

We've all felt *Roseanne* producer Jeff Harris's pain. When he resigned from the troubled TV show (after an alleged scuffle with Roseanne Barr's husband Tom Arnold during a disagreement over a script), he did so by taking out a full-page advertisement in *Variety* magazine:

To my friends at Carsey-Werner Company, ABC, to the cast, crew and staff of *Roseanne*: My sincere and heartfelt thanks to all of you. I have chosen not to return to the show next season. Instead, my wife and I have decided to share a vacation in the relative peace and quiet of Beirut.

Pulitzer prizewinning reporter Dan Neil's *LA Times* kiss-off of 11 February 2010 was rich in detail on the job, the company and his life:

It was the beginning of the most wonderful professional experience of my life, the most fun, the most satisfying, the most intellectually challenging. This placed saved me. It made me.

But they are incidentals. The resignation's status came when he spiked the tribute with an exquisitely weary:

To [those jackasses in Chicago] I say, with as much gusto as I can muster in an email, Fuck you.

At 1 a.m. on 28 September 2011, Mark Esterhuysen, a young newsreader for South Africa's EWN 702 radio station, was reading the morning's first news bulletin. Halfway through, he stopped. In the earpiece, the producer prompted him to go on. Then Esterhuysen spoke into the airwaves.

Good morning, I'm Mark Esterhuysen.
F*** racism. F*** the pigs who killed Andries Tatane. F*** the AWB. F*** racism. We are all wild animals meant to live free.

F*** capitalism. F*** fascism. F*** this f***ing wage

slavery graveyard shit. F*** domestication. F*** Malema.
F*** the state. F*** the petrol-economic growth on a finite
planet. This is the only f***ing planet we have . . .

If you don't agree with me please see my blog. Peace, love,
respect, anarchy. Follow me on Twitter: Mark Esterhuysen.
You can see me on Facebook as well: Mark Esterhuysen.

Security?

Tell the corporation to go f*** themselves.

Goodbye

It looks impressive enough, but read aloud, it's a riot –
teetering so close to raging inarticulacy that it turns into
something like music. The worst bits are where he actually
has to deliver information, such as his Twitter handle,
though he redeems that by rushing through it as he sees
the guards advancing on him, and with that final swerve
into the on-air payoff. Esterhuysen was ejected from the
station – that final call of 'Security?' was no drill – and began
campaigning for greater monitoring of police corruption
and electioneering in South Africa. Tracked down later, he
said he had 'No regrets – all's fair in love and war.'

This wonderful, spontaneous explosiveness, in which
language becomes so percussive that syntax finally
becomes redundant altogether, is what puts the fuck-you
in a different league from the planned truth attack.

It's also what makes the fuck-you so fundamentally
democratic: you aren't Václav Havel, and you don't have
a column in today's *New York Times*. This isn't a manifesto,
and no one's going to pick your grammar apart. You can be
blue-collar, white-collar or no-collar at all; a footballer or a
flight attendant.

In years to come, the name Steven Slater will be forgotten. But the flight attendant who one day, after a quarter-century of service, wigs out spectacularly, resigns over the intercom, then escapes down the crash chute and goes on the run, is now part of our cultural memory. Slater was an air steward on Jet Blue flight 1052 from Pittsburgh to New York in August 2010. After the plane had landed and was still taxiing, one passenger stood up too early and began to remove her baggage from the overhead compartment. When Slater asked her to remain in her seat, she was said to have called him a 'motherfucker' and continued to remove her baggage, knocking him on the head as she did so.

Slater, who had earlier been telling crew and passengers about his 'bad day' and how he was fed up with rude passengers, commandeered the plane's public address system and, according to witnesses, resigned with the words:

> OK, I've had it. To the passenger who called me a mother******, **** you! Those of you who have shown dignity and respect these last 20 years, thanks for a great ride, but I've been in this business for 28 years and I've had it. That's it. I'm done, mother******.

As the captain, cabin crew and control tower took in his resignation, Slater grabbed his bag and two beers from the trolley, and pulled the lever of the plane's emergency chute, throwing his bags out. He dodged the grasp of the plane's First Officer Scott Bienz and slid down the chute onto the tarmac. Once on the ground, Slater took the A-train shuttle to the parking lot, collected his silver Jeep

Wrangler, and calmly drove home. He was arrested there in a helicopter-led SWAT team raid later that evening.

The unlikely nature of his resignation – and the fact that it was provoked by the rudeness of his customers – made Slater an instant folk hero in the US. Fox News called 'the end of his 28-year career' his 'great escape', and within hours there were two different 'Ballad of Steven Slater' protest songs, two Free Steven Slater campaigns, a Facebook fan group and an 'I Hate The Mother****** Who Called Steven Slater A Mother******' web campaign. Slater was bailed for $2,500 on charges of criminal mischief and reckless endangerment.

As I write, Slater is hoping for a return to the skies, perhaps with another airline. He will get another job, move on, and forget his moment. But his resignation is full of words for the working man and woman to live by.

We have bought the spiel that there are no more jobs for life; that there's no such thing as 'society'; that we're commodities, competing with everyone else in a free market for labour. The result: moments like this are often as close as we get to pushing back at those scoundrels William Faulkner warned us about.

And perhaps this is the reason for the mania of joy and liberation that accompanies these resignations; the seeming inability to stop the torrent once it breaks; the weird playfulness that manifests itself as we grab coolers of beer, emergency slide ripcords, our national coach's lapels, anything to hand, and delight awhile in our personal liberation.

An excellent example of the 'Fuck you and goodbye' came from insurance-company worker Darren Tomlinson to his HR officer, in August 2011. Like Slater's, Tomlinson's moment came just as the job was bearing down on him. And nothing feels better than giving The Man the slip.

30th August 2011
Subject: Disciplinary

Dear [REDACTED],

Thank you for the invite to my own disciplinary hearing.

As much as I would like to attend this momentous event, unfortunately after considerable deliberation I will have to decline your polite offer due to more pressing matters, as my Cineworld Unlimited card apparently does have limits after all. As from midnight tonight it will expire, and I still haven't seen the final instalment of *Harry Potter* or *Planet of the Apes*.

I hope you appreciate the dilemma, predicament and pressure this has put me under, but I'm hoping as a compassionate and empathetic person you understand my decision to prioritise and spend the day at Cineworld instead.

I sincerely wish you all the best at [REDACTED], send my love to [REDACTED] with the black hair, and I hope we will meet again under better circumstances, but until the next time, stay beautiful stay bold. X

Yours sincerely,

Darren 'The Hammerhead' Tomlinson

It's a great letter. Rather than anger or rebellion, it casually demonstrates a change in the writer's priorities. On the one hand, official disciplinary procedures, career ladders, HR files, line managers. On the other, well, *Planet of the Apes* looks good. Choose life, or choose your film. No contest.

Today, affable 37-year-old Glaswegian Tomlinson describes the moment as 'liberating'. It all comes back to that realization on the building site I left in West Germany: the knowledge that sometimes the big changes don't come from people rallying to a flag – or even attacking one – but from people just walking off to do other things. It's the secret archetype, there all along, shadowing history.

The '90s collapse of the communist East. Dropping out and 60s counterculture. The Mississippi plantation worker's travellin' shoes. The European tradition in which a serf or villein could earn free status simply by absconding; disappearing and living for one year off his own wits in a nearby town. The refusenik. The *Aussteiger*. The slacker. The non-participant. And finally, the email that says: My disciplinary? Your narrative about me? Thanks, but no thanks. I've got my own.

If, to paraphrase Havel's *The Power of the Powerless* (and co-opt him for the age of the corporate disciplinary bulldozer), 'You can now say anything you want, but you can never, as a matter of principle, expect to be heard', then who wouldn't rather hit Cineworld instead?

Californian law graduate Taylor Grey Meyer expected to be heard, at first. She had applied for more than thirty positions with the San Diego Padres baseball club – including a minimum-wage job selling tickets at the ground. Her applications had never even been entertained. Then one day, she received a letter. The Padres were 'inviting' her to a Sports Sales Combine – an employment training day for people looking for jobs in sales – where they said networking opportunities might open up positions. There was a fee, of course.

But Meyer was ready with a counter-offer. You might say she got her resignation in first.

Aug 5, 2012

Hi [REDACTED],

I wanted to thank you for reaching out to me when thinking of ways to meet your quota for the Sports Sales Combine.

After careful review I must decline. I realize I may be burning a bridge here, but in the spirit of reciprocity, I would like to extend you a counter-offer to suck my dick. Clearly, I don't have one of these, so my offer makes about as much sense as yours. But for the price you're charging to attend the event, I'm sure I would have no problem borrowing one.

Managers like you have found this to be the most authentic training available. Real, hands-on experience getting you on your way to perfecting the techniques you will need to climb the corporate ladder. In these tough economic times, it's always good to widen your skill set.

Let's talk about why I wasn't a good fit with your organization. Was it my extensive education that made me less of a fit, that now paying $500 will allow me to overcome? My graduate work in sports commerce? Being a law student, working toward becoming an agent? Was it my past experience overseeing the execution of national and international events? Wait, I know, maybe it was my previous internship with Major League Soccer, and that I actually got my 'start' in professional sports at the age of 15 when

I volunteered at a minor league ballpark in my hometown.

And given all that, I chose to apply with the Padres, at least 30 times since moving to San Diego. Persevering through countless anonymous email rejections, I continued to submit my resume despite never even being granted the courtesy of a face-to-face interview. All for the joy of making $30K a year.

Maybe you're right. Maybe I'm not the best fit for your company. But here's a nice fit, my foot in your ass.

All the best,

Taylor

Every time I read it, I just have to allow myself a moment to go back over the high points. My favourite is the part that got talked about the least, just because everyone was still gaping at that stunning opening shot. There it is: paragraph three. Their standard-form words, spoken back to them; completely straight, no jokes. They sit there, and look as hollow and oily and scammy as Meyer thinks they will. Phoney, brandspeak narrative meets honest, heartfelt response head-on. It's a massacre.

Today, Meyer tells me her response began as an unconscious monologue she began rattling off in the kitchen having received the email offer, and that a friend told her, 'What you just said: write it down.' You can hear it. The rest is almost like jazz in the lyrical, unselfconscious way it switches from voice to voice: the CV, presented as an exercise in absurdity; the sarcastic gasp as the magic payment allows her to suddenly become suitable; the feeling of grossing out on the whole tawdry deal; the closer.

The first sign Meyer had that her kiss-off had struck a

chord was when she awoke the following morning to an email from rival team the San Francisco 49ers, expressing their admiration. Then another, from the Kansas City Chiefs. Then another, and another, until finally it became clear her email had worked its way round the NFL. Even a source from the Padres office said it was 'impressive, more than anything else'. She was courted by the national media and TV companies nibbled, then passed. Today Meyer is between jobs and preparing to move to South Korea, just like that anonymous Whole Foods resigner, to teach English. She says the responses she enjoyed most were the ones from other unemployed, bullied, passed-over or downtrodden blue-collar workers. 'They say they pin my email up on their wall,' she smiles. She made it count. She says that she has no regrets: 'People have to stand up for themselves.'

It's got all the fuck-you letter's usual bottled-up rage. But its most appealing quality is its utter lack of fear. Losing out means having nothing to lose. Meyer talked to a corporation she'd wanted to work for in the same way most people would only dare talk to a feckless ex, or a friend. Screw formality, this needs saying. Alienation as leveller. The power of the powerless? It's to tell it as you see it.

If the truth bomb is the dissident, the insider hit is the avenging ghoul, then the fuck-you is the joker in the pack. The riddler. The berserker. The holy madman. Maybe the worst of the lot. Unstoppable. They can catch you out, make your company look slow, irrelevant and heavy-footed, simply because they are past caring about any blowback. They are resignation as uncontrolled happening; Acid Test;

a truly creative enterprise. The pitch, shoot and premiere of our own story. Fear the man – or woman – with nothing to lose.

No wonder that we prepare them so thoroughly, running through the scenarios at 3 a.m. in our beds. In the darkness, nothing comes. Then, as we dream, we understand that this time, a reasoned argument, a challenge, a plan, is not what we need. Sometimes, we only need two words.

But all things pass. And even when the darkest hour arrives, unexpected things can happen . . .

7:

The Grace Note

'A man shall knowe his frende best in adversite, for then all flaterers lightly departith.'
– fifteenth-century schoolbook, British Museum Manuscript Arundel 29

'What is this power then, which cannot banish the nagging of worry or the pin-prick of fear?'
– Boethius, *The Consolation of Philosophy*, Book III

'He who learns must suffer. Drop, drop – in our sleep, upon the heart sorrow falls, memory's pain, and to us, though against our very will, even in our own despite, comes wisdom by the awful grace of God.'
– Aeschylus, *Agamemnon*

'Acting is the expression of a neurotic impulse. It's a bum's life. Quitting – that's the sign of maturity.'
– Marlon Brando

Pia Beathe Pedersen sat down at her microphone, as she did every morning. But this morning, she was shaking. The newsreader for Norway's NRK radio station looked at her producer across the studio. He nodded. The light went on, as it did every day. It was her cue to read the headlines.

But she wasn't going to read the headlines, not today. She breathed in.

> 'Good morning! My name is Pia Beathe Pedersen. What I am about to do now is really scary. I am being disobedient, and I might get a serious bollocking, but I can't see any other way of doing this . . . '

Pedersen talked and talked. She found the voice underneath her usual radio-friendly sheen. She forgot where she was. She talked about the way things had been at the station. About the stress, the terrible conflicts, the toll both physical and emotional, the job was causing her. Then she signed off: 'The news will not be read today, but I can tell you that nothing important happened. I hereby resign and leave the premises. Thank you and goodbye.' There was no revenge. No score-settling. No agenda. Pedersen got up, took off her earphones. And she was free.

In the tangled undergrowth of human self-deception, vanity, pride, ambition and vengefulness, it's easy to forget the oases and clearings. Sometimes a resignation letter hides nothing, protests nothing, represents nothing, seeks to persuade nobody. Rarely, a quality arises that you don't often see in business, politics, the media or anywhere else: *grace*, rather than *disgrace*.

In 669, St Chad was accused by the Archbishop of Canterbury of having acted in the role of bishop without being properly appointed, as he had been given the position by the King.

His response, created to avoid causing division in the Church, was, for all its sophistication, beautifully simple:

> If you know that I have not received Episcopal ordination,
> I willingly resign the office. I never thought myself worthy
> of it; but, though unworthy, for obedience sake I submitted,
> when bidden to undertake it.

His humility in resigning so impressed the Archbishop that he was reinstalled as a bishop right away.

An ABC News researcher's mix-up during the 2000 US Presidential Election saw the TV network announce to a bemused America that seventh-century St Chad was the patron saint of disputed elections.

Still, there's something for everyone in the contrasting stories of the hanging chads and resigning Chad: two career politicians fighting over a handful of voter slips in an effort to grasp power, and a man willing to resign to avoid division and rancour.

This chapter focuses on a very rare, very special, very quiet kind of resignation – the letters, speeches, or just the noiseless sentences at the heart of a letter or press release, that nobody else seems to notice.

There are no famous last words; no witty quips or sound-bites. From Winston Churchill's last farewell to Downing Street, to *New Yorker* whizzkid and plagiarist Jonah Lehrer's final confession, they have consistently been the least-reported utterances in the resigners' careers. They are the sound of a case closing, unworthy of further investigation. In their acceptance of responsibility, their capitulation to fate, they look very much like dead ends to angle-hungry news editors. Yet that very sense of completion has always made them look oddly beautiful too.

We have seen six different ways to make an exit, and

they usually take some form of personal attack or defence. In the seventh, there is only acceptance, capitulation, and sometimes, self-knowledge.

★ ★ ★

The model for the grace note has already slipped past us. General Dwight Eisenhower's short, unsent letter that he kept in his pocket on D-Day, just in case he failed. His was no ordinary job, and no ordinary resignation. In this scenario, he knew his day's work would end with the deaths of thousands of his own men and more in occupied Europe. He simply takes full responsibility, with none of Yeltsin or Blair's self-dramatizing confession of human weakness. If Eisenhower's note is a confession at all, it is a death-bed whisper.

If there is an echo of Chad or a foretaste of Eisenhower in this next resignation, it is in its humility. But this is humility born of a terrible, unrightable failure.

One night in November 1938, a team of semi-skilled labourers at the British Museum were discovered 'improving' some priceless sections of the Greek Parthenon sculptures with acid and copper scourers. Amid accusations of a cover-up and growing scandal, the investigation led straight to the top, and one of the most respected scholars of antiquity in Europe, head curator R P Hinks. This is an extract from Hinks' resignation to his colleague, Bernard Ashmole.

My dear Ashmole . . .
    You will remember that I was absent from the Museum on sick leave from the end of September 1936 until the middle

of March 1937, except for a short interval in December. On returning to duty, my first care was to make up as far as I could for the time lost during my illness by devoting myself principally to the tasks which the Keeper had entrusted to me: namely, the redecoration and rearrangement of the Bronze Room and the revision of the Catalogue of Bronzes.

Events have unhappily shown that during the Keeper's absence on subsequent occasions I should have given more general and more constant supervision to the work in progress in the masons' shops; and I wish to take this opportunity of expressing my profound regret for the damage which, through this failure of mine, was done to the Parthenon sculpture during the time when I had charge of the Department [. . .]

I believe that the Trustees will expect me to tender my resignation. I should have done so before, had I not been reluctant to leave the Department without a Keeper; but since you have very generously consented to take charge of it, I beg that you will ask the Director to place my position unreservedly in the hands of the Trustees.

Hinks' letter is quite humbling to read. It is empty of equivocation, or manoeuvring; or indeed, of any awareness of the conventions for resigning. There is no talk of distractions, of drawing a line, or of the stress of the enquiry. An archaeologist first, he just seems so immensely sad that the sculptures have been damaged, and that the failure was his.

The vocabulary is so full of passion and despair as to feel almost religious – there is care, devotion, unhappiness, failure, profound regret, belief, and surrendering to the hands of a Trust. The job is the least of his worries; the museum exhibits are all he wants to protect, even if it must be from himself.

In this company, resignation statements by the usual suspects found in this chapter – young journalists exposed as plagiarists, a spin doctor and an evangelical US Republican caught with his trousers down – might look positively lightweight. As Tony Blair discovered, grace is never, ever something a resignation can achieve on purpose. You aim for it, you lose it.

Yet sometimes, grace – spurred on by a crushing combination of self-awareness, humility, honesty and total capitulation – erupts into a resignation halfway through, taking even the resigner by surprise.

Bible Belt Republican politician Mark Souder was most famous for his tough stance on 'fornicators' and the videos he and his wife produced the virtues of Christian sexual abstinence. Then he was exposed as a philanderer. His resignation from the House of Representatives came on 18 May 2010.

Opening with the usual press-conference formalities and thanking his colleagues, Souder decided to explain himself. He had sinned in his affair with a female member of his staff. But external factors were to blame. Washington was poisonous, he was feeling stressed, his ideas were right, his enemies twisted his words, same old same old.

In the poisonous environment of Washington, DC, any personal failing is seized upon, often twisted, for political gain. I am resigning rather than to put my family through that painful, drawn-out process.

Diane and my family were more than willing to stand here with me. We are a committed family. But the error is mine and I should bear the responsibility. Not only am I thankful for a loving family but for a loving God. My comfort is that God is a gracious and forgiving God to those who sincerely seek his forgiveness as I do. But I am so ashamed to have hurt those I love. I am so sorry to have let so many friends down, people who have fought so hard for me.

The ideas we advocate are still just and right. America will survive and thrive when anchored in those values. Human beings, like me, will fail, but our cause is greater than individuals. It is based upon eternal truths. By stepping aside, my mistake cannot be used as a political football in a partisan attempt to undermine the cause for which I have labored all my adult life.

Then something unusual happened. Having read out the letter, Souder was seized with the need to say just one more thing. And that one more thing was so unusual, and so honest, that it made you believe that, in spite of everything, Souder was a better man than his resignation, or indeed his behaviour, suggested.

As he left the lectern, he deviated from his prepared remarks to deliver a parting shot at his own party colleagues.

My family were more than willing to stand here with me – we are a committed family. But the error is mine, and I should bear the responsibility. [*Pause*] And, quite frankly, I'm sick of politicians who drag their spouses up in front of the cameras, rather than confronting the problem that they have caused. Thank you and goodbye.

Likewise, Labour spin doctor Jo Moore's resignation letter to Transport Secretary Stephen Byers looks at first sight very much like the standard form. As the World Trade Center was hit by the two hijacked airliners on 11 September 2001, she sent an email to the press office of her department which read: 'It's now a very good day to get out anything we want to bury. Councillors' expenses?' Moore apologized on television, but it was already too late to save her career.

As she stepped aside with a note to Byers on 15 February, there were tiny cracks in the studiedly smooth surface of the resignation letter.

I have today decided to offer my resignation as your Special Adviser. Last September I made a terrible error of judgement by sending an e-mail for which I have been rightly condemned.

I had hoped that my apology would be accepted for the genuine, heartfelt apology it was and that I would be able to continue my work for you and our Labour government. But it has become increasingly obvious to me that this is not possible.

Clearly there are some individuals in the department who are not prepared to work with me and are even prepared to invent stories about me as they have done this week [. . .]

It therefore seems to me that the right thing to do is resign . . .

'Error of judgement' is a stock phrase used by politicians to limit their admission to that one call, that one time and place in a million; yet Moore appends the word 'terrible', adding that she deserved her condemnation, and that colleagues were now unwilling to work with her. She finally runs dry of responses, reiterating the resignation she has already given in the first line – a draining, stunned rerun of that endless moment when she realized that this particular bollocking wasn't about coming up with a solution. It is her own verdict – not that of others – which has pushed her over the edge. The rest is silence.

★ ★ ★

But the inner court that convicts also frees.

Something about seeing a person wriggling on a pin like a butterfly genuinely appals most of us – perhaps because, with age and experience comes the knowledge of pain and of our own foolishness. And in these cases – public or not – when the moment of resignation and release comes, it feels like long-winded exhalation.

In June 2012 a young and prodigiously talented science journalist named Jonah Lehrer was exposed on multiple counts of plagiarism, of fabricating quotes (by Bob Dylan, of all the high-profile obsessive-magnets to pick), of recycling old articles as new, and of lying to cover it up. He resigned from the *New Yorker* with this statement:

> This was a lie spoken in a moment of panic [. . .] I continued to lie, and say things I should not have said.
>
> The lies are over now. I understand the gravity of my position. I want to apologize to everyone I have let down, especially my editors and readers. I also owe a sincere apology to [the journalist who first exposed me]. I will do my best to correct the record and ensure that my misquotations

and mistakes are fixed. I have resigned my position as staff writer at the *New Yorker*.

There's something odd about the way Lehrer speaks here: throughout his preamble, as he retraces events leading up to his transgression, there seems to be no emotion. It's so tightly controlled, it's like a police report or post-mortem. It even feels as if he's using his journalistic voice to report on himself as a subject; or perhaps, as if he's protesting, even in his language as he steps down, that he is a dispassionate, honest and objective writer after all

Then comes the crack: 'The lies are over now.' That's the only line you couldn't have predicted; it's extraordinarily naked.

'One must never forget just how flimsy the self is,' Lehrer had written in his final *Wired* column. And here, it feels as if two selves are fighting for control. The dispassionate science journalist, reporting back on his failings as he would any other subject; and a young man, sincerely sorry, who just wants it to stop.

These tormented, merciless, almost pleading reports on the failings of the self are everywhere. Part of the current orthodoxy is that we must stand critically and really understand our failings – and demonstrate that we have understood them in order to move on. It's the twelve-step programme by way of the Cultural Revolution's denunciation meetings.

This internal court of judgement can be almost comically powerful.

Berlin Deputy, Party of Democratic Socialism leader and German Economics Minister Gregor Gysi may be the last politician to have investigated himself, found himself guilty, and been forced to resign from office, all without anyone else saying a word.

Gysi is a garrulous figure on the left in German politics. A former communist party reformer in the GDR and a mainstay of the reunified Bundestag through the 1990s, he has been a rambunctious figure of fun for many voters. Despite questions over the nature of his relationship to the Stasi in the 1980s, he was generally felt by Germans on all sides to be a man of huge integrity. And so it would prove.

In 2002, Gysi developed a nagging private suspicion that he may have redeemed some frequent flyer air miles accrued on government trips during his own holidays. Without a word from the political opposition – or indeed his colleagues – he investigated himself, found himself guilty, and reported back with his own resignation from politics.

6 August 2002

Today I tender my resignation as mayor and senator of Berlin and surrender my mandate as a Deputy. With regard to my private use of bonus air miles accrued while on business trips as a member of the Bundestag, they are a mistake for which I cannot forgive myself.

Throughout my political work in the PDS, in the People's Parliament, the Bundestag and the Berlin Senate, I have always attached great importance to moral rectitude, and have only ever used privileges to the extent necessary. I have tried to avoid becoming dependent on them

Nevertheless, I have made this error: using frequent flyer miles.

It is not a dramatic event, that is for sure. There's nothing illegal about it, and nothing that goes against any regulations.

But there is a moral imperative in politics, if you do not want to be considered beyond all social realities.

The fact that I did this regardless shows me that I have set myself apart from my voters; that I have started to take privileges for granted. It also shows me that in making distinctions like 'authorized' and 'unauthorized', I can't rely hundred per cent on instinct.

And yet I never wanted to be tainted with the loss of prestige and credibility.

In short, I am afraid of the changes in my personality.

The fact that not even members of Berlin's opposition are calling for my resignation, has helped me to reach the right decision under my own steam.

My decision last year to withdraw from public office was correct; going back on that decision and remaining in office – as I now know – was a mistake. Therefore, I hereby resign from my political offices.

I hope that my Secretary of State, as well as my team and staff, will look favourably to my successor, or find other, rewarding paths.

Finally, I would like to thank all those who, over the years, have stood with me in solidarity, or at least in fair-mindedness.

In the light of the UK MPs' expenses scandal, Jeremy Hunt's BSkyB bid-mongering, Maria Miller's infamous thirty-two-second apology for expenses infractions in the Commons, and Downing Street's pass-the-parcel over blame for everything from tabloid cronyism to lobbying, this is hugely impressive stuff. If you're a British politician, pin it on your office wall and read it to yourself every single morning.

Gysi's is deep and critical self-examination taken to the extreme. To declare that the letter of the law (or code of conduct) is *irrelevant* – to declare that, if you even have to start thinking in terms like that, then you've lost the game – feels almost radically pure in today's politics.

It would be wrong to imply that graceful exits are always made by suffering souls when many are warm, happy or even jovial. But all of them share a sense of willed closure.

In the words of US journalist John Mecklin on 29 April 2011:

> I am resigning as editor in chief of *Miller-McCune* magazine today, primarily because I'd recently begun to feel – how to say it precisely? – done.

By 1918, American author Sherwood Anderson was finally ready to resign from his copywriting job at Chicago-based agency Taylor Critchfield. But instead of entering into a discussion about it, he figured he would make a case for firing himself.

Chicago
June 25, 1918

Dear Barton:

> You have a man in your employ that I have thought for a long time should be fired. I refer to Sherwood Anderson. He is a fellow of a good deal of ability, but for a long time I have been convinced that his heart is not in his work.

There is no question but that this man Anderson has in some ways been an ornament to our organization. His hair, for one thing, being long and mussy gives an artistic carelessness to his personal appearance that somewhat impresses such men as Frank Lloyd Wright and Mr Curtenius of Kalamazoo when they come into the office.

But Anderson is not really productive. As I have said his heart is not in his work. I think he should be fired and if you will not do the job I should like permission to fire him myself.

I therefore suggest that Anderson be asked to sever his connections with the Company on August 1st. He is a nice fellow. We will let him down easy but let's can him.

Respectfully submitted,

Sherwood Anderson

The self-sacking is an ingenious way to vanish cleanly. The humour defuses the tension; the relegation to 'sacked' begins a process of convivial erasure.

It's all the more crucial when your disappearance from the stage would otherwise be cause for national concern. Having offered his resignation to the Queen, Winston Churchill penned a formal letter of resignation as Prime Minister to the head of his local Conservative Association on 6 April 1955. After talking about his advanced age and commending Sir Anthony Eden's 'long and distinguished service' and his mission to 'sustain the highest interests and tradition of Britain and uphold the causes of Tory democracy', he signs off with the most elegant of fade outs.

I look forward to supporting him whenever the Election comes, and will appeal to the electors of Woodford to entrust me with the task and confer upon me the honour of representing them in the House of Commons as they have done during the last thirty years.

The proudly humble note in 'looking forward to supporting' seems to prefigure his wartime Comrade Dwight Eisenhower's valediction six years later. He would be taking the step up to proud supporter and private citizen, not down. Steering the country is someone else's worry now.

The same sense of freedom in the step off the wheel is found in the sudden resignation of Silicon Valley whizzkid and outdoor aficionado Evan Bigall, who in April 1998 stepped off the career fast-track at Rational Software to live the life of a beach bum in Thailand with a resignation letter that read:

A well known Yosemite climbing bum once said: At each end of the social spectrum there is a leisure class. I've decided to try the other end.

But moving on without regret can spur tabloid outrage too. After fourteen years, Wolfgang Roch, an engineer at the Town Hall surveyor's office in Zoff, North Rhine-Westphalia, resigned in March 2012, pocketing a reported €745,000 in pensions and other payments. When it was leaked to the papers, his resignation email caused national soul-searching about Germany's notoriously well-looked-after civil servants and stretched public finances.

Today will be my last Thursday here.

For that reason, I'd like to thank those of you who, around 14 years ago, reorganized the technical department, and gave me a steady, peaceful time of it.

I've been here since 1998 – in a sense. That is, I've been physically present, though I haven't really been 'here'. So I'm already pretty well-trained for entering retirement!

I have, since I took this job, done more or less nothing.

Bye.

But Churchill's letter, Sherwood Anderson's tongue-in-cheek self-sacking and even Roch's gently humorous resignation are happy affairs.

What they share is the same (almost Chad-like) sense of self-erasure; that the narrative ends with this last letter. Anderson supplies the 'other side', settling the case for their disappearance in the minds of their employers. Winston Churchill simply recasts himself – the man who led Britain to victory in the Second World War – as a 'servant', a small link in a chain of greater souls, of which his successor would be the next. Perhaps this almost cosmic perspective acts as midwife to humility and grace.

On 27 January 2011, Kansas City Royals pitcher Gil Meche responded to a run of poor form with a stunning – and rather beautiful – resignation. Something about it feels less like he's leaving a job than restarting his life.

When I signed my contract, my main goal was to earn it. Once I started to realize I wasn't earning my money, I felt bad. I was making a crazy amount of money for not even pitching. Honestly, I didn't feel like I deserved it. I didn't want to have those feelings again.

This isn't about being a hero – that's not even close to what it's about. It's just me getting back to a point in my life where I'm comfortable. Making that amount of money from a team that's already given me over $40 million for my life and for my kids, it just wasn't the right thing to do.

I want to get back to what I remember as a kid, the way of life here in Louisiana. We tend to think we live a little differently down here. It's a lot of culture, a lot of French culture. Everywhere I've been in the country, for some reason, this is the place I can't get away from.

Cartoonist Carl Barks's 9 November 1942 resignation note to Hal Adelquist at Disney studios shares Meche's sense that the career is a dream from which he must awake. Life is elsewhere. To step away from the pseudo-nocturnal existence of the worker in a darkened office, and get back to reality – that thing, out there, where plants grow, perspective arrives with the morning horizon. And everything will be OK.

Dear Sir:

I tried to see you last Friday to tell you that I have decided to leave the studio and try farming at my San Jacinto estate (five acres of Russian thistles). I had not planned to leave so suddenly, in fact, I might have stuck around indefinitely had not gasoline rationing forced me to move while it is still possible to do so. My reasons for leaving are several, the chief one being that I spent too many years in too dark a room. Walt could make money growing mushrooms in 2-D 1.

Seriously speaking, I have become tired of working for wages and have decided to make one reckless effort to survive on my own. I hope that my farm and chickens will support me while I build up an income from free-lance cartooning. I feel that with more time to develop my long-neglected knack for drawing human figures I may be able to break into the comic magazine field. Probably I won't have enough on the ball to click in that racket, but if I don't give it a try I will never know . . .

This is not the maddening, circling missive from a trapped auditor, but an indie film in miniature. Perhaps it's even *The Matrix*. This sense of finished business is the moment of calm surrender – of grace itself. It's the difference between attack (or defence) and acceptance. John Mecklin perhaps put it best as he resigned.

I'm not sure getting older necessarily means getting wiser, in a general sense, but I have learned a few things during my decades in journalism. One of them involves the close parallel between houseguests and editors. The best of them make sure never to stay too long. [. . .]

So I have decided that, rather than staying all the way through the metaphorical weekend, I will be a thoughtful guest and leave.

There is something weirdly transcendent in these resignations; this cycle is complete, with no hanging code, no unanswered questions, no regrets.

You find that quality in the difference between the two resignations, twenty-six years apart, by Apple's Steve Jobs.

The first, coming on 17 September 1985 as the digital age dawned, saw Jobs in his whizzkid guise blasting the misleading noises coming from a board that had out-manoeuvred him, and was now forcing him out. The letter was addressed to vice-chairman Mike Markkula – the venture capitalist who had invested in Jobs back in the 1970s, and whom Jobs now perceived to be the one pushing him from the company.

'This morning's papers carried suggestions that Apple is considering removing me as Chairman,' thundered Jobs. 'I don't know the source of these reports but they are both misleading to the public and unfair to me. Accordingly, I must insist upon the immediate acceptance of my resignation.'

Jobs may have been more upset at the idea that he'd be viewed as damaged goods in Silicon Valley than by leaving the company. Young and with another venture boiling away in his mind already, this was all about protecting Brand Jobs. 'I would hope that in any public statement it feels it must issue, the company will make it clear that the decision to resign as Chairman was mine,' he says. 'As you know, the company's recent reorganization left me with no work to do and no access even to regular management reports. I am but 30 and want still to contribute and achieve.'

This is the sound of a young man, full of righteous fire and hungry for absolute transparency.

Twenty-six years after this first resignation, we see a different Steve Jobs – and a different attitude towards transparency. Having returned in the 1990s and made Apple the world's most successful and cash-rich brand, Jobs was terminally ill with a pancreatic endocrine tumour, and had been increasingly absent from the company.

His second resignation – again, issued as a combined press release and company memo – displays a far more complex attitude towards truth and disclosure. While in his 1985 letter Jobs rages and manoeuvres, his 2011 resignation has a calm detachment, an almost floating quality.

> I have always said if there ever came a day when I could no longer meet my duties and expectations as Apple's CEO, I would be the first to let you know. Unfortunately, that day has come.
>
> I hereby resign as CEO of Apple. I would like to serve, if the Board sees fit, as Chairman of the Board, director and Apple employee.

Then, as if the first item of the meeting agenda had been dealt with, the tone lightens, hardens, becomes the one we know from all those product unveilings. Jobs recommends that the company 'execute our succession plan' and name the next CEO. This is all part of the plan. It's a step forwards for the company. A new beginning, not an end.

Then, before moving on to personal farewells to friends and colleagues, Jobs circles back for another go at the transition he's about to make. He sounds forced – almost theatrically optimistic – as he reiterates that he and Apple are far from done with each other.

I believe Apple's brightest and most innovative days are ahead of it. And I look forward to watching and contributing to its success in a new role.

When you know that his cancer would kill him just six weeks later on 5 October, the clash of different voices in his final parting shot is both typically stock-market smart and almost unbearably poignant.

Whether it's a consequence of age and a deeper, more travelled personality, or the fact that he is inside the corporation rather than throwing stones from the exit, the memo is an exercise in absence, in leaving truth out and embracing fuzziness. Jobs is trying not to disrupt the smooth running of the company. But does he succeed?

It is the end scene, in which our hero mounts his horse and heads off into the haze, leaving the townspeople to carry on what he's started. We are directed to consider what he leaves behind, not his next move, or any of the unanswered questions of the previous few months. No drama, just succession and erasure.

★ ★ ★

The best of these resignations show what we can do, faced with whatever is intolerable, impossible and final. The end also brings freedom from envy; or covetousness, or whatever you want to call it. The feeling that – for whatever reason – the game is thrown over and left to others. That the time for the game itself has passed, maybe.

This odd, elusive quality can transform even the most templated resignation statements into something else entirely. In November 2012, after leaked emails revealed his affair with a female member of the Washington press corps, General David Petraeus resigned as Director of the CIA. Petraeus had been well regarded, but his exposure – complete with media guessing-games and the republishing of interviews between him and his lover in the press – caused a sensation.

Everybody knew what his resignation would say. Everybody knew how it would have to say it. It would be issued as a formatted CIA release. Yet that Statement to Employees of 9 November is included here because it's rather extraordinary.

> After being married for over 37 years, I showed extremely poor judgment by engaging in an extramarital affair. Such behavior is unacceptable, both as a husband and as the leader of an organization such as ours. This afternoon, the President graciously accepted my resignation . . .
>
> Teddy Roosevelt once observed that life's greatest gift is the opportunity to work hard at work worth doing. I will always treasure my opportunity to have done that with you and I will always regret the circumstances that brought that work with you to an end.

What's so extraordinary here is what is *missing* – there is no waffle about becoming the focus of media intrusion hurting family and colleagues, no smokescreen about becoming a distraction. But it's also extraordinary for what is there. Personal elements such as 'After being married for 37 years and 'such as ours' seem to have been parachuted into the middle of a standard paragraph.

Had they not been there, nobody would have batted

an eyelid; the world knew what those personal reasons were. Indeed, most public resignations take advantage of this and skip the gory details. Hardened Downing Street spokesmen talk vaguely of 'becoming the story'; Donald Rumsfeld couldn't even bring himself to mutter the word 'Iraq'; but Petraeus chose to go further than he had to into his failings. There is honour in his exit: he talks of other people's extraordinary work, not his own; his own failure, not theirs. He has squared his conscience before pressing 'send'.

On 7 November 2012, just as Petraeus was composing his letter, and just a few short miles from where he sat, an employee only identified as Mrs X resigned from the Washington, DC offices of the law firm Clifford Chance. The writer's name never emerged – the firm itself was tight-lipped. The media called it a *cri de coeur*. But I think it's something far more interesting.

CLIFFORD CHANCE – A MOTHER'S DEPARTURE MEMO
A day in the life of Ms X (and many others here, I presume):

4:00am: Hear baby screaming, hope I am dreaming, realize I'm not, sleep walk to nursery, give her a pacifier and put her back to sleep

4:45am: Finally get back to bed

5:30am: Alarm goes off, hit snooze

6:00am: See the shadow of a small person standing at my bedroom door, realize it is my son who has wet the bed (time to change the sheets)

6:15am: Hear baby screaming, make a bottle, turn on another excruciating episode of *Backyardigans*, feed baby

7:00am: Find some clean clothes for the kids, get them dressed

7:30am: Realize that I am still in my pajamas and haven't showered, so pull hair back in a ponytail and throw on a suit

8:00am: Pile into the car, drive the kids to daycare

8:15am: TRAFFIC

9:00am: finally arrive at daycare, baby spits up on suit, get kids to their classrooms, realize I have a conference call in 15 minutes

9:20am: Run into my office, dial-in to conference call 5 minutes late and realize that no one would have known whether or not I was on the call, but take notes anyway

9:30am: Get an email that my time is late, Again! Enter my time

10:00am: Team meeting; leave with a 50-item to-do list

11:00am: Attempt to prioritize to-do list and start tasks; start an email delegating a portion of the tasks (then, remember there is no one under me)

2:00pm: Realize I forgot to eat lunch, so go to the 9th floor kitchen to score some leftovers

2:30pm: Get a frantic email from a client needing an answer to a question by COB today

2:45pm: postpone work on task number 2 of 50 from to-do list and attempt to draft a response to client's question

4:30pm: send draft response to Senior Associate and Partner for review

5:00pm: receive conflicting comments from Senior Associate and Partner (one in new version and one in track changes); attempt to reconcile; send redline

5:30pm: wait for approval to send response to client;

realize that I am going to be late picking up the kids from daycare ($5 for each minute late)

5:50pm: get approval; quickly send response to client

6:00pm: race to daycare to get the kids (they are the last two there)

6:30pm: TRAFFIC with a side of screaming kids who are starving

7:15pm: Finally arrive home, throw chicken nuggets in the microwave, feed the family

7:45pm: Negotiate with husband over who will do bathtime and bedtime routine; lose

8:00pm: Bath, pajamas, books, bed

9:00pm: Kids are finally asleep, check blackberry and have 25 unread messages

9:15pm: Make a cup of coffee and open laptop; login to Citrix

9:45pm: Citrix finally loads; start task number 2

11:30pm: Wake up and realize I fell asleep at my desk; make more coffee; get through task number 3

1:00am: Jump in the shower (lord knows I won't have time in the morning)

1:30am: Finally go to bed

REPEAT

'Needless to say,' it winds up, 'I have not been able to simultaneously meet the demands of career and family, so have chosen to leave private practice, and the practice of law (at least for now) . . .'

The note sparked a lot of debate – around childcare provisions, around corporate culture, even around the marriage and homelife of the anonymous executive. What didn't ignite much debate – but of course, it's my field – was the resignation statement itself.

It's an odd one. It sounds, for most of its length, as if it's about to become a protest – even a truth bomb. The logging of details, the times, even the expenses incurred, seem to be building a case. Then nothing. The case is there – you can almost see the spreadsheet – then you look up and she's waving goodbye.

The letter went around the building, then the company, then America, then the world. But who was the real recipient?

To me, this looks like one half of one of those two-column checklists you draw up when you have a difficult decision to make. You do it, really, to explain it to yourself. To rationalize something you know you have to do. On one side, all of these reasons. What's missing is the other side. But then we all know what that is.

That 'other side' is the same for every one of us when our turn comes. It's invisible here, simply because she knows only too well, as we all know, what it says.

Family.
Job Security.
Financial Stability.
Career Path.
Fulfilment.
Status.
Work Benefits.
Friends.
Life.

Here's the same letter – only in different words – from Kenneth Grahame, author of *The Wind In The Willows*, pushed to breaking point by his boss at the Bank of England more than a century earlier, in 1908.

> For some time past I have been forced to realize that the constant strain entailed upon me by a post of much responsibility is telling on me in a way that makes me very anxious, both as to my ability to continue rendering proper and efficient service, and as to the wisdom of facing further deterioration of brain and nerve: and I feel strongly that even at heavy cost I ought to seek relief from the burden.

There are resignations as petition for sanctuary. Sometimes resigning isn't the dangerous, uncertain and self-destructive path after all – staying is.

That danger is real. The annihilation we risk by staying on is of the spirit, of our selves. Sometimes, of our bodies too. When King Idris of Libya abdication from the throne in 1969, he did so amid a *coup d'etat*, led by a young army officer named Muammar Gaddafi. On 4 August, from exile in Greece – he had fled there to pre-empt the passing of a death sentence by the army – he wrote a phrase that sums up the sense of entropy in these resignations; the sense that, eventually for all of us, things fall apart.

> The carrying-out of duties and affairs have worn me down. And in the words of the poet, 'Life and its demands have become wearisome.'

They are always the same, these inner voices. And the truth is that it's them, and not our conscience or the knowledge of what we need to do, that whisper and twist and torture us through those silent, small hours.

For them, we make our exits, give our statements, send our emails and talk into our microphones. In the end, every resignation is about making ourselves at ease with them; reconciling ourselves to letting go of the things that seemed so important.

In a way, we have to envy the ones who can kid themselves it's really just about press intrusion, or becoming a distraction, or bad luck, or shareholders, or timing. We envy the public figures who talk a good game: Tony Blair, the lawyer; Charles Taylor, the showman; Donald Rumsfeld, entering peaceful repose, shrugging off the guilt with a few words about unknown unknowns.

But here, in the grace notes struck by those who've been forced to reckon with themselves and their weakness, there is something hopeful. The end didn't kill them. In the end, failure wasn't failure at all, but a kind of success.

Try writing your own resignation letter – just for fun, you don't have to send it – just to know that you're suddenly holding the key to your own future in your hand. As the great philosopher George Clinton once said, 'Free your mind . . . and your ass will follow.'

Epilogue
The Last Goodbye

When I started collecting together my notes for this book – looking back over thousands of resignations – I never imagined that I would be writing myself out of the very line of business I had once written myself into.

As this labour of love built, over the years of collation and months of writing, it felt like a journey through an alternate history; a safari park of parting shots. You can get right up close, get a sense of how they lived and evolved, the habitat. Wander from area to area, peer through the glass – taking an occasional flash of the life, a brief whiff of the adrenalin, a sense of the world that bore them. All without having actually to draft and submit your own resignation.

At times, you feel more like a natural historian, or palaeontologist. Specialist subject: disappearances and extinctions.

But you can spend too long in the zone. You can spend so much time with departures – curating them, pinning and analysing them, looking for clues, tracing this hidden version of history; so long watching for endings, that it becomes hard to take a fresh start at face value. The moment a new government is elected, a new venture announced, a new appointment made, one's inner stopwatch begins ticking. Looking for ends even in beginnings, you start to see the skull beneath the skin.

You find yourself speculating on the most abundant harvests, the most rewarding departures, like a wine buyer or a futures trader. And the more resignations you write, read, witness and collect, the more they seem like anguished howls from the figures in some Hieronymus Bosch painting. Those cries of dissidence that felt so liberating at first – the protests, the truth attacks – now sound to me like the 'Buy' and 'Sell' of a trading floor. They want in or out, change or not, but they're all still playing the game.

As I prepared the last chapter, something happened that I hadn't foreseen. I was taken with the idea that the letters there have a weird and unique peacefulness to them. Against everything the other chapters tell me – the resignations from those who have nothing to lose – those who give every shred of their future hopes, their ambition, their plotted career path up to the wind, and simply walk away, started to speak loudest.

If you're one of the many people who consulted with me, I hope it works out well for you.

To everyone else reading this: I hope you're OK. Really, I do. Getting to the point where you want to resign with a statement of any kind means you're kicking against the pricks, and it's the toughest feeling. So here's my advice, for what it's worth.

Don't let it take over your free time. If you wake up at night, remember no matter how trapped you feel, there are other jobs. Walking out is OK: you're not leaving the story, you're writing your own version. Take care. This book is for you. You might want to see it as your primer for dealing in departures yourself; if you fancy entering my line of work, there's now a vacancy.

And as I finish the last paragraph of the last letter of my twenty-five-year secret sideline in resignations, I find myself wishing I could tell you more of the mysteries in which I've been privileged to gain understanding. But it's late, and we all know handover notes are never as clear as you hope they'll be anyway. So good luck, and here's to finding an answer to the question when your moment comes.

See you on the other side.

Sources and Selected Bibliography

Chris Abbott, *21 Speeches That Shaped Our World*, Rider. London, 2012

Aeschylus, *The Oresteia*, Penguin, 1977

Jonathan Aitken, *Pride and Perjury: An Autobiography*, Continuum, London 2000

Anthony Armov/Howard Zinn (Ed), *Voices of a People's History of the United States*, Seven Stories Press, USA, 2004

Ambrose Bierce, *Ghost & Horror Stories*, Dover, London, 1964

Black Hawk (ed. J.B.Patterson) The Autobiography of Ma-Ka-Tai-Me-She-Kia-Kiak, or Black Hawk, Embracing the Traditions of his Nation, Various Wars In Which He Has Been Engaged, and His Account of the Cause and General History of the Black Hawk War of 1832, His Surrender, and Travels Through the United States. Also Life, Death and Burial of the Old Chief, Together with a History of the Black Hawk War, Press of the Continental Printing Co., St Louis, 1832

Tony Blair, *A Journey*, Arrow, London, 2011

Boethius, *The Consolation of Philosophy*, Penguin, London, 1989

Edmund Burke, *Reflections on the Revoution in France, and on Proceedings in Certain Societies in London Relative to that Event*, Penguin, London, 1968

Davison L. Budhoo, *Enough Is Enough: Dear Mr. Camdessus. . . Open Letter of Resignation to the Managing Director of the International Monetary Fund*, New Horizons Press, New York, 1990

Fidel Castro, *Che: A Memoir*, Ocean, UK, 2006

William R Clark, *Petrodollar Warfare: Oil, Iraq & the Future of the Dollar*, New Society, USA, 2005

Robin Cook, *The Point of Departure*, Simon & Schuster, London, 2007

Giles Coren, *Anger Management For Beginners*, Hodder, London, 2010

J.A.E. Curtis, *Mikhail Bulgakov, Manuscripts Don't Burn: A Life In Letters & Diaries*, Bloomsbury, 2012

Richard Davenport-Hines, *An English Affair: Sex, Class & Power In The Age Of Profumo*, HarperPress, London, 2013

Charles Dickens, A Christmas Carol and Other Writings, Penguin Classics, London, 2010

Peter Elkind & Bethany McLean, *The Smartest Guys In The Room: The Amazing Rise And Scandalous Fall Of Enron*, Penguin, London, 2004

Andrew Feinstein, *The Shadow World: Inside The Global Arms Trade*, Penguin, London, 2012

Kelly Flinn, *Proud to Be: My Life, The Airforce, The Controversy*, Diane, USA, 1997

Francis Fukuyama, *The End of History And The Last Man*, Simon & Schuster, New York, 1992

Neal Gabler, *Walter Winchell: Gossip, Power & the Culture of Celebrity*, Pan Macmillan, London, 1994

Bradley Graham, *By His Own Rules: The Ambitions, Successes & Ultimate Failures of Donald Rumsfeld*, Public Affairs, New York, 2008

Dennis Grube, *Prime Ministers and Rhetorical Governance*, Palgrave, London, 2013

J.H. Hatfield, *Fortunate Son, George W Bush & The Making of an American President*, Vision, USA, 2004

Václav Havel, *The Power of the Powerless*, Hutchinson, London, 1985

Václav Havel, *Living In Truth*, Faber, London, 1990

Sir Geoffrey Howe, *Conflict of Loyalty*, Pan, London, 1995

Karen J Jacobsen, 'Economic Hauntings: Wealth and class in Edith Wharton's Ghost Stories', *West Chester University Journal*, Vol.35, Issue 1 Winter 2008

Michael Janeway, *Republic of Denial: Press, Politics & Public Life*, Yale University Press, US, 2001

John Keegan, *The American Civil War*, Vintage, London, 2010

Rashid Khalidi, *Resurrecting Empire: Western Footprints and America's Perilous Path in the Middle East*, IB Tauris, UK, 2004

John Brady Kiesling, *Diplomacy Lessons: Realism for an Unloved Superpower*, Potomac, USA, 2006

Rudyard Kipling, *The Mark of the Beast and Other Fantastical Tales*, Gollancz, London, 2010

Naomi Klein, *No Logo*, Flamingo, London, 2000

Naomi Klein, *The Shock Doctrine: The Rise of Disaster Capitalism*, Knopf, Canada, 2007

Peter de Krassel: *Custom Maid Spin for New World Disorder: Political Dust Storms, Corrosive Money and Slick Oil*, Cal Books, USA, 205

Sources and Selected Bibliography

V.I. Lenin, *What Is To Be Done?* Penguin 20th Century Classics, London, 1989

Brian MacArthur (ed.), *The Penguin Book of Modern Speeches*, Penguin, London, 2012

Karl Marx, *Das Kapital: A Critique of Political Economy*, Penguin, London, 1990

Taylor Grey Meyer & Michelle Duckworth, *A Wig For Ally*, Createspace, 2010

Evgeny Morozov, *The Net Delusion: How Not To Liberate The World*, Penguin, London, 2012

Friedrich Nietzsche, *Twilight of the Idols/The Anti-Christ*, Penguin, London, 1972

Paul Oliver, *Blues Fell This Morning: Meaning In The Blues*, Cambridge University Press, Cambridge, 1990

Paul Ormerod, *Why Most Things Fail*, Faber, London, 2005

George Orwell: *A Life In Letters*, Penguin Modern Classics, London, 2011

Charles Osgood, *Funny Letters from Famous People*, Crown Archetype, New York, 2003

Matthew Parris, *Great Parliamentary Scandals: Four Centuries of Calumny, Smear & Innuendo*, Robson, London, 1995

Giles Radice, *Trio: Inside the Blair, Brown, Mandelson Project*, I. B. Tauris & Co Ltd, London, 2010

Richard Reeves, *President Nixon: Alone in the White House*, Simon & Schuster, New York, 2002

Christopher Ricks & Leonard Michaels, *The State of the Language*, Faber, London, 1990

Peter Saunders, *Unequal But Fair? A Strudy of Class Barriers In Britain*, Civitas, London, 1996

Greg Smith, *Why I Left Goldman Sachs*, Grand Central Publishing, New York, 2012

Jean Edward Smith, *Eisenhower in War & Peace*, Random House, London, 2013

Joseph Stiglitz, *Globalization & Its Discontents*, Norton, New York, 2002

Margaret Thatcher, *The Downing Street Years*, HarperPress, London, 2012

David A. Thomas, *Churchill, The Member for Woodford*, Routledge, Abingdon, 2013

John B. Thompson, *Politcal Scandal: Power and Visibility in the Media Age*, Politey Press, New York 2000

Shaun Usher, *Letters of Note: Correspondence Deserving of a Wider Audience*, Canongate, 2013

Elijah Wald, *Escaping The Delta: Robert Johnson & the Invention of the Blues*, Amistad, NYC, 1990

Alan J. Whiticker, *Speeches That Reshaped The World*, New Holland, Australia, 2009

Michael Young, *The Rise of the Meritocracy, 1877-2033*, Pelican, Harmondsworth, 1958

In addition, the following resources have been invaluable:

The public Enron email archive (www.enron-mail.com).

Soccer Ireland's web resource dedicated to the Roy Keane incident in Saipan: http://www.soccer-ireland.com/saipan/

The US Navy Department Archive for its facsimile letters from the Civil War (www.history.navy.mil/library/online/going_south.htm).

Gawker (http://gawker.com) – the first to break the story behind the now-viral Whole Foods resignation.

The FDR Library and the US Government's various public domain archives.

Credits

There is no literature of the resignation to speak of – or rather, this is it. So I have largely relied on my own collection of clippings, as well as friends, contacts, libraries, universities, gumshoe work and digitized document research.

I have also, at various points along the way, been helped and encouraged by the high-profile resigners featured here.

My personal and professional gratitude goes to Richard Peppiatt for allowing me not just to quote his letter, but for being so forthcoming and generally a lovely bloke. His show *One Rogue Reporter* was fantastic too. (www.richpeppiatt.com).

Also to Taylor Grey Meyer, who is as funny, charming and smart in person as she is in print. Her book, *A Wig for Ally*, is beautiful. (http://taylorgreymeyer.com/a-wig-for-ally).

Laurie Garrett, Mark Schlueb, Jom Romenesko and a number of others who prefer not to be named have been more gracious and helpful than I had any right to expect.

Darren Tomlinson is a lovely guy who gave freely of his time. How nice a guy is he? I asked him how I could thank him for all his assistance, and he asked me to plug two of his mates' projects instead of his own. They are a band (http://martinandjames.com/fr_tourdates.cfm) and a photographer (http://macqueenphotography.com/Artist.asp?ArtistID=28948&Akey=FGY2FKRY.)

Stewart Butterfield, formerly of Flickr/Yahoo, now of the rather excellent Tinyspeck.com (via tinsmithing) has also been a gent.

My thanks to all those who volunteered resignation stories. Paul Colbert, Ian Belcher, Matt Beaven, Janae Jones, and others too many to mention.

I have made repeated, unsuccessful attempts to contact Millard Peck, Ron Keys, and others, either directly or through associates, cold trails, businesses and so on. If you are out there, I'd still love to talk.

The final quotation in the book is a nod to George Clinton, whose Funkadelic album *Free Your Mind . . . And Your Ass Will Follow* (Westbound Records, 1971) is not only his claim to the title of great philosopher, but is extremely funky.

Author's Note on the Text

This book quotes from a huge number of resignations. Some I quote in part, some in full; almost all
are quoted within the scope of fair comment and review
– within the context of this book, which is a discussion and
analysis of the resignations featured within the context of
our age's broader cultural and industrial history; with the
permission of the writer; and/or public domain and as
items of historic public interest. In some cases, and despite
efforts to identify them, the authors remain unknown. In
others, as with the joke/apocryphal kiss-offs, authorship
is either unclear or diffuse. Where resignations have been
brought to light thanks to the work of a particular source,
and where that source has been identifiable by me at this
temporal remove during the production of this book, I
have sought to credit that source either in the text or in the
bibliography or acknowledgements.

I have tried to be fair and reasonable in my discussion
of these resignations. I also hope that the reader will
understand: this is a book on resignations, and does not seek

to join or pass judgement on the organizations, colleagues, superiors, shareholders or associates mentioned within the context of those resignations. However, it is worth reiterating that the points of view expressed in resignations featured in this book do not necessarily reflect my opinions, and by quoting or discussing them here I do not make any suggestion that the claims in them in respect of their reasons for resigning; the behaviours of their co-workers or their organization; or of any other party mentioned in the resignations, is either necessarily true or to be taken at face value.

I am committed to reporting and historical analysis such as that contained in this book as an ongoing, organic process. I will continue to publish any responses and clarifications arising at my website (www.mattpotterbooks.com), and to incorporate updates as appropriate into future editions.

www.mattpotterbooks.com
Follow me on Twitter: @MattPotter

Acknowledgements

Special thanks to Humfrey Hunter at Hunter Profiles; Rebecca Watson at Valerie Hoskins Associates; Andreas Campomar at Little, Brown; Andrew Hirsch at John Brown Media whose support and encouragement have been invaluable; Dr Kelly Hignett of Leeds Metropolitan University; Annie Machon; and too many others who have helped this book take shape. I would like to thank all of the patients, friends, contacts and go-betweens who have kept me in resignations – discussed, read, delivered, mooted, collected, analysed and bottled out of – over the past twenty-five years.

My gratitude and love to David, Linda and Andrea Potter.

For Lila, Elliot and Flynn. Everything, always.